Czech

phrasebooks
and
Richard Nebeský

Czech phrasebook
2nd edition – March 2007

Published by
Lonely Planet Publications Pty Ltd ABN 36 005 607 983
90 Maribyrnong St, Footscray, Victoria 3011, Australia

Lonely Planet Offices
Australia Locked Bag 1, Footscray, Victoria 3011
USA 150 Linden St, Oakland CA 94607
UK 2nd fl, 186 City Rd, London, EC1V 2NT

Cover illustration
Drinking the holy waters of Prague by Michael Ruff

ISBN 978 1 74104 047 0

text © Lonely Planet Publications Pty Ltd 2007
cover illustration © Lonely Planet Publications Pty Ltd 2007

Printed through Colorcraft Ltd, Hong Kong. Printed in China

10 9 8 7 6 5 4

All rights reserved. No part of this publication may be reproduced,
stored in a retrieval system or transmitted in any form by any means,
electronic, mechanical, photocopying, recording or otherwise, except
brief extracts for the purpose of review, without the written permission
of the publisher.

Lonely Planet does not allow its name or logo to be appropriated by
commercial establishments, such as retailers, restaurants or hotels.
Please let us know of any misuses: www.lonelyplanet.com/ip

Lonely Planet and the Lonely Planet logo are trade marks of Lonely
Planet and are registered in the U.S. Patent and Trademark Office and
in other countries.

**Although the authors and Lonely Planet try to make the infor-
mation as accurate as possible, we accept no responsibility
for any loss, injury or inconvenience sustained by anyone
using this book.**

acknowledgments

Editor Branislava Vladisavljevic would like to acknowledge the following people for their contributions to this phrasebook:

Richard Nebeský for the comprehensive translations and the cultural information included in this book.

Richard spent the first decade or so of his life in the bilingual environment of Czechoslovakia, where he also studied Russian in primary school. He moved to Australia, where French was added to his curriculum in high school, and he studied linguistics at Monash University. After graduating, extensive travels in many European and Asian countries as well as working in Austria, Switzerland and the USA broadened his linguistic horizons further. Richard has authored many European and Asian titles for Lonely Planet as well as the Czech chapter for the first editions of both the Central Europe and Eastern Europe phrasebooks.

Richard would like to thank his wife Romana for many devoted hours spent on the project fine-tuning phrases and proofing; his mother Jitka for tirelessly proofing the entire manuscript; Daniel Mourek for his assistance and Dr Pavel Sturza and his wife Stana for proofing the Health chapter.

Thanks also to Michael Ruff for the inside illustrations.

Lonely Planet Language Products

Publishing Manager: Chris Rennie
Commissioning Editor: Karin Vidstrup Monk
Editor: Branislava Vladisavljevic
Assisting Editors: Vanessa Battersby & Francesca Coles
Managing Editor: Annelies Mertens

Layout Designers: Pablo Gastar & David Kemp
Senior Layout Designer: Sally Darmody
Series Designer: Yukiyoshi Kamimura
Cartographer: Wayne Murphy
Production Manager: Jennifer Bilos
Project Manager: Adam McCrow

make the most of this phrasebook ...

Anyone can speak another language! It's all about confidence. Don't worry if you can't remember your school language lessons or if you've never learnt a language before. Even if you learn the very basics (on the inside covers of this book), your travel experience will be the better for it. You have nothing to lose and everything to gain when the locals hear you making an effort.

finding things in this book

For easy navigation, this book is in sections. The Tools chapters are the ones you'll thumb through time and again. The Practical section covers basic travel situations like catching transport and finding a bed. The Social section gives you conversational phrases, pick-up lines, the ability to express opinions – so you can get to know people. Food has a section all of its own: gourmets and vegetarians are covered and local dishes feature. Safe Travel equips you with health and police phrases, just in case. Remember the colours of each section and you'll find everything easily; or use the comprehensive Index. Otherwise, check the two-way traveller's Dictionary for the word you need.

being understood

Throughout this book you'll see coloured phrases on each page. They're phonetic guides to help you pronounce the language. Start with them to get a feel for how the language sounds. The pronunciation chapter in Tools will explain more, but you can be confident that if you read the coloured phrase, you'll be understood. As you become familiar with the spoken language, move on to using the actual text in the language which will help you perfect your pronunciation.

communication tips

Body language, ways of doing things, sense of humour – all have a role to play in every culture. 'Local talk' boxes show you common ways of saying things, or everyday language to drop into conversation. 'Listen for ...' boxes supply the phrases you may hear. They start with the language (so a local can find the phrase they want and point it out to you) and then lead in to the phonetic guide and the English translation.

introduction 8

tools 11

practical 45

social 107

CONTENTS

7

czech

Germany

Poland

Děčín
Teplice · Liberec
Chomutov · Ústí nad Labem
· Most
Karlovy Vary · Kladno
· Mladá Boleslav
· Hradec Králové
Plzeň
· Prague (Praha)
· Pardubice

Karviná
Ostrava
Havířov
Český Těšín
Jablunkov

CZECH REPUBLIC

Olomouc
Frýdek-Místek
Prostějov
Přerov
Jihlava
Brno
Zlín

České Budějovice

Germany

Slovakia

Austria

0 ———— 100 km
0 ———— 60 mi

■ **official language**
For more details, see the **introduction**.

Denmark · Kaliningrad (Russia)

Germany · Poland

CZECH REPUBLIC

Slovakia

Austria · Hungary

Italy · Slovenia

If the Czech language was a person, she could be excused for needing serious therapy. The Czech Republic may now be one of the most stable and well-off Eastern European countries, but over the centuries the land and the language have been regularly swallowed and regurgitated by their neighbours. Most recently, in 1993 the Velvet Divorce ended the patched-together affair that was Czechoslovakia, and allowed Czech to go its own way after being tied to Slovak for over 70 years.

Both Czech and Slovak belong to the western branch of the Slavic language family, pushed westward with the Slavic people by the onslaught of the Huns, Avars, Bulgars and Magyars in the 5th and 6th centuries. Czech is also related to Polish, though not as closely as to Slovak – adults in Slovakia and the Czech Republic can generally understand one another, although younger people who have not been exposed to much of the other language may have difficulty in communication.

at a glance ...

language name:
Czech

name in language:
*Čeština chesh·*tyi·nuh

language family:
Slavic

approximate number of speakers: 12 million

close relatives:
Polish, Slovak

donations to English:
dollar, howitzer, pistol, robot

The earliest written literature dates from the 13th century upswing in Czech political power, which continued for several centuries. In the 17th century, however, the Thirty Years War nearly caused literature in Czech to become extinct. Fortunately, the national revival of the late 18th century brought it to the forefront again, at least until the 20th century, when first Nazi and then Communist rule pressed it into a subordinate place once more.

introduction

Many English speakers flinch when they see written Czech – especially words like *prst* prst (finger) and *krk* krk (neck) with no apparent vowels, and the seemingly unpronounceable clusters of consonants in phrases like *čtrnáct dní* chtr·natst dnyee (fortnight). Don't despair! With a little practice and the coloured pronunciation guides in this book you'll be enjoying the buttery mouthfeel of Czech words in no time. Czech also has one big advantage in the pronunciation stakes – unlike English, each Czech letter is always pronounced exactly the same way, so once you've got the hang of the Czech alphabet you'll be able to read any word put before you with aplomb. Thank religious writer and martyr Jan Hus for this – he reformed the spelling system in the 15th and 16th centuries and introduced the *háček* ha·chek (ˇ) and the various other accents you'll see above Czech letters.

This book will give you all the practical phrases you need to explore the countryside, visit Golden Prague, and tour castles and mountains worthy of the Brothers Grimm (in fact, the 2005 movie of that name was filmed here). It also contains all the fun phrases you need to connect with local people and get a better understanding of the country and its culture. Local knowledge, new relationships and a sense of satisfaction are on the tip of your tongue. So don't just stand there – say something!

abbreviations used in this book

a	adjective	n (after Czech)	neuter
adv	adverb	n (after English)	noun
f	feminine	pl	plural
inf	informal	pol	polite
lit	literally	sg	singular
m	masculine	v	verb

Most of the sounds in Czech are also found in English, and of the few that aren't, only one can be a little tricky to master – the infamous rzh (written *ř*). You can take comfort, however, from the fact that even some Czechs have difficulty with it! If you find it something of a struggle even after a bit of practice, don't worry – people will generally be able to understand you regardless (and they'll probably sympathise as well).

Czech letters always have the same pronunciation, so once you've mastered them you're ready to go. To make sure you're understood, always stress the first syllable of a word – this is indicated with italics in this book, so just follow the coloured pronunciation guides next to each phrase and you'll be fine.

Czech has a number of different regional dialects, as well as a formal variety (based on medieval Czech) that's used in books and the media. The pronunciation in this phrasebook is that of standard Czech as spoken in the Prague area in everyday communication. Using it you'll be understood by Czech speakers everywhere.

vowel sounds

Czech vowel sounds are similar to those found in the English words in the table on the following page. Just be aware that in the transliteration air only the vowel should be pronounced, (unlike in American English), not the r sound. You'll also notice that Czech has a number of vowel sound combinations (so-called diphthongs).

symbol	english equivalent	czech example	transliteration
a	father	*já*	ya
ai	aisle	*krajka*	*krai*·kuh
air	hair	*veliké*	ve·lee·**kair**
aw	law	*balcón*	*bal*·**kawn**
e	get	*pes*	pes
ee	bee	*prosím*	*pro*·**seem**
ey	hey	*dej*	d**ey**
i	bit	*kolik*	ko·lik
o	hot	*noha*	*no*·huh
oh	oh	*koupit*	*koh*·pit
oo	moon	*ústa*	*oo*·stuh
oy	toy	*výstroj*	vee·str**oy**
ow	how	*autobus*	**ow**·to·bus
u	put	*muž*	muzh
uh	run	*nad*	n**uh**d

consonant sounds

The consonants in Czech are mostly the same as in English, with the exception of the kh sound (which is pronounced in the back of the throat as in the Scottish word *loch*), the r sound (which is rolled as it is in Spanish) and the rzh sound (a rolled r followed quickly by a zh sound as in the word 'leisure').

The sounds r, s and l can be used as quasi-vowels – hence the existence of those infamous Czech words that appear to have no vowels, like *krk* krk (neck), *osm* o·sm (eight) or *vlk* vlk (wolf). The r in the first word, for example, is pronounced like the 'r' in the American way of saying 'third'. If you find these clusters of consonants intimidating, just try putting a tiny uh sound between them.

Note also that some consonants are words in their own right – such as the prepositions *k* k (to), *s* s (with) or *v* v (in). They're usually joined with the following word in pronunciation.

symbol	english equivalent	czech example	transliteration
b	big	*bláto*	*bla*·to
ch	cheer	*odpočinek*	ot·po·**chi**·nek
d	dive	*nedávný*	*ne*·dav·nee
f	fin	*vyfotit*	*vi*·fo·tit
g	gate	*vegetarián*	ve·ge·tuh·ri·an
h	hit	*zahrady*	zuh·hruh·di
k	skin	*navěky*	na·vye·**ki**
kh	loch	*kuchyně*	ku·**khi**·nye
l	loud	*loni*	*lo*·nyi
m	man	*menší*	*men*·shee
n	no	*nízký*	*nyeez*·kee
p	pause	*dopis*	*do*·pis
r	rolled, as in Spanish *rapido*	*rok*	rok
rzh	rolled r followed by zh	*řeka*	*rzhe*·kuh
s	side	*slovo*	*slo*·vo
sh	shoe	*pošta*	*posh*·tuh
t	tell	*fronta*	*fron*·tuh
ts	lets	*co*	tso
v	van	*otvor*	*otvor*
y	yes	*již*	yizh
z	zero	*zmiz*	zmiz
zh	measure	*už*	uzh
'	a slight y sound	*promiňte, déšť, teď*	*pro*·min'·te, dairsht', ted'

word stress

Word stress in Czech is easy – it's always on the first syllable of the word. Stress is marked with italics in the coloured pronunciation guides in this book as a reminder.

reading & writing

The Czech alphabet has 42 letters and is based on the Latin alphabet. The alphabet is entirely phonetic and letters are always pronounced the same. For spelling purposes (eg if you need to spell your name when booking a hotel room) we've included the pronunciation of each letter.

Czech has a long and a short version of each vowel – the long vowel always has an acute accent on it in the written language (eg é), and in the case of u, there are two letters for the long vowel, ú and ů. Note also that d, n and t, when followed in writing by ě, i or í, are pronounced with a slight 'y' sound after them – just like ď, ň and ť are always pronounced with that sound.

alphabet					
A a	uh	I i	ee	S s	es
Á á	a	Í í	*dloh*·hair ee	Š š	esh
B b	bair	J j	yair	T t	tair
C c	tsair	K k	ka	Ť ť	tyair
Č č	chair	L l	el	U u	u
D d	dair	M m	em	Ú ú	*dloh*·hair u
Ď ď	dyair	N n	en	Ů ů	u s *krohzh*·kem
E e	e	Ň ň	en'	V v	vair
É é	*dloh*·hair air	O o	o	W w	*dvo*·yi·tair vair
Ě ě	e s *hach*·kem	Ó ó	*dloh*·hair o	X x	iks
F f	ef	P p	pair	Y y	*ip*·si·lon
G g	gair	Q q	kair	Ý ý	*dloh*·hee *ip*·si·lon
H h	ha	R r	er	Z z	zet
Ch ch	cha	Ř ř	erzh	Ž ž	zhet

contents

The list below shows the grammatical structures you can use to say what you want. Look under each function – given in alphabetical order – for information on how to build your own phrases. For example, to tell the taxi driver where your hotel is, look for **giving instructions** and you'll be directed to information on **case**, **demonstratives**, etc. A **glossary** of grammatical terms is included at the end of this chapter to help you. Abbreviations like **nom** and **acc** in the literal translations for each example refer to the case of the noun or pronoun – this is explained in the **glossary** and in **case**.

making statements

naming people/things

negating

pointing things out

possessing

adjectives & adverbs

Adjectives come before the noun, and change their gender, number and case endings to agree with the nouns they describe. In the **dictionaries** and word lists in this phrasebook, adjectives are given in the masculine form and nominative case (see **case**, **gender** and **plurals**). The most common endings in the nominative case are *-ý* -ee for the masculine, *-á* -a for the feminine and *-é* -air for the neuter gender. These endings become *-í* -ee m, *-é* -air f and *-á* -a n in the plural.

wonderful liqueur   *báječný likér* m   *ba*·yech·nee *li*·ker
  (lit: wonderful liqueur)
wonderful vodka   *báječná vodka* f   *ba*·yech·na *vod*·kuh
  (lit: wonderful vodka)
wonderful beer   *báječné pivo* n   *ba*·yech·nair *pi*·vo
  (lit: wonderful beer)

Adverbs are formed by removing the nominative adjective ending (*-ý* or *-í*, both pronounced -ee) and replacing it with *-o* -o, *-e* -e or *-ě* -ye. Adverbs come after the verb, and they don't change to match the verb at all.

She cooks wonderfully.
  Ona vaří báječně.   onuh *vuh*·rzhee *ba*·yech·nye
  (lit: she cooks wonderfully)

articles

There are no equivalents for the words 'a' and 'the' in Czech – *pivo* pi·vo can mean both 'a beer' or 'the beer', depending on the context.

be

describing people/things · making statements

The verb *být* beet (be) changes to match the person and number of the subject. Below are the present tense forms of *být*. See also **negatives** and **verbs**.

be – present tense			
I	am	*jsem*	ysem
you sg inf	are	*jsi*	ysi
you sg pol	are	*jste*	yste
he/she/it	is	*je*	ye
we	are	*jsme*	ysme
you pl	are	*jste*	yste
they	are	*jsou*	ysoh

I'm a businessperson.
> *Jsem obchodník.* m&f   ysem *op*·khod·nyeek
> (lit: I-am businessperson)

I'm tired.
> *Jsem unavený/á.* m/f   ysem *u*·nuh·ve·nee/a
> (lit: I-am tired-m/f)

case

doing things · giving instructions · indicating location · naming people/things · possessing

Czech has a system of seven case endings (shown opposite), which are used to indicate the role of nouns, pronouns and adjectives in a sentence. The word lists, **culinary reader** and **dictionaries** in this phrasebook provide words in the nominative case – this will generally be understood, even when another case would normally be used within a sentence.

TOOLS

case

nominative nom – shows the subject of a sentence

The palace is beautiful.
Palác je krásný.   puh·lats ye *kras*·nee
(lit: palace-nom is beautiful)

accusative acc – shows the direct object of a sentence

Did you see the performance?
Viděli jste to představení?   vi·dye·li yste to przheds·tuh·ve·nyee
(lit: saw you-are-pol that performance-acc)

genitive gen – shows possession 'of'

Where's Franz Kafka's grave?
Kde je hrob Franze Kafky?   gde ye hrob *fruhn*·ze *kuhf*·ki
(lit: where is grave Franz-gen Kafka-gen)

dative dat – shows the indirect object of a sentence

I gave my passport to the policeman.
Dal/Dala jsem můj pas   duhl/*duh*·luh ysem mooy puhs
policajtovi. m/f   po·li·tsai·to·vi
(lit: gave-m/f I-am my passport policeman-dat)

locative loc – used with prepositions to show location

Does it stop in Prague?
Staví v Praze?   sta·vee f *pruh*·ze
(lit: stops in Prague-loc)

instrumental inst – shows how something is done

I came by train.
Přijel/Přijela jsem   przhi·yel/przhi·ye·la ysem
vlakem. m/f   *vluh*·kem
(lit: came-m/f I-am train-inst)

vocative voc – used to address someone

Hi Emil, what's new?
Ahoj Emile co je nového?   uh·hoy e·mi·le tso ye *no*·vair·ho
(lit: hi Emil-voc what is new)

The genitive case is also used with many prepositions (such as 'to', 'from' or 'at'). See also **prepositions**.

from May	*od kvetna*	od *kvyet*·nuh
to June	*do cervna*	do *cher*·vnuh
	(lit: from May-gen to June-gen)	

demonstratives

giving instructions · indicating location ·
naming people/things · pointing things out

Czech uses the same word for both 'this' and 'that'. This word
changes in gender, number and case to agree with the noun it
refers to. The different forms in the nominative and accusative
case are shown below. See also **case**, **gender** and **plurals**.

this & that	singular			plural		
case	m	f	n	m	f	n
nom	*ten* ten	*ta* tuh	*to* to	*ti/ty* * ti/ti	*ty* ti	*ta* tuh
acc	*toho* to·ho	*tu* tu	*to* to	*ty* ti	*ty* ti	*ta* tuh

* animate/inanimate (for an explanation, see **gender**)

That's my seat.
 To je moje místo.   to ye *mo·ye mees·*to
 (lit: that-nom-n-sg is my-nom-n-sg seat-nom)

gender

naming people/things

Czech nouns have gender – masculine m, feminine f or neuter n. The masculine gender is further divided into 'animate'
(anything living that can move) and 'inanimate' (anything not
living or not able to move, like rocks or plants).

 You need to learn the grammatical gender for each noun as
you go, but you can often recognise it by the noun's ending –
masculine nouns generally end in a consonant, feminine ones
in -*a* -uh, -*e* -e or a 'soft' consonant (those with diacritical marks,
such as *ť* or *š*), and neuter nouns in -*o* -o, -*e* -e or -*i* -i. You need
to know gender to form adjectives and past tense verbs.

TOOLS

The nouns in this book's lists, **dictionaries** and **culinary reader** all have their gender marked.

castle	*hrad* m	hruhd
statue	*socha* f	so·khuh
city	*město* n	myes·to

See also **adjectives & adverbs**, **demonstratives** and **verbs**.

have

possessing

An easy way of expressing possession in Czech is to use the verb *mít* meet (have).

I have a lot of luggage.
    Mám mnoho zavazadel.   mam *mno*·ho *zuh*·vuh·zuh·del
    (lit: I-have much luggage-**acc**)

The present tense forms of 'have' are shown in the following table. See also **possessives**.

have – present tense			
I	have	*mám*	mam
you sg inf	have	*máš*	mash
you sg pol	have	*máte*	ma·te
he/she/it	has	*má*	ma
we	have	*máme*	ma·me
you pl	have	*máte*	ma·te
they	have	*mají*	muh·yee

negatives

Making negatives in Czech is very simple – you just attach the prefix *ne-* ne- (no) to the verb:

I'm English.
Jsem Angličan/   ysem *uhn*·gli·chuhn/
Angličanka. m/f   *uhn*·gli·chuhn·kuh
(lit: I-am English-m/f)

I'm not Czech.
Nejsem Čech/Češka. m/f   *ney*·sem chekh/*chesh*·kuh
(lit: no-I-am Czech-m/f)

See also **verbs**.

nouns

Czech nouns have many forms – various endings are used to show their role in the sentence. For more information, see **case**, **gender** and **plurals**.

personal pronouns

**doing things • making statements •
naming people/things • possessing**

Personal pronouns ('I', 'you', etc) aren't generally necessary in Czech, as the case endings make it clear what the role of each person or thing in a sentence is (eg whether it's a subject or an object). Their main use is for emphasis:

No, I had the goulash, you had the dumplings.
Ne, já jsem měl/měla   ne ya ysem myel/*mye*·luh
guláš a ty knedlíky. m/f   *gu*·lash uh ti *kne*·dlee·ki
(lit: no I I-am had-m/f goulash-acc and you-inf dumplings-acc)

The nominative and accusative cases of personal pronouns, used for the subject and the object of the sentence respectively, are shown in the following two tables. Czech has both an informal and a polite word for 'you' – basically, unless you know the person very well, use the polite form, *vy* vi and the second-person plural form of the verb. See the box **all about you** on page 172 for more information.

subject (nominative case) pronouns					
I	*já*	ya	we	*my*	mi
you sg inf	*ty*	ti	you pl	*vy*	vi
you sg pol	*vy*	vi			
he	*on*	on		*oni* m	o·nyi
she	*ona*	o·nuh	they	*ony* f	o·ni
it	*ono*	o·no		*ona* n	o·nuh

object (accusative case) pronouns					
me	*mne/mě*	m·ne/mye	us	*nás*	nas
you sg inf	*tebe/tě*	te·be/tye	you pl	*vás*	vas
you sg pol	*vás*	vas			
him	*jeho/ něho*	ye·ho/ nye·ho		*je/ně* m	ye/nye
her	*ji/ni*	yi/nyi	them	*je/ně* f	ye/nye
it	*je/ně*	ye/nye		*je/ně* n	ye/nye

Where there are two versions of the pronoun separated by a slash, the second version is for using with prepositions ('to him' etc).

See also **case**, **gender** and **plurals**.

plurals

Plurals are formed with a variety of word endings – the most common are *-y* -ee, *-a* -uh, *-e* -e and *-i* -i. If the singular word ends in a vowel, the vowel is replaced with the plural ending. If it ends in a consonant, just add the ending to form the plural.

singular			plural		
map	*mapa* f	*muh*·puh	maps	*mapy* f	*muh*·pi
bag	*zava-zadlo* n	*zuh*·vuh·zuhd·lo	bags	*zava-zadla* n	*zuh*·vuh·zuhd·luh
bed	*postel* f	*pos*·tel	beds	*postele* f	*pos*·te·le
thing	*věc* f	vyets	things	*věci* f	*vye*·tsi

possessives

As in English, possession can be shown in Czech by using the verb 'have' (see **have**) or by using words like 'my' and 'your'. The words for 'his' (*jeho* ye·ho), 'her' (*její* ye·yee) and 'their' (*jejich* ye·yikh) are always the same. The Czech versions of 'my', 'your' and 'our', however, change to match the case, number and gender of the noun they go with. Whether the form used is singular or plural depends on the number of the object (what's possessed), not the subject (who's possessing). The nominative case, which you'll hear and use most often, is listed in the tables opposite.

my friend
  můj/moje kamarád(ka) m/f   mooy/*mo*·ye *kuh*·muh·rad(·kuh)
  (lit: my-m/f friend-m/f)

my children
  moje děti n pl   *mo*·ye *dye*·tyi
  (lit: my-n-pl children)

possessive adjectives – singular

	masculine		feminine		neuter	
my	*můj*	mooy	*moje*	mo·ye	*moje*	mo·ye
your sg inf	*tvůj*	tvooy	*tvoje*	tvo·ye	*tvoje*	tvo·ye
your sg pol	*váš*	vash	*vaše*	vuh·she	*vaše*	vuh·she
our	*náš*	nash	*naše*	nuh·she	*naše*	nuh·she
your pl	*váš*	vash	*vaše*	vuh·she	*vaše*	vuh·she

possessive adjectives – plural

	masculine		feminine		neuter	
my	*moji*	mo·yi	*mé*	mair	*moje*	mo·ye
your sg inf	*tvoji*	tvo·yi	*tvé*	tvair	*tvoje*	tvo·ye
your sg pol	*vaši*	vuh·shi	*vaše*	vuh·she	*vaše*	vuh·she
our	*naši*	nuh·shi	*naše*	nuh·she	*naše*	nuh·she
your pl	*vaši*	vuh·shi	*vaše*	vuh·she	*vaše*	vuh·she

See also **case**, **gender** and **plurals**.

prepositions

giving instructions • indicating location • pointing things out

Prepositions are used to show relationships between words in a sentence, just like in English. In Czech, where the meaning is already clear from the case that's used, they may be left out (see **case** for more information). Some useful ones are shown on the next page.

prepositions					
about	*o*	o	in	*v*	v
at	*u*	u	on	*na*	nuh
from	*z*	z	to	*do*	do

questions

asking questions

You can change a statement into a yes/no question in Czech by swapping the verb and the subject, as you would in English:

They're going to Brno.
> *Oni/Ony jedou do Brna.* m/f   *o*·nyi/*o*·ni *ye*·doh do *br*·nuh
> (lit: they-m/f go to Brno-gen)

Are they going to Brno?
> *Jedou oni/ony do Brna?* m/f   *ye*·doh *o*·nyi/*o*·ni do *br*·nuh
> (lit: go they-m/f to Brno-gen)

To get specific information, use a question word at the start of a sentence.

question words					
How?	*Jak?*	yuhk	Where?	*Kde?*	gde
What?	*Co?* inf *Prosím?* pol	tso *pro*·seem	Who?	*Kdo?*	gdo
When?	*Kdy?*	gdi	Why?	*Proč?*	proch

verbs

doing things · making statements

Czech has three tenses – past, present and future. Past and present tenses are formed by taking the infinitive (or 'dictionary form') of the verb, dropping the -*t* ending, and adding the appropriate tense ending.

present

The present tense endings used depend on the verb class. There are four classes: the verbs in the first class end in *-at* -uht or *-át* -at, the second in *-ovat* -o·vuht, *-ít* -eet or *-ýt* -eet, the third in *-it* -it, *-et* -et or *-ět* -yet, and the fourth includes all other endings. Here are the endings for the verb 'drink', *pít* peet.

pít (drink) – present tense			
I	drink	*piju*	*pi·yu*
you sg inf/pol	drink	*piješ/pijete*	*pi·yesh/pi·ye·te*
he/she/it	drinks	*pije*	*pi·ye*
we	drink	*pijeme*	*pi·ye·me*
you pl	drink	*pijete*	*pi·ye·te*
they	drink	*pijí*	*pi·yee*

I don't drink alcohol.
   Nepiju alkohol.   *ne·pi·yu uhl·ko·hol*
   (lit: I-not-drink alcohol-**acc**)

past

To form the past tense, take the *-t* -t off the end of the infinitive, and replace it with an ending that matches the gender and number of who or what is performing the action (the subject):

dělat (do) – past tense						
m sg	*-l*	*dělal*	*dye·luhl*	m pl	*-li*	*dělali*	*dye·luh·li*
f sg	*-la*	*dělala*	*dye·luh·luh*	f pl	*-ly*	*dělaly*	*dye·luh·li*
n sg	*-lo*	*dělalo*	*dye·luh·lo*	n pl	*-la*	*dělala*	*dye·luh·luh*

Add the present tense form of *být* beet (be), unless the subject is 'he/she/it' or 'they', in which case *být* is omitted. See also **be**.

We did that last year.
   Udělali jsme to minulý rok.   *u·dye·luh·li ysme to mi·nu·lee rok*
   (lit: did-**m-pl** we-are that-**acc-n-sg** last year)

He did it yesterday.
    Udělal to včera.   u·dye·luhl to *fche·*ruh
    (lit: he-did-**m-sg** that-**acc-n-sg** yesterday)

If you're female, of course, 'I/she did' is *udělala* u·dye·luh·luh.

future

Future tense is formed with the future tense of *být* beet (be), shown in the table below, followed by the infinitive of the verb.

be – future tense			
I	will be	budu	bu·du
you sg inf/pol	will be	budeš/budete	bu·desh/bu·de·te
he/she/it	will be	bude	bu·de
we	will be	budeme	bu·de·me
you pl	will be	budete	bu·de·te
they	will be	budou	bu·doh

Will you go out with me?
    Budeš se mnou chodit?   bu·desh se mnoh *kho·*dyit
    (lit: you-will-**inf** with me go-out)

word order

making statements

Word order in Czech is flexible, because the case endings and verb endings make it clear who's doing what to whom. However, the default order of a simple sentence is still subject–verb–object, as in English. If you change this order, it puts a strong emphasis on whatever comes first in the sentence.

It doesn't fit.
    Nepadne mi to.   *ne·*puhd·ne mi to
    (lit: not-fit me that-**acc-n-sg**)

glossary

accusative (case)	type of *case marking*, used to show the *direct object* of the sentence – 'Czechs celebrate **beer drinking** at numerous festivals'
adjective	a word that describes something – '**Czech brewing** traditions go back many centuries'
adverb	a word that explains how an action was done – 'with Czech beer, you can drink **freely** and not worry about ill effects'
article	the words 'a', 'an' and 'the'
case (marking)	word ending which tells us the role of a thing or person in the sentence
dative (case)	type of *case marking* which shows the *indirect object* – 'local breweries are important to **Czechs** as part of their national culture'
demonstrative	a word that means 'this' or 'that'
direct object	the thing or person in the sentence that has the action directed to it – 'Czech breweries use only **natural ingredients** for the fermentation process'
gender	classification of *nouns* into classes (masculine, feminine and neuter), requiring other words (eg *adjectives*) to belong to the same class
genitive (case)	type of *case marking* which shows ownership or possession – 'Czech beer is one of the **world's** finest'
indirect object	the person or thing in the sentence that is the recipient of the action – 'Czechs usually return beer bottles to **the seller** for a refund'

infinitive	the dictionary form of a *verb* – 'they say it's impossible to **get** a hangover from Czech beer'
instrumental (case)	type of *case marking* which shows how something is done – 'Czech beer is fermented by **a bottom method**'
locative (case)	type of *case marking* used to show where the *subject* is – 'there are no chemicals in **Czech beer**'
nominative (case)	type of *case marking* used for the *subject* of the sentence – '**Czech beer** is served at cellar temperature'
noun	a thing, person or idea – '**Czechs** have many **sayings** about **beer**'
number	whether a word is singular or plural – 'there are over 60 **breweries** in the Czech Republic'
personal pronoun	a word that means 'I', 'you', etc
possessive adjective	a word that means 'my', 'your', etc
preposition	a word like 'for' or 'before' in English
subject	the thing or person in the sentence that does the action – '**people** in the Czech Republic consume an ocean of beer every year'
tense	form of a *verb* that tells you whether the action is in the present, past or future – eg 'drink' (present), 'drank' (past), 'will drink' (future)
verb	the word that tells you what action happened – 'many beer-inspired competitions **are organised** in the Czech Republic '

language difficulties
jazykové problémy

Do you speak (English)?
Mluvíte (anglicky)?   mlu·vee·te (*uhn·*glits·ki)

Does anyone speak (English)?
Mluví tady někdo   mlu·vee tuh·di nye·gdo
(anglicky)?   (*uhn·*glits·ki)

Do you understand?
Rozumíte?   ro·zu·mee·te

Yes, I understand.
Ano, rozumím.   uh·no ro·zu·meem

No, I don't understand.
Ne, nerozumím.   ne ne·ro·zu·meem

I speak (English).
Mluvím (anglicky).   mlu·veem (*uhn·*glits·ki)

I don't speak (Czech).
Nemluvím (česky).   ne·mlu·veem (*ches·*ki)

I speak a little.
Mluvím trochu.   mlu·veem tro·khu

I'd like to practise (Czech).
Rád/Ráda bych si procvičil/   rad/*ra·*duh bikh si prots·vi·chil/
procvičila (češtinu). **m/f**   prots·vi·chi·luh (*chesh·*tyi·nu)

Let's speak (Czech).
Mluvme (česky).   mluf·me (*ches·*ki)

---

tongue torture

Czech is famous for its absence of vowels – many words
lack them totally, and there's a well-known tongue twister
composed entirely of consonants:

Strč prst skrz krk.   **Stick your finger**
   strch prst skrz krk   **through your neck.**

Pardon?
   Promiňte?   pro·min'·te

What does (knedlík) mean?
   Co znamená (knedlík)?   tso znuh·me·na (kned·leek)

How do you ...?	*Jak se ...?*	yuhk se ...
pronounce this	*toto vyslovuje*	toh·to vis·lo·vu·ye
write (krtek)	*píše (krtek)*	pee·she (kr·tek)

Could you	*Prosím,*	pro·seem
please ...?	*můžete ...?*	moo·zhe·te ...
repeat that	*to opakovat*	to o·puh·ko·vuht
speak more	*mluvit*	mlu·vit
slowly	*pomaleji*	po·muh·le·yi
write it down	*to napsat*	to nuhp·suht

---

false friends

There are a number of Czech words that look or sound very similar to English words, but have a completely different meaning. For example:

fakt m   fuhkt   fact
  not 'fucked', which is *z kurvený* s kur·ve·nee

med n   med   honey
  not 'mad', which is *šílený* shee·le·nyee

mít   meet   have
  not 'meet', which is *potkat* pot·kuht

police f pl   po·li·tse   shelves
  not 'police', which is *policie* po·li·tsi·ye

pórek m   paw·rek   leek
  not 'pork', which is *vepřové* ve·przho·vair

svit   svit   shine
  not 'sweet', which is *sladký* sluhd·kee

trafika f   truh·fi·kuh   tobacconist
  not 'traffic', which is *doprava* do·pruh·vuh

cardinal numbers

Czech numbers from 21 to 29, 31 to 39 and so on, have two forms – both are used in everyday speech.

0	*nula*	*nu·luh*
1	*jeden/jedna/*	*ye·den/yed·na/*
	jedno m/f/n	*yed·no*
2	*dva* m	*dvuh*
	dvě f&n	*dvye*
3	*tři*	*trzhi*
4	*čtyři*	*chti·rzhi*
5	*pět*	*pyet*
6	*šest*	*shest*
7	*sedm*	*se·dm*
8	*osm*	*o·sm*
9	*devět*	*de·vyet*
10	*deset*	*de·set*
11	*jedenáct*	*ye·de·natst*
12	*dvanáct*	*dvuh·natst*
13	*třináct*	*trzhi·natst*
14	*čtrnáct*	*chtr·natst*
15	*patnáct*	*puht·natst*
16	*šestnáct*	*shest·natst*
17	*sedmnáct*	*se·dm·natst*
18	*osmnáct*	*o·sm·natst*
19	*devatenáct*	*de·vuh·te·natst*
20	*dvacet*	*dvuh·tset*
21	*dvacet jedna/*	*dvuh·tset yed·nuh/*
	jednadvacet	*yed·nuh·dvuh·tset*
22	*dvacet dva/*	*dvuh·tset dvuh/*
	dvaadvacet	*dvuh·uh·dvuh·tset*

30	třicet	*trzhi*·tset
40	čtyřicet	*chti*·rzhi·tset
50	padesát	*puh*·de·sat
60	šedesát	*she*·de·sat
70	sedmdesát	*se*·dm·de·sat
80	osmdesát	*o*·sm·de·sat
90	devadesát	*de*·vuh·de·sat
100	sto	sto
200	dvěstě	*dvye*·stye
1000	tisíc	*tyi*·seets
1,000,000	milión	*mi*·li·yawn

as simple as one, two, three

Most numbers in Czech have just one form, regardless of the noun's gender, and are followed by the noun in the genitive case and in the plural:

devět jelenů m pl   *de*·vyet *ye*·le·noo   **nine deers**

There are only two exceptions to this rule. The number 'one' and numbers ending in 'one' are followed by the nominative singular form of a noun. The word 'one' has three forms, to agree with the gender of the noun that follows it (see the **phrasebuilder** for more on case, gender and number):

jeden stan m sg	*ye*·den stuhn	**one tent**
jedna hruška f sg	*yed*·nuh *hrush*·kuh	**one pear**
jedno auto n sg	*yed*·no *ow*·to	**one car**

The number 'two' also agrees with the gender of the following noun (it has one form for the masculine gender and another for both the feminine and neuter gender). The following noun is in the nominative or accusative plural form:

dva roky m pl	dvuh *ro*·ki	**two years**
dvě motorky f pl	dvye *mo*·tor·ki	**two motorcycles**
dvě vajíčka n pl	dvye *vuh*·yeech·kuh	**two eggs**

Of course, when counting in Czech, the forms used are simply *jeden, dva, tři ye*·den dvuh trzhi – 'one, two, three …'

ordinal numbers

Ordinal numbers are generally formed by adding the ending -*(t)ý* -(t)ee to cardinal numbers. The exceptions are shown below. They're abbreviated in writing as the numeral followed by a full stop (eg '1.' or '18.') and are used to write dates, just like in English – so '18th October' is written as *18. října*.

1st	*první*	prv·nyee
2nd	*druhý*	dru·hee
3rd	*třetí*	trzhe·tyee
4th	*čtvrtý*	chtvr·tee
5th	*pátý*	pa·tee
6th	*šestý*	shes·tee
7th	*sedmý*	sed·mee
8th	*osmý*	os·mee
9th	*devátý*	de·va·tee
10th	*desátý*	de·sa·tee

fractions & decimals

a quarter	*čtvrtina*	chtvr·tyi·nuh
a third	*třetina*	trzhe·tyi·nuh
a half	*polovina*	po·lo·vi·nuh
three-quarters	*třičtvrtina*	trzhi·chtvr·tyi·nuh
all	*všechno*	fshe·khno
none	*nic*	nyits

Decimals are generally written as in English, except on price tags, where a comma is used instead of the full stop – eg 'eight crowns and fifty heller' is written as 8,50 Kč.

3.14	*tři celé čtrnáct*	trzhi tse·lair chtr·natst
4.2	*čtyři celé dvě*	chti·rzhi tse·lair dvye
5.1	*pět celých jedna*	pyet tse·leekh yed·nuh

useful amounts

How much/many?	*Kolik?*	ko·lik
Please give me ...	*Prosím dejte mi ...*	pro·seem *dey*·te mi ...
100 grams	*deset deka*	de·set *de*·kuh
a dozen	*tucet*	*tu*·tset
half a dozen	*půl tuctu*	pool *tuts*·tu
a kilo	*kilo*	*ki*·lo
half a kilo	*půl kila*	pool *ki*·luh
a bottle	*láhev*	*la*·hef
a jar	*sklenici*	*skle*·nyi·tsi
a packet	*balíček*	*buh*·lee·chek
a slice	*plátek*	*pla*·tek
a tin	*plechovku*	*ple*·khof·ku
a few	*několik*	*nye*·ko·lik
less	*méně*	*mair*·nye
(just) a little	*trochu*	*tro*·khu
a lot	*hodně*	*hod*·nye
many	*mnoho*	*mno*·ho
more	*více*	*vee*·tse
some	*několik*	*nye*·ko·lik

For more amounts, see **self-catering**, page 174.

a couple of things about pairs

In spoken Czech, the word *pár* par (pair) doesn't necessarily mean 'two' – rather, it's used in the sense of 'a few' or 'several'. For example, *pár dnů* par dnoo is 'a few days' (not strictly two days).

The word *párek* pa·rek (lit: little pair) is a diminutive of *pár* (diminutives are words used to express the 'smallness' of something or affection – eg 'doggy' in English). You might hear it in a phrase such as *To je hezký párek!* to ye *hez*·kee *pa*·rek, which means 'What a nice couple!'

telling the time

Officially (eg in timetables and shop hours), Czechs use the 24-hour clock – so '2pm' is *14.00 hodin* (*čtrnáct hodin chtr*·natst *ho*·dyin). However, the 12-hour clock is still used in everyday speech. The Czech word for both 'hour' and 'o'clock' is *hodina ho*·dyi·nuh when used with 'one', *hodiny ho*·dyi·ni with 'two', 'three' and 'four' and *hodin ho*·dyin with higher numbers.

When it comes to shorter time segments, Czechs look ahead at the coming hour – 'quarter past ten' and 'half past ten' becomes 'quarter of eleven' (*čtvrt na jedenáct* chtvrt nuh *ye*·de·natst) and 'half eleven' (*půl jedenácté* pool *ye*·de·nats·tair).

What time is it?
  Kolik je hodin?   *ko*·lik ye *ho*·dyin

It's one o'clock.
  Je jedna hodina.   ye *yed*·nuh *ho*·dyi·nuh

It's (ten) o'clock.
  Je (deset) hodin.   ye (*de*·set) *ho*·dyin

Five past (ten).
  (Deset hodin) a pět minut.   (*de*·set *ho*·dyin) a pyet *mi*·nut
  (lit: ten hours and five minutes)

Quarter past ten.
  Čvrt na jedenáct.   chtvrt nuh *ye*·de·natst

Half past ten.
  Půl jedenácté.   pool *ye*·de·nats·tair

Quarter to (eleven).
Třičtvrtě na (jedenáct).   trzhi·chtvr·tye nuh (ye·de·natst)
(lit: three-quarters of eleven)

Twenty to (eleven).
Za pět minut třičtvrtě   zuh pyet *mi*·nut *trzhi*·chtvr·tye
na (jedenáct).   nuh (ye·de·natst)
(lit: in five minutes
three-quarters of eleven)

am (midnight-8am)	*ráno*	*ra*·no
am (8am-noon)	*dopoledne*	*do*·po·led·ne
pm (noon-7pm)	*odpoledne*	*ot*·po·led·ne
pm (7pm-midnight)	*večer*	*ve*·cher

At what time?	*V kolik hodin?*	f *ko*·lik *ho*·dyin
At (five).	*V (pět).*	f (pyet)
At (7.57pm).	*V (sedm padesát*	f (*se*·dm *puh*·de·sat
	sedm večer).	*se*·dm *ve*·cher)

the calendar

kalendář

days

Monday	*pondělí* n	*pon*·dye·lee
Tuesday	*úterý* n	*oo*·te·ree
Wednesday	*středa* f	*strzhe*·duh
Thursday	*čtvrtek* m	*chtvr*·tek
Friday	*pátek* m	*pa*·tek
Saturday	*sobota* f	*so*·bo·tuh
Sunday	*neděle* f	*ne*·dye·le

months

January	*leden* m	*le·den*
February	*únor* m	*oo·nor*
March	*březen* m	*brzhe·zen*
April	*duben* m	*du·ben*
May	*květen* m	*kvye·ten*
June	*červen* m	*cher·ven*
July	*červenec* m	*cher·ve·nets*
August	*srpen* m	*sr·pen*
September	*září* n	*za·rzhee*
October	*říjen* m	*rzhee·yen*
November	*listopad* m	*li·sto·puht*
December	*prosinec* m	*pro·si·nets*

the poetry of nature

Unlike most European languages, Czech doesn't use the Latin-based words to name months. The Czech names for months have Slavic roots dating from before the onset of Christianity and reflect the seasonal changes in the world of nature. Some of these poetic meanings are obvious, while others have been forgotten and can only be guessed.

January	*leden*	Month of Ice (from *led* led – 'ice', as it's the coldest month of the year)
May	*květen*	Month of Blooming Flowers (from *květ* kvyet – 'flower', as most flowers bloom in May)
August	*srpen*	Month of the Sickle (from *srp* srp – 'sickle', a tool used during harvest time to cut plants)
November	*listopad*	Month of Falling Leaves (from *list* list – 'leaf' and *padat* puh·duht – 'to fall')

dates

When numerals are used for writing dates, they are followed by
a full stop in Czech – eg '18th October' is written as *18. října.*

What date is it today?
   Kolikátého je dnes?   ko·li·ka·tair·ho ye dnes

It's (18 October).
   Je (osmnáctého října).   ye (o·sm·nats·tair·ho *rzheey*·nuh)

seasons

spring	*jaro* n	*yuh*·ro
summer	*léto* n	*lair*·to
autumn	*podzim* m	*pod*·zim
winter	*zima* f	*zi*·muh

present

now	*teď*	teď
today	*dnes*	dnes
tonight	*večer*	ve·cher
this	*dnes ...*	dnes ...
morning (early)	*ráno*	ra·no
morning (late)	*dopoledne*	do·po·led·ne
afternoon	*odpoledne*	ot·po·led·ne
this ...	*tento ...*	ten·to ...
week	*týden*	tee·den
month	*měsíc*	mye·seets
year	*rok*	rok

past

day before yesterday	*předevčírem*	*przhe*·def·chee·rem
(three days) ago	*před (třemi dny)*	przhet (*trzhe*·mi dni)
since (May)	*od (května)*	od (*kvyet*·nuh)
last night	*včera v noci*	*fche*·ruh v *no*·tsi
last week	*minulý týden*	*mi*·nu·lee *tee*·den
last month	*minulý měsíc*	*mi*·nu·lee *mye*·seets
last year	*vloni*	*vlo*·nyi
yesterday ...	*včera ...*	*fche*·ruh ...
morning (early)	*ráno*	*ra*·no
morning (late)	*dopoledne*	*do*·po·led·ne
afternoon	*odpoledne*	*ot*·po·led·ne
evening	*večer*	*ve*·cher

future

day after tomorrow	*podelzítří*	*po*·del·zeet·rzhee
in (six days)	*za (šest dnů)*	zuh (shest dnoo)
until (June)	*do (června)*	do (*cher*·vnuh)
next ...	*příští ...*	*przheesh*·tyee ...
week	*týden*	*tee*·den
month	*měsíc*	*mye*·seets
year	*rok*	rok
tomorrow ...	*zítra ...*	*zee*·truh ...
morning (early)	*ráno*	*ra*·no
morning (late)	*dopoledne*	*do*·po·led·ne
afternoon	*odpoledne*	*ot*·po·led·ne
evening	*večer*	*ve*·cher

during the day

afternoon	odpoledne n	ot·po·led·ne
dawn	svítání n	svee·ta·nyee
day	den m	den
evening	večer m	ve·cher
midday/noon	poledne n	po·led·ne
midnight	půlnoc f	pool·nots
morning	ráno n	ra·no
night	noc f	nots
sunrise	východ slunce m	vee·khod slun·tse
sunset	západ slunce m	za·puhd slun·tse

festival fun

The most important festivals in the Czech Republic are the modern-day setting for some colourful local traditions:

The Burning of the Witches

Pálení Čarodějnic   pa·le·nyee *chuh*·ro·dyey·nyits

On 30 April, friends in towns gather to make big bonfires (*hranice hruh*·nyi·tse), and in the countryside the whole village has one big, communal bonfire. This end of winter celebration was originally a pagan ritual during which people cleaned their houses and then burned their brooms on top of the nearest hill to ward off evil spirits, especially witches (*čarodějnice chuh*·ro·dyey·nyi·tse).

The Devil and St Nicholas Day

Čert a Mikuláš   chert uh *mi*·ku·lash

Celebrated on the eve of 5 December (the day of St Nicholas, the patron saint of children, falls on the next day). Three people dress up as St Nicholas, the devil (*čert* chert) and an angel (*anděl uhn*·dyel) and visit children to see if they've been good during the year. They give the good children chocolate and fruit – the naughty children get coal or potatoes.

Since the Czech Republic has joined the European Union in 2004, the government is expecting to change its currency from the Czech crown (*Česká koruna* ches·ka ko·ru·nuh) to the euro (*euro* e·u·ro) by 2010.

How much is it?
Kolik to stojí? — ko·lik to sto·yee

Can you write down the price?
Můžete mi napsat cenu? — moo·zhe·te mi nuhp·suht tse·nu

Do I have to pay?
Mám zaplatit? — mam zuh·pluh·tyit

There's a mistake in the bill.
Na účtu je chyba. — nuh ooch·tu ye khi·buh

I'd like to …, please.	Chtěl/Chtěla bych …, prosím. m/f	khtyel/khtye·luh bikh … pro·seem
cash a cheque	proplatit šek	pro·pluh·tyit shek
change a travellers cheque	vyrměnit cestovní šek	vi·mye·nyit tses·tov·nyee shek
change money	vyměnit peníze	vi·mye·nyit pe·nyee·ze
get a cash advance	zálohu v hotovosti	za·lo·hu v ho·to·vos·tyi
get change for this note	drobné za tuto bankovku	drob·nair zuh tu·to buhn·kof·ku
transfer money	převést peníze	przhe·vairst pe·nyee·ze
withdraw money	vybrat peníze	vi·bruht pe·nyee·ze

Where's …?	Kde je …?	gde ye …
an ATM	bankomat	buhn·ko·muht
a foreign exchange office	směnárna	smye·nar·nuh

What's the ...?	Jaký je ...?	yuh·kee ye ...
charge	poplatek	po·pluh·tek
exchange rate	devizový kurz	de·vi·zo·vee kurz
It's ...	Je to ...	ye to ...
free	bez poplatku	bez po·pluht·ku
(12) crowns	(dvanáct) korun	(dvuh·natst) ko·run
(5) euros	(pět) eur	(pyet) e·ur
Do you	Může se	moo·zhe se
accept ...?	platit ...?	pluh·tyit ...
credit cards	kreditními	kre·dit·nyee·mi
	kartami	kuhr·tuh·mi
debit cards	platebními	pluh·teb·nyee·mi
	kartami	kuhr·tuh·mi
travellers	cestovními	tses·tov·nyee·mi
cheques	šeky	she·ki
I'd like ...,	Chtěl/Chtěla bych	khtyel/khtye·luh bikh
please.	..., prosím. m/f	... pro·seem
a receipt	účtenku	ooch·ten·ku
a refund	vrátit peníze	vra·tyit pe·nyee·ze
my change	mé drobné	mair drob·nair
to return this	vrátit toto	vra·tyit to·to

For more money-related phrases, see **banking**, page 91.

For more money-related phrases, see **banking**, page 91.

money talk

One of the most common slang words for 'money' in Czech is *prachy* pruh·khi (lit: dust). Slang words are also used for specific denominations:

kačka f	*kuhch·kuh*	one crown
(lit: ducky)		
bůra n	*boo·ruh*	five crowns
(no literal meaning)		
kilo n	*ki·lo*	a hundred crowns
(lit: kilogram)		
litr m	*li·tr*	a thousand crowns
(lit: litre)		

TOOLS

44

getting around

cestování po okolí

On public transport, most young people readily give up their seats for the elderly or disabled, and pregnant women. When entering a train compartment, it's customary to greet the other passengers with *dobrý den* dob·ree den (good day), and when leaving, to say *nashledanou* nuhs·khle·duh·noh (goodbye).

Which ...	*Který/á ...*	kte·ree/a ...
goes to (České Budějovice)?	*jede do (Českých Budějovic)?* m/f	ye·de do (ches·keekh bu·dye·yo·vits)
bus	*autobus* m	ow·to·bus
train	*vlak* m	vluhk
tram	*tramvaj* f	truhm·vai
trolleybus	*trolejbus* m	tro·ley·bus
Is this the ... to (Mělník)?	*Jede tento/tato ... do (Mělníka)?* m/f	ye·de ten·to/tuh·to ... do (myel·nyee·kuh)
bus	*autobus* m	ow·to·bus
train	*vlak* m	vluhk
tram	*tramvaj* f	truhm·vai
trolleybus	*trolejbus* m	tro·ley·bus
When's the ... (bus)?	*V kolik jede ... (autobus)?*	f ko·lik ye·de ... (ow·to·bus)
first	*první*	prv·nyee
last	*poslední*	po·sled·nyee
next	*příští*	przhee·shtyee

What time does the bus/train leave?

| V kolik hodin odjíždí autobus/vlak? | f ko·lik ho·dyin od·yeezh·dyee ow·to·bus/vluhk |

What time does the bus/train get to (Plzeň)?

| V kolik hodin přijede autobus/vlak do (Plzně)? | f ko·lik ho·dyin przhi·ye·de ow·to·bus/vluhk do (pl·znye) |

How long will it be delayed?

| Jak dlouho bude mít zpoždění? | yuhk dloh·ho bu·de meet zpozh·dye·nyee |

Is this seat available?

| Je toto místo volné? | ye to·to mees·to vol·nair |

That's my seat.

| To je mé místo. | to ye mair mees·to |

Please tell me when we get to (Přerov).

| Prosím vás řekněte mi kdy budeme v (Přerově). | pro·seem vas rzhek·nye·te mi kdi bu·de·me f (przhe·ro·vye) |

Please stop here.

| Prosím vás zastavte. | pro·seem vas zuhs·tuhf·te |

How long do we stop here?

| Jak dlouho zde budeme stát? | yuhk dloh·ho zde bu·de·me stat |

---

listen for ...

automat na lístky m	ow·to·muht nuh leest·ki	ticket machine
cestovní kancelář f	tses·tov·nyee kuhn·tse·larzh	travel agent
jízdní řád m	yeezd·nyee rzhad	timetable
nástupiště n	na·stu·pish·tye	platform
obsazeno	op·suh·ze·no	full
pokladna n	po·kluh·dnuh	ticket window
tamten	tuhm·ten	that one
tenhle	ten·hle	this one
zpoždění	zpozh·dye·nyee	delayed
zrušen	zru·shen	cancelled

tickets

Where do I buy a ticket?
   Kde koupím jízdenku?   gde koh·peem yeez·den·ku

Do I need to book?
   Potřebuji místenku?   pot·rzhe·bu·yi mees·ten·ku

A ... ticket	*... do (Telče),*	*... do (tel·che)*
to (Telč), please.	*prosím.*	*pro·seem*
1st-class	*Jízdenku*	*yeez·den·ku*
	první třídy	*prv·nyee trzhee·di*
2nd-class	*Jízdenku*	*yeez·den·ku*
	druhé třídy	*dru·hair trzhee·di*
child's	*Dětskou*	*dyets·koh*
	jízdenku	*yeez·den·ku*
one-way	*Jednosměrnou*	*yed·no·smyer·noh*
	jízdenku	*yeez·den·ku*
return	*Zpáteční*	*zpa·tech·nyee*
	jízdenku	*yeez·den·ku*
student	*Studentskou*	*stu·dents·koh*
	jízdenku	*yeez·den·ku*

I'd like a/an	*Chtěl/Chtěla*	khtyel/*khtye·luh*
... seat.	*bych ...* m/f	bikh ...
aisle	*místo v uličce*	*mees·to f u·lich·tse*
nonsmoking	*nekuřácké*	*ne·ku·rzhats·kair*
	místo	*mees·to*
smoking	*kuřácké*	*ku·rzhats·kair*
	místo	*mees·to*
window	*místo u okna*	*mees·to u ok·nuh*

I'd like to ...	*Chtěl/Chtěla*	khtyel/*khtye·luh*
my ticket,	*bych ... mojí*	bikh ... *mo·yee*
please.	*jízdenku,*	*yeez·den·ku*
	prosím. m/f	*pro·seem*
cancel	*zrušit*	*zru·shit*
change	*změnit*	*zmye·nyit*
collect	*vyzvednout*	*vi·zved·noht*
confirm	*potvrdit*	*pot·vr·dyit*

Is there (a) …?	Je tam …?	ye tuhm …
air conditioning	klimatizace	kli·muh·ti·zuh·tse
blanket	deka	de·kuh
sick bag	sáček při nevolnosti	sa·chek przhi ne·vol·nos·tyi
toilet	toaleta	to·uh·le·tuh

Can I get a couchette/sleeping berth?
Mohu si koupit   mo·hu si koh·pit
lehátko/lůžko?   le·hat·ko/loozh·ko

How much is it?
Kolik to stojí?   ko·lik to sto·yee

How long does the trip take?
Jak dlouho trvá cesta?   yuhk dloh·ho tr·va tses·tuh

Is it a direct route?
Je to přímá cesta?   ye to przhee·ma tses·tuh

What time should I check in?
V kolik hodin se mám   f ko·lik ho·dyin se mam
dostavit k odbavení?   do·stuh·vit k od·buh·ve·nyee

luggage

zavazadla

Where can I find a/the …?	Kde mohu najít …?	gde mo·hu nuh·yeet …
baggage claim	výdej zavazadel	vee·dey zuh·vuh·zuh·del
left-luggage office	úschovnu zavazadel	oos·khov·nu zuh·vuh·zuh·del
luggage locker	zavazadlová schránka	zuh·vuh·zuhd·lo·va skhran·kuh
trolley	vozík	vo·zeek

Can I have some coins/tokens?

Můžete mi dát několik mincí/žetonů?		*moo·zhe·te mi dat nye·ko·lik min·tsee/zhe·to·noo*

My luggage has been ...	*Moje zavazadlo bylo ...*	*mo·ye zuh·vuh·zuhd·lo bi·lo ...*
damaged	*poškozeno*	*posh·ko·ze·no*
lost	*ztraceno*	*ztruh·tse·no*
stolen	*ukradeno*	*u·kruh·de·no*

backpack	*batoh* m	*buh·tawh*
bag	*taška* t	*tuhsh·kuh*
box	*krabice* f	*kruh·bi·tse*
rucksack	*ruksak* m	*ruk·suhk*
suit bag	*vak na oblek* m	*vuhk nuh o·blek*
suitcase	*kufr* m	*ku·fr*
toiletry bag	*necesér* m	*ne·tse·ser*

kabinové zavazadlo n	kuh·bi·no·vair zuh·vuh·zuhd·lo	carry-on baggage
nadměrné zavazadlo n	nuhd·myer·nair zuh·vuh·zuhd·lo	excess baggage
palubní vstupenka f	puh·lub·nyee vstu·pen·kuh	boarding pass
pas m	puhs	passport
přestup m	przhes·tup	transfer
tranzit m	tran·zit	transit
žeton m	zhe·ton	token

plane

letadlo

Where does flight (OK25) arrive?
Kam přiletí let (OK25)? kuhm *przhi*·le·tyee let (*aw*·ka *dvuh*·tset pyet)

Where does flight (OK25) depart?
Kde odlítá let (OK25)? gde *od*·lee·ta let (*aw*·ka *dvuh*·tset pyet)

Where's (the) ...?	Kde je ...?	gde ye ...
airport shuttle	letištní kyvadlová doprava	le·tyisht·nyee ki·vuhd·lo·va do·pruh·vuh
arrivals hall	příletová hala	przhee·le·to·va huh·luh
departures hall	odletová hala	od·le·to·va huh·luh
duty-free shop	prodejna bezcelního zboží	pro·dey·nuh bez·tsel·nyee·ho zbo·zhee
gate (8B)	východ k letadlu (8B)	vee·khod k le·tuhd·lu (o·sm bair)

bus & coach

Is this a bus stop?
Je toto autobusová   ye *to*·to *ow*·to·bu·so·va
zastávka?   zuh·staf·kuh

How often do buses come?
Jak často jezdí   yuhk *chuh*·sto *yez*·dyee
autobusy?   *ow*·to·bu·si

Does it stop at (Klatovy)?
Staví v (Klatovech)?   *sta*·vee v (*kluh*·to·vekh)

What's the next stop?
Která je příští   *kte*·ra ye *przheesh*·tyee
zastávka?   zuhs·taf·kuh

How many stops to (the market)?
Kolik je zastávek (na trh)?   *ko*·lik ye *zuhs*·ta·vek (nuh trh)

I'd like to get off at (Příbram).
Chtěl/Chtěla bych   khtyel/*khtye*·luh bikh
vystoupit v (Příbrami). m/f   *vi*·stoh·pit f (*przhee*·bruh·mi)

How much is it to (Brno)?
Kolik stojí jízdenka   *ko*·lik *sto*·yee *yeez*·den·kuh
do (Brna)?   do (*br*·nuh)

... **bus**	... *autobus*	... *ow*·to·bus
city	*městský*	*myest*·skee
intercity	*meziměstský*	*me*·zi·myest·skee
hotel	*hotelový*	*ho*·te·lo·vee
local	*místní*	*meest*·nyee

departure bay	*nástupiště* n	*nas*·tu·pish·tye
local bus	*místní*	*meest*·nyee
station	*autobusové*	*ow*·to·bu·so·vair
	nádraží n	*na*·dra·zhee
long distance	*autobusové*	*ow*·to·bu·so·vair
bus station	*nádraží* n	*na*·dra·zhee
timetable	*tabule jízdního*	*tuh*·bu·le yeezd·nyee·ho
display	*řádu* f	*rzha*·du

bus & train station signs

Čekárna	che·kar·nuh	**Waiting Room**
Informace	in·for·muh·tse	**Information**
Jízdní řády	yeezd·nye rzha·di	**Timetables**
Metro	me·tro	**Underground**
Mezinárodní	me·zi·na·rod·nye	**International**
Místenkové	mees·ten·ko·vair	**Reservations**
pokladny	po·kluhd·ni	
Nádraží	na·dra·zhee	**Station**
Nástupiště	nas·tu·pish·tye	**Platform**
Nouzový východ	noh·zo·vee vee·khod	**Emergency Exit**
Odjezdy	od·yez·di	**Departures**
Pokladna	po·kluhd·nuh	**Ticket Office**
Příjezdy	przhee·yez·di	**Arrivals**
Úschovna	oos·khov·nuh	**Left-luggage**
zavazadel	zuh·vuh·zuh·del	**Office**
Vchod	vkhod	**Entrance**
Vnitrostraní	vnyi·tros·truh·nye	**Domestic**
Vstup Zakázán	vstup zuh·ka·zan	**No Entry**
Zákaz	za·kuhz	**No Smoking**
Kouření	koh·rzhe·nye	

train & metro

vlak & metro

What's the next station?
Která je příští stanice? — kte·ra ye przheesh·tyee stuh·nyi·tse

Does it stop at (Cheb)?
Zastaví to v (Chebu)? — zuhs·tuh·vee to f (khe·bu)

Do I need to change?
Musím přestupovat? — mu·seem przhes·tu·po·vuht

Which carriage is for (Domažlice)?
Který vagon jede do (Domažlic)? — kte·ree vuh·gon ye·de do (do·muh·zhlits)

PRACTICAL

Which carriage is (for) ...?	Který vagon má ...?	kte·ree *vuh*·gon ma ...
1st class	první třídu	prv·nyee trzhee·du
dining	jídelní část	yee·del·nyee chast
smoking	kuřácké místa	ku·rzhats·kair *mees*·tuh

Is it (a/an)...?	Je to ...?	ye to ...
EuroCity	EC	e·tsair
express	rychlík	rikh·leek
fast train	spěšný vlak	spyesh·nee vluhk
InterCity	IC	i·tsair
local train	osobní vlak	o·sob·nyee vluhk
SuperCity	SC	es·tsair

taxi

taxík

I'd like a taxi ...	Potřebuji taxíka ...	po·trzhe·bu·yi tuhk·see·kuh ...
at (9am)	v (devět hodin dopoledne)	f (de·vyet ho·dyin do·po·led·ne)
now	teď	ted'
tomorrow	zítra	zee·truh

Where's the taxi rank?
Kde je taxi stanoviště?   gde ye tuhk·si stuh·no·vish·tye

Is this taxi available?
Je tento taxík volný?   ye ten·to tuhk·seek vol·nee

Please take me to (this address).
Prosím odvezte mě na (tuto adresu).   pro·seem od·ves·te mye na (tu·to uh·dre·su)

Please put the meter on.
 Prosím zapněte   pro·seem *zuhp*·nye·te
 taxametr.   *tuhk*·suh·me·tr

How much is it to …?
 Kolik stojí jízdenka   ko·lik *sto*·yee *yeez*·den·kuh
 do …?   do …

How much is the flag fall/hiring charge?
 Kolik je nástupní sazba? ko·lik ye *nas*·tup·nye *suhz*·buh

Please …	*Prosím …*	pro·seem …
come back at	*přijeďte zpět*	*przhi*·yed'·te spyet
(10 o'clock)	*v (deset hodin)*	f (*de*·set *ho*·dyin)
slow down	*zpomalte*	*spo*·muhl·te
stop here	*zastavte zde*	*zuhs*·tuhf·te zde
wait here	*počkejte zde*	*poch*·key·te zde

For other useful phrases, see **directions**, page 63 and **money**, page 43.

car & motorbike

auto & motorka

car & motorbike hire

I'd like to hire	*Chtěl/Chtěla bych*	khtyel/*khtye*·luh bikh
a/an …	*si půjčit … m/f*	si *pooy*·chit …
4WD	*auto s*	*ow*·to s
	náhonem na	*na*·ho·nem nuh
	čtyři kola	*chti*·rzhi *ko*·luh
automatic	*auto s*	*ow*·to s
	automatickou	*ow*·to·muh·tits·koh
	převodovkou	*przhe*·vo·dof·koh
car	*auto*	*ow*·to
manual	*auto s*	*ow*·to s
	manuální	*muh*·nu·al·nyee
	převodovkou	*przhe*·vo·dof·koh
motorbike	*motorku*	*mo*·tor·ku

PRACTICAL

with ...   *s ...*   *s ...*

  air conditioning *klimatizací* *kli·muh·ti·zuh·tsee*

  a driver *řidičem* *rzhi·dyi·chem*

How much for daily/weekly hire?
Kolik stojí půjčení   *ko·lik sto·yee pooy·che·nyee*
na den/týden?   nuh den/*tee*·den

Does that include insurance?
Je v tom započítané   ye f tom *zuh*·po·chee·tuh·nair
pojištění?   *po*·yish·tye·nyee

Does that include mileage?
Jsou v tom započítané   ysoh f tom *zuh*·po·chee·tuh·nair
najeté kilometry?   nuh·ye·tair *ki*·lo·me·tri

Do you have a guide to the road rules (in English)?
Máte příručku   *ma*·te *przhee*·ruch·ku
dopravních předpisů   *do*·pruhv·nyeekh *przhed*·pi·soo
(v angličtině)?   (f *uhn*·glich·tyi·nye)

Do you have a road map?
Máte automapu?   *ma*·te *ow*·to·muh·pu

road signs

Jednosměrný	yed·nos·myer·nee	**One Way**
provoz	pro·voz	
Objížďka	ob·yeezhd'·kuh	**Detour**
Průjezd	proo·yezd	**No Through**
zakázán	zuh·ka·zan	**Traffic Allowed**
Úsek měření	oo·sek mye·rzhe·nyee	**Speed Detection**
rychlosti	rikh·los·tyi	**Sector**
Vjezd	vyezd	**Entrance**
Východ	vee·khod	**Exit**
Zákaz	za·kuhz	**No Parking**
parkování	puhr·ko·va·nyee	
Zákaz vjezdu	za·kuhz vyez·du	**No Entry**

on the road

What's the speed limit?
Jaká je povolená rychlost?   yuh·ka ye po·vo·le·na rikh·lost

Is this the road to (Cheb)?
Vede tato silnice do   ve·de tuh·to sil·ni·tse do
(Chebu)?   (khe·bu)

Where's a petrol station?
Kde je benzinová pumpa?   gde ye ben·zi·no·va pum·puh

Can you check the ...?	*Můžete zkontrolovat ...?*	moo·zhe·te zkon·tro·lo·vuht ...
oil	*olej*	o·ley
tyre pressure	*tlak vzduchu v pneumatikách*	tluhk vzdu·khu f pne·u·muh·ti·kakh
water	*vodu*	vo·du

How long can I park here?
Jak dlouho zde mohu   yuhk dloh·ho zde mo·hu
parkovat?   puhr·ko·vuht

Can I park here?
Mohu zde parkovat?   mo·hu zde puhr·ko·vuht

Do I have to pay?
Musím platit?   mu·seem pluh·tyit

Can I have a receipt for my fine payment?
Můžete mi dát   moo·zhe·te mi dat
potvrzení za   pot·vr·ze·nyee zuh
zaplacenou pokutu?   zuh·pluh·tse·noh po·ku·tu

listen for ...

bez poplatku	bez po·pluht·ku	**free**
dálniční známka f	dal·nyich·nyee znam·kuh	**motorway pass**
parkovací automat m	puhr·ko·vuh·tsee ow·to·muht	**parking meter**
řidičský průkaz m	rzhi·dyich·skee proo·kuhz	**drivers licence**

address it right

Addresses in Czech are written in a different way from English. The number of the house or apartment block is written after the street name, not before. Although each apartment has a number, these are rarely used. Instead, a person's name is written next to the bell at the main entrance and on the main door to the apartment.

Aleš Nový	name
Žižkova 24	street & number
903 20 Palcátov 2	postcode & suburb
Tábor	town
Česká republika	country

As shown above, Czechs don't use the words 'street' (*ulice* u·li·tse), 'lane' (*ulička* u·lich·kuh) or 'avenue' (*třída* trzhee·duh), after the actual name in addresses and on maps, but they do use the words *náměstí* na·myes·tyee (square) and *nábřeží* na·brzhe·zhee (quay):

Karlovo náměstí	Charles Square
Dvořákovo nábřeží	Dvořák Quay

problems

I need a mechanic.
    Potřebuji mechanika.   pot·rzhe·bu·yi *me*·khuh·ni·kuh

I've had an accident.
    Stala se mi dopravní   stuh·luh se mi *do*·pruhv·nyee
    nehoda.   ne·ho·duh

The car has broken down (at Třebíč).
    Porouchalo se mi auto   po·roh·khuh·lo se mi *ow*·to
    (v Třebíči).   (f *trzhe*·bee·chi)

The motorbike has broken down (at Třebíč).
    Porouchala se mi   po·roh·khuh·luh se mi
    motorka (v Třebíči).   mo·tor·kuh (f *trzhe*·bee·chi)

The car/motorbike won't start.
 Auto/Motorka nechce   ow·to/mo·tor·kuh nekh·tse
 nastartovat.   nuhs·tuhr·to·vuht

I have a flat tyre.
 Mám defekt.   mam de·fekt

I've lost my car keys.
 Ztratil/Ztratila jsem   ztruh·tyil/ztruh·tyi·luh ysem
 své klíče od auta. m/f   svair klee·che od ow·tuh

I've locked the keys inside.
 Zamknul/Zamknula jsem   zuhm·knul/zuhm·knu·luh ysem
 si uvnitř klíče. m/f   si uv·nyi·trzh klee·che

I've run out of petrol.
 Došel mi benzin.   do·shel mi ben·zin

Can you fix it (today)?
 Můžete to opravit (dnes)?   moo·zhe·te to o·pruh·vit (dnes)

How long will it take?
 Jak dlouho to bude trvat?   yuhk dloh·ho to bu·de tr·vuht

petrol
benzin m
ben·zin

windscreen
přední sklo n
przhed·nyee sklo

battery
baterie f
buh·te·ri·ye

engine
motor m
mo·tor

tyre
pneumatika f
pne·u·muh·ti·kuh

headlight
reflektor m
re·flek·tor

bicycle

I'd like to … a bicycle.	Chtěl/Chtěla bych si … kolo. m/f	khtyel/khtye·luh bikh si … ko·lo
buy	koupit	koh·pit
hire	půjčit	pooy·chit

I'd like a … bike.	Chtěl/Chtěla bych … kolo. m/f	khtyel/khtye·luh bikh … ko·lo
mountain	horské	hors·kair
racing	závodní	za·vod·nyee
second-hand	použité	po·u·zhi·tair

How much is it per …?	Kolik to stojí na …?	ko·lik to sto·yee nuh …
hour	hodinu	ho·dyi·nu
day	den	den

Do I need a helmet?
Potřebuji helmu?   pot·rzhe·bu·yi *hel*·mu

Are there bicycle paths?
Jsou tam cyklistické trasy?   ysoh tuhm *tsi*·klis·tits·kair *truh*·si

Is there a bicycle-path map?
Existuje mapa   ek·sis·tu·ye *muh*·puh
cyklistické trasy?   tsi·klis·tits·kair *truh*·si

I have a puncture.
Mám defekt.   mam *de*·fekt

I'd like my bicycle repaired.
Potřebuji opravit kolo.   pot·rzhe·bu·yi o·pruh·vit *ko*·lo

lonely letters

The single consonants in our coloured pronunciation guides haven't been pushed out of an overcrowded Czech word by mistake. They're Czech versions of some common prepositions (eg 'with', 'in') and are usually joined in pronunciation with the following word. You'll see v or f for the sound of the letter v, k for k and s or z for the letters s and z. For more on prepositions, see the **phrasebuilder**, page 25.

Finding those strange Czech letters a bit intimidating? Maybe the consonants aren't rolling easily off your tongue? If you're having trouble and the locals don't understand you, the best solution is to practice your pronunciation.

Start with some of the most useful words for a traveller – common placenames. Here's a list of placenames you'll probably need while making your way around the Czech Republic – in particular, remember to say *Praha pruh*·huh, not 'Prague', when admiring the Golden City!

Brno	*br*·no	**Brno**
Cheb	tsheb	**Cheb**
České	*ches*·kair	**České**
Budějovice	bu·dye·yo·vi·tse	**Budějovice**
Český Krumlov	*ches*·kee *krum*·lof	**Český Krumlov**
Český Těšín	*ches*·kee *tye*·sheen	**Český Těšín**
Děčín	*dye*·cheen	**Děčín**
Domažlice	*do*·muh·zhli·tse	**Domažlice**
Havířov	*huh*·vee·rzhov	**Havířov**
Hradec Králové	*hruh*·dets *kra*·lo·vair	**Hradec Králové**
Karlovy Vary	*kuhr*·lo·vi *vuh*·ri	**Karlovy Vary**
Karlštejn	*kuh*·rl·shteyn	**Karlštejn**
Kutná Hora	*kut*·na *ho*·ruh	**Kutná Hora**
Mělník	*myel*·neek	**Mělník**
Olomouc	*o*·lo·mohts	**Olomouc**
Plzeň	*pl*·zen'	**Plzeň**
Praha	*pruh*·huh	**Prague**
Přerov	*przhe*·rov	**Přerov**
Rožnov Pod	*rozh*·nov pod	**Rožnov Pod**
Radhoštěm	*ruhd*·hosh·tyem	**Radhoštěm**
Třebíč	*trzhe*·beech	**Třebíč**
Telč	telch	**Telč**

border crossing

hraniční přechod

I'm here …	Jsem zde …	ysem zde …
in transit	v tranzitu	f *truhn*·zi·tu
on business	na služební cestě	nuh *slu*·zheb·nyee *tses*·tye
on holiday	na dovolené	nuh *do*·vo·le·nair

I'm here for …	Jsem zde na …	ysem zde nuh …
(10) days	(deset) dní	(*de*·set) dnyee
(three) weeks	(tři) týdny	(trzhi) *teed*·ni
(two) months	(dva) měsíce	(dvuh) *mye*·see·tse

I'm going to (Valtice).
  Jedu do (Valtic).   *ye*·du do (*vuhl*·tyits)

I'm staying at the (Hotel Špalíček).
  Jsem ubytovaný/á   ysem *u*·bi·to·vuh·nee/a
  v (Hotelu Špalíček). m/f   v (*ho*·te·lu *shpuh*·lee·chek)

The children are on this passport.
  Děti jsou zapsané   *dye*·tyi ysoh *zuhp*·suh·nair
  v tomto pasu.   f *tom*·to *puh*·su

listen for …

pas m	puhs	**passport**
rodina f	*ro*·dyi·nuh	**family**
sám/sama m/f	sam/*suh*·ma	**alone**
skupina f	*sku*·pi·nuh	**group**
vízum n	*vee*·zum	**visa**

at customs

I have nothing to declare.
Nemám nic k proclení.   ne·mam nyits k *prots*·le·nyee

I have something to declare.
Mám něco k proclení.   mam *nye*·tso k *prots*·le·nyee

Do I have to declare this?
Musím to nahlásit   mu·seem to nuh·hla·sit
k proclení?   k *prots*·le·nyee

I didn't know I had to declare it.
Nevěděl/Nevěděla   ne·vye·dyel/ne·vye·dye·luh
jsem že to musím   ysem zhe to *mu*·seem
nahlásit k proclení. m/f   nuh·hla·sit k *prots*·le·nyee

That's mine.
To je moje.   to ye *mo*·ye

That's not mine.
To není moje.   to ne·nyee *mo*·ye

Do I need an export permit?
Potřebuji vývozní   pot·rzhe·bu·yi *vee*·voz·nyee
povolení?   po·vo·le·nyee

I have an export permit.
Mám vývozní povolení.   mam *vee*·voz·nyee po·vo·le·nyee

I have a Tax-Free shopping voucher.
Mám poukázku   mam *poh*·kaz·ku
nepodléhající dani.   ne·pod·lair·huh·yee·tsee *duh*·nyi

For phrases on payments and receipts, see **money**, page 43.

signs		
Celnice	tsel·ni·tse	**Customs**
Duty-Free	dyu·ti free	**Duty-Free**
Karanténa	kuh·ruhn·tair·nuh	**Quarantine**
Passová kontrola	puh·so·va kon·tro·luh	**Passport Control**

PRACTICAL

62

Where's the (market)?
Kde je (trh)? — gde ye (trh)

What's the address?
Jaká je adresa? — yuh·ka ye uh·dre·suh

Can you show me (on the map)?
Můžete mi to ukázat (na mapě)? — moo·zhe·te mi to u·ka·zuht (nuh muh·pye)

How far is it?
Jak je to daleko? — yuhk ye to duh·le·ko

How do I get there?
Jak se tam dostanu? — yuhk se tuhm dos·tuh·nu

It's ...	*Je to ...*	ye to ...
behind ...	*za ...*	zuh ...
far	*daleko*	duh·le·ko
here	*zde*	zde
in front of ...	*před ...*	przhed ...
near	*blízko*	bleez·ko
next to ...	*vedle ...*	ved·le ...
on the corner	*na rohu*	nuh ro·hu
opposite ...	*naproti ...*	nuh·pro·tyi ...
straight ahead	*přímo*	przhee·mo
there	*tam*	tuhm

Turn ...	*Odbočte ...*	od·boch·te ...
at the corner	*za roh*	zuh rawh
at the traffic lights	*u semaforu*	u se·muh·fo·ru
left	*do leva*	do le·vuh
right	*do prava*	do pruh·vuh

north	*sever* m	*se*·ver
south	*jih* m	yih
east	*východ* m	*vee*·khod
west	*západ* m	*za*·puhd
by bus	*autobusem*	*ow*·to·bu·sem
by taxi	*taxikem*	*tuhk*·si·kem
by train	*vlakem*	*vluh*·kem
on foot	*pěšky*	*pyesh*·ki
What ... is this?	*Jak se jmenuje ...?*	yuhk se *yme*·nu·ye ...
square	*toto náměstí*	*to*·to *na*·myes·tyee
street	*tato ulice*	*tuh*·to *u*·li·tse
village	*tato vesnice*	*tuh*·to *ves*·nyi·tse
avenue	*třída* f	*trzhee*·duh
quay	*nábřeží* n	*nab*·rzhe·zhee
square	*náměstí* n	*na*·myes·tyee
street	*ulice* f	*u*·li·tse

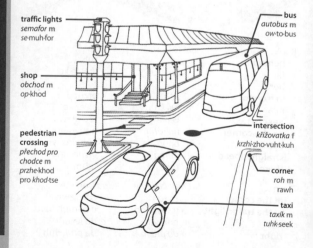

traffic lights
semafor m
se·muh·for

shop
obchod m
op·khod

pedestrian crossing
přechod pro chodce m
przhe·khod pro *khod*·tse

bus
autobus m
ow·to·bus

intersection
křižovatka f
krzhi·zho·vuht·kuh

corner
roh m
rawh

taxi
taxík m
tuhk·seek

finding accommodation

The 'international' terms hostel *hos·tel* (youth hostel) and *auto-kemp ow·to·kemp* (camping ground) are used in addition to the more complicated Czech phrases for these accommodation options given in the list below. The German phrase *Zimmer frei* (rooms available) is often found on signs for private accommodation around the country, for the attention of many German-speaking visitors.

Where's (a) ...?	*Kde je ...?*	gde ye ...
camping ground	*tábořiště*	ta·bo·rzhish·tye
guesthouse	*penzion*	pen·zi·on
hotel	*hotel*	ho·tel
some private accommodation	*privát*	pri·vat
student hostel	*studentská noclehárna*	stu·dents·ka nots·le·har·nuh
youth hostel	*mládežnická ubytovna*	mla·dezh·nyits·ka u·bi·tov·nuh
Can you recommend somewhere ...?	*Můžete mi doporučit něco ...?*	moo·zhe·te mi do·po·ru·chit nye·tso ...
cheap	*levného*	lev·nair·ho
clean	*čistého*	chis·tair·ho
good	*dobrého*	dob·rair·ho
luxurious	*luxusního*	luk·sus·nyee·ho
nearby	*nejbližšího*	ney·blizh·shee·ho
romantic	*romantického*	ro·muhn·tits·kair·ho
safe for women travellers	*bezpečného pro cestovatelky*	bez·pech·nair·ho pro tses·to·vuh·tel·ki

I want something near the ...	Potřebuji něco blízko ...	pot·rzhe·bu·yi nye·tso bleez·ko ...
city centre	středu města	strzhe·du myes·tuh
shops	obchodů	op·kho·doo
train station	železničního nádraží	zhe·lez·nyich·nyee·ho na·druh·zhee

What's the address?
Jaká je adresa?   yuh·ka ye uh·dre·suh

For responses, see **directions**, page 63.

local talk		
dive	*pelech* m	*pe*·lekh
rat-infested	*zavšivenej*	*zuhv*·shi·ve·ney
top spot	*nóbl hotel* m	*naw*·bl *ho*·tel

booking ahead & checking in

I'd like to book a room, please.
Chtěl/Chtěla bych   khtyel/*khtye*·luh bikh
rezervovat pokoj, prosím. m/f   re·zer·vo·vuht *po*·koy *pro*·seem

I have a reservation.
Mám rezervaci.   mam *re*·zer·vuh·tsi

My name's ...
Mé jméno je ...   mair *ymair*·no ye ...

For (three) nights/weeks.
Na (tři) noci/týdny.   nuh (trzhi) *no*·tsi/*teed*·ni

From (2 July) to (6 July).
Od (druhého července)   od (*dru*·hair·ho *cher*·ven·tse)
do (šestého července).   do (*shes*·tair·ho *cher*·ven·tse)

Do you have a double room?
Máte pokoj s manželskou   *ma*·te *po*·koy s muhn·zhels·koh
postelí?   *pos*·te·lee

Kolik nocí?	*ko·lik no·*tsee	**How many nights?**
doklad	*dok·*luhd	**identification**
totožnosti m	*to·*tozh·nos·tyi	
obsazeno	*op·*suh·ze·no	**full**
pas m	puhs	**passport**

Do you have a ... room?	*Máte ... pokoj?*	*ma·*te ... *po·*koy
single	*jednolůžkový*	*yed·*no·loozh·ko·vee
twin	*dvoulůžkový*	*dvoh·*loozh·ko·vee
How much is it per ...?	*Kolik to stojí ...?*	*ko·*lik to *sto·*yee ...
night	*na noc*	nuh nots
person	*za osobu*	zuh o·so·bu
week	*na týden*	nuh *tee·*den

Can I see it?
Mohu se na něj podívat? *mo·*hu se na nyey *po·*dyee·vuht

I'll take it.
Vezmu ho. *vez·*mu ho

Do I need to pay upfront?
Musím zaplatit dopředu? *mu·*seem *zuh·*pluh·tyit *dop·*rzhe·du

Can I pay by ...?	*Mohu zaplatit ...?*	*mo·*hu *zuh·*pluh·tyit ...
credit card	*kreditní kartou*	*kre·*dit·nyee *kuhr·*toh
travellers cheque	*cestovním šekem*	*tses·*tov·nyeem *she·*kem

For other methods of payment, see **money**, page 43, and **banking**, page 91.

Koupelna	*koh·pel·nuh*	**Bathroom**
Kuchyň	*ku·khin'*	**Kitchen**
Obsazeno	*ob·suh·ze·no*	**No Vacancy**
Prádlo	*prad·lo*	**Laundry**
Recepce	*re·tsep·tse*	**Reception**
Snídaně	*snyee·duh·nye*	**Breakfast**
Volné pokoje	*vol·nair po·ko·ye*	**Vacancy**
WC	*vair·tsair*	**Toilet**
Dámy/Ženy	*da·mi/zhe·ni*	**Women**
Páni/Muži	*pa·ni/mu·zhi*	**Men**

requests & queries

žádosti & dotazy

Is breakfast included?
Je to včetně snídaně?   ye to *fchet*·nye *snyee*·duh·nye

When is breakfast served?
V kolik se podává   f *ko*·lik se *po*·da·va
snídaně?   *snyee*·duh·nye

Where is breakfast served?
Kde se podává   gde se *po*·da·va
snídaně?   *snyee*·duh·nye

Is there hot water all day?
Teče teplá voda po   *te*·che *tep*·la *vo*·duh po
celý den?   *tse*·lee den

Please wake me at (seven).
Prosím probuďte mě   *pro*·seem *pro*·buď'·te mye
v (sedm).   f (*se*·dm)

Can I use the ...?	*Mohu použít ...?*	*mo*·hu *po*·u·zheet ...
kitchen	*kuchyň*	*ku*·khin'
laundry	*prádelnu*	*pra*·del·nu
telephone	*telefon*	*te*·le·fon

Do you have a/an ...?	Máte ...?	ma·te ...
elevator	výtah	vee·tah
laundry service	prádelní službu	pra·del·nyee sluzh·bu
message board	tabuly na vzkazy	tuh·bu·li nuh fskuh·zi
safe	trezor	tre·zor
swimming pool	bazén	buh·zairn

Could I have ..., please?	Můžete mi dát ..., prosím?	moo·zhe·te mi dat ... pro·seem
a receipt	stvrzenku	stvr·zen·ku
my key	můj klíč	mooy kleech

Do you arrange tours here?
Organizujete zde zájezdy? or·guh·ni·zu·ye·te zde za·yez·di

Do you change money here?
Měníte zde peníze? mye·nyee·te zde pe·nyee·ze

Is there a message for me?
Je tam pro mě vzkaz? ye tuhm pro mye fskuhz

Can I leave a message for someone?
Mohu nechat pro někoho vzkaz? mo·hu ne·khuht pro nye·ko·ho fskuhz

I'm locked out of my room.
Zaboúchl/Zaboúchla jsem si dveře. m/f zuh·boh·khl/zuh·boh·khluh ysem si dve·rzhe

---

listen for ...

klíč m	kleech	key
recepce f	re·tsep·tse	reception

accommodation

69

complaints

It's too …	Je moc …	ye mots …
bright	*světlý*	*svyet*·lee
cold	*studený*	*stu*·de·nee
dark	*tmavý*	*tmuh*·vee
expensive	*drahý*	*druh*·hee
noisy	*hlučný*	*hluch*·nee
small	*malý*	*muh*·lee

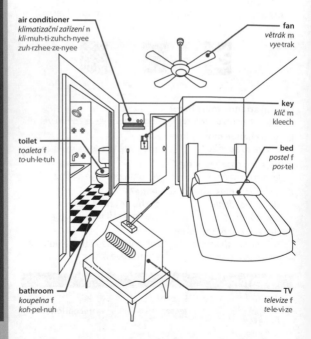

air conditioner
klimatizační zařízení n
kli·muh·ti·zuhch·nyee
zuh·rzhee·ze·nyee

fan
větrák m
vye·trak

key
klíč m
kleech

toilet
toaleta f
to·uh·le·tuh

bed
postel f
pos·tel

bathroom
koupelna f
koh·pel·nuh

TV
televize f
te·le·vi·ze

The ... doesn't work.	... nefunguje.	... ne·fun·gu·ye
air conditioner	Klimatizace	kli·muh·ti·zuh·tse
fan	Větrák	vye·trak
heater	Ohřívač	o·hrzhee·vuhch
toilet	Toaleta	to·uh·le·tuh

Can I get another (blanket)?
Mohu dostat další (deku)? — *mo·hu dos·tuht duhl·shee (de·ku)*

This (pillow) isn't clean.
Tento (polštář) neni čistý. — *ten·to (pol·shtarzh) ne·nyi chis·tee*

There's no hot water.
Neteče teplá voda. — *ne·te·che tep·la vo·duh*

---

a knock at the door ...

Who is it?	Kdo je to?	gdo ye to
Just a moment.	Počkejte chvíli.	poch·key·te khvee·li
Come in.	Vstupte.	vstup·te
Come back later, please.	Vraťte se později, prosím.	vruht'·te se poz·dye·yi pro·seem

---

checking out

What time is checkout?
V kolik hodin máme vyklidit pokoj? — *f ko·lik ho·dyin ma·me vi·kli·dyit po·koy*

Can I have a late checkout?
Můžem vyklidit pokoj později? — *moo·zhem vi·kli·dyit po·koy poz·dye·yi*

Can you call a taxi for me (for 11 o'clock)?
Můžete mi zavolat taxika (na jedenáctou hodinu)? — *moo·zhe·te mi zuh·vo·luht tuhk·si·kuh (nuh ye·de·nats·toh ho·dyi·nu)*

I'm leaving now.
    Teď odjíždím.   ted' *od*·yeezh·dyeem

Can I leave my bags here?
    Mohu si zde nechat   *mo*·hu si zde ne·khuht
    zavazadla?   zuh·vuh·zuhd·luh

There's a mistake in the bill.
    Na účtu je chyba.   nuh *ooch*·tu ye *khi*·buh

I had a great stay, thanks.
    Měl/Měla jsem   myel/*mye*·luh ysem
    báječný pobyt. m/f   ba·yech·nee po·bit

Could I have	*Můžete mi*	moo·zhe·te mi
my ..., please?	*vratit ..., prosím?*	*vra*·tyit ... pro·seem
deposit	*zálohu*	za·lo·hu
passport	*pas*	puhs
valuables	*cennosti*	*tse*·nos·tyi

I'll be back ...	*Vrátím se ...*	vra·tyeem se ...
in (three) days	*za (tři) dny*	zuh (trzhi) dni
on (Tuesday)	*v (úterý)*	f (oo·te·ree)

camping

táboření

Who do I ask to stay here?
    Koho se mám zde zeptat   ko·ho se mam zde zep·tuht
    na ubytování?   nuh u·bi·to·va·nyee

Can I ...?	*Mohu ...?*	mo·hu ...
camp here	*zde stanovat*	zde stuh·no·vuht
park next to	*parkovat*	puhr·ko·vuht
my tent	*vedle mého*	ved·le mair·ho
	stanu	stuh·nu

How much is it per …?	Kolik to stojí …?	ko·lik to sto·yee …
caravan	za karavan	zuh kuh·ruh·vuhn
person	na osobu	nuh o·so·bu
tent	za stan	zuh stuhn
vehicle	za vůz	zuh vooz

Do you have …?	Máte …?	ma·te …
a laundry	prádelnu	pra·del·nu
a site	místo na stanování	mees·to nuh stuh·no·va·nyee
electricity	elektrický proud	e·lek·trits·kee prohd
shower facilities	sprchové zařízení	spr·kho·vair zuh·rzhee·ze·nyee
tents for hire	stany na pronajmutí	stuh·ni nuh pro·nai·mu·tyee

Is it coin-operated?
Je to automat na mince?　　ye to ow·to·muht nuh min·tse

Is the water drinkable?
Je ta voda pitná?　　ye tuh vo·duh pit·na

Could I borrow …?
Mohu si půjčit …?　　mo·hu si pooy·chit …

renting

Do you have a/an … for rent?	Pronajímáte …?	pro·na·yee·ma·te …
cabin	chatu	khuh·tu
house	dům	doom
room	pokoj	po·koy
villa	vilu	vi·lu

I'm here about the (apartment) for rent.
Přišel/Přišla jsem　　przhi·shel/przhi·shluh ysem
ohledně pronájmu　　o·hled·nye pro·nai·mu
(bytu). m/f　　(bi·tu)

Is there a bond?	Platí se záloha?	pluh·tyee se za·lo·huh
Are bills extra?	Jsou účty zvlášť?	ysoh ooch·ti zvlasht'
furnished	zařízený	zuh·rzhee·ze·nee
partly	částečně	chas·tech·nye
furnished	zařízený	zuh·rzhee·ze·nee
unfurnished	nezařízený	ne·zuh·rzhee·ze·nee

staying with locals

Czechs are traditionally polite and conservative people. You'll be expected to use the formal 'you' form (vy vi) when addressing your hosts, unless you're told otherwise. As hosts, Czechs are very generous and will ply you with food and drink – it's polite to consume a lot to show them that you really enjoy it.

Can I stay at your place?
   Mohu u vás zůstat?　　mo·hu u vas zoos·tuht

Is there anything I can do to help?
   Mohu s něčím pomoci?　mo·hu s nye·cheem po·mo·tsi

I have my own ...	Mám ...	mam ...
mattress	svoji matraci	svo·yi muh·truh·tsi
sleeping bag	svuj spací	svuy spuh·tsee
	pytel	pi·tel

Can I ...?	Mohu ...?	mo·hu ...
bring anything	přinést něco	przhi·nairst nye·tso
for the meal	k jídlu	k yeed·lu
do the dishes	umýt nádobí	u·meet na·do·bee
set/clear the	prostřít/	prost·rzheet/
table	uklidit stůl	u·kli·dyit stool
take out the	vynést odpadky	vi·nairst ot·puht·ki
rubbish		

Thanks for your hospitality.
   Děkuji za pohoštění.　　dye·ku·yi zuh po·hosh·tye·nyee

To compliment your hosts' cooking, see **eating out**, page 166.

PRACTICAL

looking for ...

Are shops open on (Czechoslovakian Foundation Day)?
Jsou obchody otevřené   ysoh *op*·kho·di *o*·tev·rzhe·nair
na (Den vzniku   na (den *vzny*i·ku
Československa)?   *ches*·ko·slo·vens·kuh)

What hours are the shops open?
Jaká je otvírací   *yuh*·ka ye *ot*·vee·ruh·tsee
doba obchodů?   *do*·buh *ob*·kho·doo

Where can I buy (a padlock)?
Kde si mohu koupit   gde si *mo*·hu *koh*·pit
(zámek)?   (*za*·mek)

Where's a ...?	*Kde je ...?*	gde ye ...
convenience store	*večerka*	*ve*·cher·kuh
grocery store	*konzum*	*kon*·zum
department store	*obchodní dům*	*op*·khod·nyee doom
market	*tržnice*	*trzh*·nyi·tse
shopping centre	*nákupní centrum*	*na*·kup·nyee *tsen*·trum
souvenir shop	*obchod se suvenýry*	*op*·khod se *su*·ve·nee·ri
supermarket	*samoobsluha*	*suh*·mo·op·slu·huh

For more items and shopping locations, see the **dictionary**.

making a purchase

I'm just looking.
Jenom se dívám.   *ye*·nom se *dyee*·vam

I'd like to buy (an adaptor plug).
Chtěl/Chtěla bych koupit   khtyel/*khtye*·la bikh *koh*·pit
(adapter do zásuvky). m/f   (*uh*·duhp·ter do *za*·suf·ki)

How much is it?
Kolik to stojí?   *ko*·lik to *sto*·yee

Can you write down the price?
Můžete mi napsat cenu?   moo·zhe·te mi *nuhp*·suht *tse*·nu

Do you have any others?
Máte ještě jiné?   ma·te *yesh*·tye *yi*·nair

Can I look at it?
Mohu se na to podívat?   *mo*·hu se nuh to *po*·dyee·vuht

Is this (240) volts?
Má to (dvěstě čtyřicet)   ma to (*dvye*·stye *chti*·rzhi·tset)
voltů?   *vol*·too

Do you accept …?	*Mohu platit …?*	*mo*·hu *pluh*·tyit …
credit cards	*kreditními kartami*	*kre*·dit·nyee·mi *kuhr*·tuh·mi
debit cards	*platebními kartami*	*pluh*·teb·nyee·mi *kuhr*·tuh·mi
travellers cheques	*cestovními šeky*	*tses*·tov·nyee·mi *she*·ki
Could I have a …, please?	*Můžete mi dát …, prosím?*	moo·zhe·te mi dat … *pro*·seem
bag	*tašku*	*tuhsh*·ku
receipt	*účet*	*oo*·chet

PRACTICAL

I don't need a bag, thanks.
Nepotřebuji tašku,
děkuji.
ne·pot·rzhe·bu·yi *tuhsh*·ku
dye·ku·yi

Could I have it wrapped?
Můžete mi to zabalit?
moo·zhe·te mi to *zuh*·buh·lit

Could I get a Tax-Free shopping voucher?
Mohu dostat Tax Free
poukázku?
mo·hu dos·tuht *taks*·free
poh·kaz·ku

Does it have a guarantee?
Je na to záruka?
ye nuh to *za*·ru·kuh

Can I have it sent abroad?
Můžete mi to poslat
do zahraničí?
moo·zhe·te mi to *pos*·luht
do zuh·hruh·nyi·chee

Can you order it for me?
Můžete to pro mě
objednat?
moo·zhe·te to pro mye
ob·yed·nuht

Can I pick it up later?
Mohu si to vyzvednout
později?
mo·hu si to *viz*·ved·noht
poz·dye·yi

The quality isn't good.
Není to kvalitní.
ne·nyi to *kvuh*·lit·nyee

It's faulty.
Je to vadné.
ye to *vuhd*·nair

**I'd like …,
please.**
   a refund
   my change
   to return this

Chtěl/Chtěla bych
…, prosím. m/f
   vrátit peníze
   mé drobné
   toto vrátit

khtyel/*khtye*·la bikh
… pro·seem
   vra·tyit pe·nyee·ze
   mair *drob*·nair
   to·to vra·tyit

local talk		
bargain	výhodná cena f	vee·hod·na tse·nuh
rip-off	zloděina f	zlo·dyey·nuh
sale	výprodej f	vee·pro·dey
specials	slevy f pl	sle·vi

bargaining

That's too expensive.
To je moc drahé.   to ye mots *druh*·hair

Can you lower the price?
Můžete mi snížit cenu?   moo·zhe·te mi *snyee*·zhit *tse*·nu

Do you have something cheaper?
Máte něco levnějšího?   ma·te *nye*·tso *lev*·nyey·shee·ho

What's your final price?
Jaká je vaše konečná   yuh·ka ye *vuh*·she ko·nech·na
cena?   tse·nuh

I'll give you (200 crowns).
Dám vám (dvěstě korun).   dam vam (*dvye*·stye *ko*·run)

books & reading

Is there an (English)-language …?	*Je tam … s (anglickýma) knihama?*	ye tuhm … s (*uhn*·glits·kee·muh) *knyi*·huh·muh
bookshop section	*knihkupectví sekce*	*knyih*·ku·pets·tvee *sek*·tse
Do you have …?	*Máte …?*	ma·te …
a book by (Milan Kundera)	*knihu od (Milana Kundery)*	*knyi*·hu od (*mi*·luh·nuh *kun*·de·ri)
an entertainment guide	*přehled kulturních pořadů*	*przhe*·hled *kul*·tur·nyeekh *po*·rzhuh·doo

PRACTICAL

I'd like a ...	Chtěl/Chtěla bych ... m/f	khtyel/khtye·luh bikh ...
dictionary	slovník	slov·nyeek
newspaper	noviny	no·vi·ni
(in English)	(v angličtině)	(f uhn·glich·tyi·nye)
notepad	blok	blok

Can you recommend a book for me?
Můžete mi doporučit knihu? — moo·zhe·te mi do·po·ru·chit knyi·hu

Do you have Lonely Planet guidebooks?
Máte Lonely Planet průvodce? — ma·te loh·ne·li pluh·net proo·vod·tse

listen for ...

Mohu vám pomoci? mo·hu vam po·mo·tsi	**Can I help you?**
Přejete si ještě něco? przhe·ye·te si yesh·tye nye·tso	**Anything else?**
Ne, nemáme žádné. ne ne·ma·me zhad·nair	**No, we don't have any.**

clothes

oblečení

My size is ...	Mám ... velikost.	mam ... ve·li·kost
small	malou	muh·loh
medium	střední	strzhed·nyee
large	velikou	ve·li·koh

My size is (40).
Mám číslo (čtyřicet). — mam chee·slo (chti·rzhl·tset)

Can I try it on?
Mohu si to zkusit? — mo·hu si to sku·sit

It doesn't fit.
Nepadne mi to. — ne·puhd·ne mi to

hairdressing

I'd like (a) …	Chtěl/Chtěla bych … m/f	khtyel/khtye·luh bikh …
colour	odbarvit	od·buhr·vit
foils/streaks	melírovat	me·lee·ro·vuht
haircut	ostříhat	ost·rzhee·huht
	vlasy	vluh·si
my beard	zastřihnout	zuhst·rzhih·noht
trimmed	plnovous	pl·no·vohs
my hair washed/	umýt/usušit	u·meet/u·su·shit
dried	vlasy	vluh·si
shave	oholit	o·ho·lit
trim	kaskádový	kuhs·ka·do·vee
	sestřih	sest·rzhih

Don't cut it too short.
Nestříhejte mi to
příliš na krátko.
nest·rzhee·hey·te mi to
przhee·lish nuh krat·ko

Please use a new blade.
Můžete prosím
použít novou žiletku.
moo·zhe·te pro·seem
po·u·zheet no·voh zhi·let·ku

Shave it all off!
Oholte vše!
o·hol·te vshe

I don't like this!
Nelíbí se mi to!
ne·lee·bee se mi to

I love it!
Je to úžasné!
ye to oo·zhuhs·nair

I should never have let you near me!
Nikdy jsem se neměl/
neměla nechat zde
ostříhat! m/f
nyik·di ysem se ne·myel/
ne·mye·luh ne·khuht zde
ost·rzhee·huht

music & DVD

I'd like a …	Chtěl/Chtěla bych … m/f	khtyel/khtye·luh bikh …
blank tape	prázdnou pásku	prazd·noh pas·ku
CD	CD	tsair·dairch·ko
DVD	DVD	dee·vee·deech·ko
video	video	vi·de·o

I'm looking for something by (Kabát).
Hledám něco od (Kabátu). hle·dam nye·tso od (kuh·ba·tu)

What's their best recording?
Jakou mají nejlepší nahrávku? yuh·koh muh·yee ney·lep·shee nuh·hraf·ku

Will this work on any DVD player?
Bude to hrát na jakýmkoliv DVD přehrávači? bu·de to hrat nuh yuh·keem·ko·liv dee·vee·dee przhe·hra·vuh·chi

Is this for a (PAL/NTSC) system?
Má to (PAL/NTSC) systém? ma to (puhl/en·tair·es·tsair) sis·tairm

video & photography

I need a/an …	Potřebuji …	pot·rzhe·bu·yi …
film for this camera.	film pro tento fotoaparát.	film pro ten·to fo·to·uh·puh·rat
APS	APS	a·pair·es
B&W	černobílý	cher·no·bee·lee
colour	barevný	buh·rev·nee
slide	diapozitivní	di·uh·po·zi·tiv·nye
(200) speed	film s citlivostí (dvěstě)	film s tsit·li·vos·tyee (dvye·stye)

Can you …?	Můžete …?	moo·zhe·te …
develop digital photos	vyvolat digitální fotografie	vi·vo·luht di·gi·tal·nyee fo·to·gruh·fi·ye
develop this film	vyvolat tento film	vi·vo·luht ten·to film
load my film	vložit můj film	vlo·zhit mooy film
recharge the battery for my digital camera	nabít baterii do mého digitálního fotoaparátu	nuh·beet buh·te·ri·i do mair·ho di·gi·tal·nyee·ho fo·to·uh·puh·ra·tu
transfer photos from my camera to CD	uložit fotografie z mého fotoaparátu na CD	u·lo·zhit fo·to·gruh·fi·ye z mair·ho fo·to·uh·puh·ra·tu nuh tsair·dairch·ko

Do you have (a) … for this camera?	Máte … do tohoto fotoaparátu?	ma·te … do to·ho·to fo·to·uh·puh·ra·tu
batteries	baterie	buh·te·ri·ye
flash	blesk	blesk
flash bulb	žárovku na blesk	zha·rof·ku nuh blesk
(zoom) lens	(zoomový) objektiv	(zoo·mo·vee) ob·yek·tif
light meter	expozimetr	eks·po·zi·me·tr
memory cards	paměťovou kartu	puh·mye·tyo·voh kuhr·tu
… camera	… fotoaparát m	… fo·to·uh·puh·rat
digital	digitální	di·gi·tal·nyee
disposable	jednorázový	yed·no·ra·zo·vee
underwater	podvodní	pod·vod·nyee

I need a cable to connect my camera to a computer.

Potřebuji kabel na	pot·rzhe·bu·yi kuh·bel nuh
připojení fotoaparátu	przhi·po·ye·nyee fo·to·uh·puh·ra·tu
k počítači.	k po·chee·tuh·chi

I need a cable to recharge this battery.

Potřebuji kabel na	pot·rzhe·bu·yi kuh·bel nuh
nabití této baterie.	nuh·bi·tyee tair·to buh·te·ri·ye

I need a video cassette for this camera.

Potřebuji videokazetu	pot·rzhe·bu·yi vi·de·o·kuh·ze·tu
pro tuto kameru.	pro tu·to kuh·me·ru

souvenirs

antiques	starožitnictví n pl	stuh·ro·zhit·nyits·tvee
classical music CDs	CD	tsair·dairch·ka
	s klasickou	s kluh·sits·koh
	hudbou n pl	hud·boh
crystal	křišťál m	krzhish·tyal
decorated Easter eggs	zdobená	zdo·be·na
	velikonoční	ve·li·ko·noch·nyee
	vajíčka f pl	vuh·yeech·kuh
folk decorated ceramics	malovaná	muh·lo·vuh·na
	lidová	li·do·va
	keramika f	ke·ruh·mi·kuh
folk wooden tools	dřevěné	drzhe·vye·nair
	nástroje	na·stro·ye
	lidových	li·do·veekh
	řemesel n pl	rzhe·me·sel
garnets	granáty m pl	gruh·na·ti
glassware	sklo n	sklo
lace	krajka f	krai·kuh
'onion' porcelain	cibulový	tsi·bu·lo·vee
	porcelán m	por·tse·lan
puppets	loutky f pl	loht·ki
second-hand books	antikvární	uhn·tik·var·nyee
	knihy f pl	knyi·hi
wooden toys	dřevěné	drzhe·vye·nair
	hračky f pl	hruhch·ki

When will it be ready?
   Kdy to bude hotové?   gdi to *bu*·de *ho*·to·vair

How much is it?
   Kolik to stojí?   *ko*·lik to *sto*·yee

I need a passport photo taken.
   Potřebuji fotografii   pot·rzhe·bu·yi *fo*·to·gruh·fi·i
   na pas.   nuh puhs

I'm not happy with these photos.
   Nejsem spokojený/á   *ney*·sem *spo*·ko·ye·nee/a
   s těmito fotkami. m/f   s *tye*·mi·to *fot*·kuh·mi

I don't want to pay the full price.
   Nechci platit plnou cenu.   *nekh*·tsi *pluh*·tyit *pl*·noh *tse*·nu

repairs

Can I have my … repaired here?	*Můžete zde opravit … ?*	*moo*·zhe·te zde *o*·pruh·vit …
backpack	*můj batoh*	mooy *buh*·tawh
bag	*moji tašku*	*mo*·yi *tuhsh*·ku
(video)camera	*moji (video) kameru*	*mo*·yi (*vi*·de·o) *kuh*·me·ru
(sun)glasses	*mé (slunečné) brýle*	mair (*slu*·nech·nair) *bree*·le
rucksack	*můj ruksak*	mooy *ruk*·suhk
shoes	*mé boty*	mair *bo*·ti

When will it be repaired?
   Kdy to bude opravené?   gdi to *bu*·de *o*·pruh·ve·nair

who's talking?

Masculine and feminine markers (m and f) in our phrases always refer to the subject of a sentence – in the phrase *Chtěl/Chtěla bych …* m/f khtyel/*khtye*·luh bikh … (I'd like …) the m/f refers to the gender of the speaker.

the internet

internet

Where's the local Internet café?
Kde je místní   gde ye *meest*·nyee
internetová kavárna?   in·ter·ne·to·va *kuh*·var·nuh

Do you have public Internet access here?
Máte zde přístup na   ma·te zde *przhee*·stup nuh
internet pro veřejnost?   in·ter·net pro ve·*rzhey*·nost

I'd like to …	*Chtěl/Chtěla*	khtyel/*khtye*·luh
	bych … m/f	bikh …
burn a CD	*vypálit CD*	vi·pa·lit
		tsair·dairch·ko
check my	*zkontrolovat*	skon·tro·lo·vuht
email	*můj email*	mooy *ee*·meyl
download my	*přesunout si*	*przhe*·su·noht si
photos	*mé fotografie*	mair fo·to·gruh·fi·e
get Internet	*přístup na*	*przhees*·tup nuh
access	*internet*	in·ter·net
use a printer	*použít*	po·u·zheet
	tiskárnu	*tyis*·kar·nu
use a scanner	*použít skener*	po·u·zheet *ske*·ner
Do you have …?	*Máte …?*	ma·te …
Macs	*Mackintoshe*	muh·kin·to·she
PCs	*osobní*	o·sob·nyee
	počítače	po·chee·tuh·che
a Zip drive	*ZIP mechaniku*	zip me·khuh·ni·ku

Can I connect my ... to this computer?	Mohu si připojit ... k tomuto počítači?	mo·hu si przhi·po·yit ... k to·mu·to po·chee·tuh·chi
camera	fotoaparát	fo·to·uh·puh·rat
media player	multimediální přehrávač	mul·ti·me·di·al·nyee przhe·hra·vuhch
portable hard drive	přenosný pevný disk	przhe·nos·nee pev·nee disk
USB drive	USB paměť	u·es·bair puh·myet'

How much per ...?	Kolik to stojí ...?	ko·lik to sto·yee ...
hour	na hodinu	nuh ho·dyi·nu
(five) minutes	na (pět) minut	nuh (pyet) mi·nut
page	za stránku	zuh stran·ku

How do I log on?

Jak se přihlásim? yuhk se przhi·hla·sim

Please change it to the (English)-language setting.

Prosím vás změňte nastavení na (angličtinu). pro·seem vas zmyen'·te nuh·stuh·ve·nyee nuh (uhn·glich·tyi·nu)

It's crashed.

Zhroutil se. zhroh·tyil se

I've finished.

Skončil/Skončila jsem. m/f skon·chil/skon·chi·luh ysem

phone code

In Czech, phone numbers are usually read in pairs – eg '246 576 821' is read as *dvacet čtyři, šedesát pět, sedmdesát šest, osmdesát dva, jedna* dvuh·tset chti·rzhi she·de·sat pyet se·dm·de·sat shest o·sm·de·sat dvuh yed·nuh (twenty-four, sixty-five, seventy-six, eighty-two, one).

mobile/cell phone

I'd like a …	*Chtěl/Chtěla*	ktyel/*khtye*·luh
	bych … m/f	bikh …
charger for	*nabíječku*	*nuh*·bee·yech·ku
my phone	*pro můj mobil*	pro mooy *mo*·bil
mobile/cell	*si půjčit mobil*	si *pooy*·chit *mo*·bil
phone for hire		
prepaid mobile/	*předplacenou*	*przhed*·pluh·tse·noh
cell phone	*mobil sadu*	*mo*·bil *suh*·du
SIM card for	*SIM kartu pro*	sim *kuhr*·tu pro
your network	*vaší síť*	*vuh*·shee seet'

What are the rates?
Jaké jsou tarify? yuh·kair ysoh *tuh*·ri·fi

(Seven crowns) per minute.
(Sedm korun) za (*se*·dm *ko*·run) zuh
jednu minutu. *yed*·nu *mi*·nu·tu

phone

What's your phone number?
Jaké je vaše yuh·kair ye *vuh*·she
telefonní číslo? te·le·fo·nyee *chees*·lo

Where's the nearest public phone?
Kde je nejbližší gde ye *ney*·blizh·shee
veřejný telefon? ve·rzhey·nee te·le·fon

Can I look at a phone book?
Mohu se podívat do *mo*·hu se po·dyee·vuht do
telefonního seznamu? te·le·fo·nyee·ho *sez*·nuh·mu

Can I have some coins/tokens?
Mohu dostat nějaké *mo*·hu *dos*·tuht nye·yuh·kair
mince/žetony? *min*·tse/zhe·to·ni

I want to …	Chtěl/Chtěla bych … m/f	ktyel/khtye·luh bikh …
buy a phonecard	koupit telefonní kartu	koh·pit te·le·fo·nyee kuhr·tu
call (Singapore)	telefonovat do (Singapůru)	te·le·fo·no·vuht do (sin·guh·poo·ru)
make a (local) call	si zavolat (místně)	si zuh·vo·luht (meest·nye)
reverse the charges	telefonovat na účet volaného	te·le·fo·no·vuht na oo·chet vo·luh·nair·ho
speak for (three) minutes	mluvit (tři) minuty	mlu·vit (trzhi) mi·nu·ti

How much does … cost?	Kolik stojí …?	ko·lik sto·yee …
a (three)-minute call	(tří) minutový hovor	(trzhee) mi·nu·to·vee ho·vor
each extra minute	každá další minuta	kuhzh·da duhl·shee mi·nu·tuh

What's the country code for (New Zealand)?

Jaké je národní směrové číslo (Nového Zélandu)?	yuh·kair ye na·rod·nyee smye·ro·vair chees·lo (no·vair·ho zair·luhn·du)

The number is …

Číslo je …	chees·lo ye …

It's engaged.

Je obsazeno.	ye op·suh·ze·no

I've been cut off.

Byl/Byla jsem přerušen/ přerušena. m/f	bil/bi·luh ysem przhe·ru·shen/ przhe·ru·she·nuh

The connection's bad.

Spojení je špatné.	spo·ye·nyee ye shpuht·nair

Hello.
Haló.   huh·law

Can I speak to (Mr Novák)?
Mohu mluvit s   mo·hu mlu·vit s
(panem Novákem)?   (puh·nem no·va·kem)

It's …
To je …   to ye …

My number is …
Mé telefonní číslo je …   mair te·le·fo·nyee chees·lo ye …

I don't have a contact number.
Nemám telefonní číslo.   ne·mam te·le·fo·nyee chees·lo

I'll call back later.
Zavolám později.   zuh·vo·lam poz·dye·yi

What time should I call?
V kolik hodin mám zavolat?   f ko·lik ho·dyin mam zuh·vo·luht

Can I leave a message?
Mohu nechat vzkaz?   mo·hu ne·khuht vskuhz

Please tell him/her I called. (said by a man)
Prosím sdělte jemu/jí   pro·seem sdyel·te ye·mu/yee
že jsem telefonoval.   zhe ysem te·le·fo·no·vuhl

Please tell him/her I called. (said by a woman)
Prosím sdělte jemu/jí   pro·seem sdyel·te ye·mu/yee
že jsem telefonovala.   zhe ysem te·le·fo·no·vuh·luh

For telephone numbers, see **numbers & amounts**, page 33.

---

listen for …

Kdo volá?		
gdo vo·la	**Who's calling?**	
S kým chcete mluvit?		
s keem khtse·te mlu·vit	**Who do you want to speak to?**	
Špatné číslo.		
shpuht·nair chees·lo	**Wrong number.**	
On/Ona tady není.		
on/o·nuh tuh·di ne·nyee	**He/She isn't here.**	

communications

post office

I want to send a ...	Chci poslat ...	khtsi po·sluht ...
letter	dopis	do·pis
parcel	balík	buh·leek
postcard	pohled	po·hled

I want to buy a/an ...	Chci koupit ...	khtsi koh·pit ...
aerogram	aerogram	uh·e·ro·gruhm
envelope	obálku	o·bal·ku
stamp	známku	znam·ku

customs declaration	celní prohláška f	tsel·nyee pro·hlash·kuh
mailbox	poštovní schránka f	posh·tov·nyee skhran·kuh
PO box	poštovní přihrádka f	posh·tov·nyee przhi·hrad·kuh
postcode	poštovní směrovací číslo n	posh·tov·nyee smye·ro·vuh·tsee chees·lo

Please send it by air/surface mail to (Australia).

Prosím vás pošlete to letecky/obyčejnou poštou do (Austrálie).

pro·seem vas po·shle·te to le·tets·ki/o·bi·chey·noh posh·toh do (ow·stra·li·ye)

Where's the poste restante section?

Kde je poste restante?   gde ye pos·te res·tuhn·te

snail mail		
by ... mail	... poštou	... posh·toh
express	expresní	eks·pres·nyee
registered	doporučenou	do·po·ru·che·noh
sea	lodní	lod·nyee
surface	obyčejnou	o·bi·chey·noh
by airmail	leteckou poštou	le·tets·koh posh·toh

What times/days is the bank open?

Jaké jsou úřední   yuh·kair ysoh *oo*·rzhed·nyee
hodiny/dny?   ho·dyi·ni/dni

Where can I …?	*Kde mohu …?*	gde *mo*·hu …
I'd like to …	*Chtěl/Chtěla bych … m/f*	kthyel/*khtye*·luh bikh …
cash a cheque	*proměnit šek*	pro·*mye*·nyit shek
change a travellers cheque	*proměnit cestovní šek*	pro·*mye*·nyit tses·tov·nyee shek
change money	*vyměnit peníze*	*vi*·mye·nyit pe·nyee·ze
get a cash advance	*zálohu v hotovosti*	za·lo·hu v ho·to·vos·tyi
get change for this note	*drobné za tuto bankovku*	drob·nair zuh tu·to *buhn*·kof·ku
transfer money	*převést peníze*	*przhe*·vairst pe·nyee·ze
withdraw money	*vybrat peníze*	*vi*·bruht pe·nyee·ze

What's the …?	*Jaký je …?*	yuh·kee ye …
charge for that	*poplatek za to*	po·pluh·tek zuh to
exchange rate	*devizový kurz*	de·vi·zo·vee kurz
Where's …?	*Kde je …?*	gde ye …
an ATM	*bankomat*	*buhn*·ko·muht
a foreign exchange office	*směnárna*	*smye*·nar·nuh

The ATM took my card.

Bankomat mi
nevrátil kartu.

buhn·ko·muht mi
ne·vra·tyil kuhr·tu

I've forgotten my PIN.

Zapomněl/Zapomněla
jsem svůj PIN. m/f

zuh·pom·nyel/zuh·pom·nye·luh
ysem svooy pin

Can I use my credit card to withdraw money?

Mohu si vybrat peníze
z mé kreditní karty?

mo·hu si vi·bruht pe·nyee·ze
s mair kre·dit·nyee kuhr·ti

Has my money arrived yet?

Přišly už moje peníze?

przhi·shli uzh mo·ye pe·nyee·ze

How long will it take to arrive?

Jak dlouho bude trvat
než přijdou?

yuhk dloh·ho bu·de tr·vuht
nezh przhiy·doh

---

listen for ...

občanský	*ob·chuhn·skee*	**identification**
průkaz m	*proo·kuhz*	
pas m	*puhs*	**passport**

Máme problém.
  ma·me prob·lairm — **There's a problem.**

Nezbývají vám finanční prostředky.
  nez·bee·vuh·yee vam
  fi·nuhn·chnyee prost·rzhed·ki — **You have no funds left.**

Nemůžeme to udělat.
  ne·moo·zhe·me to u·dye·luht — **We can't do that.**

Podepište se zde.
  po·de·pish·te se zde — **Sign here.**

For other useful phrases, see **money**, page 43.

PRACTICAL

I'd like a/an ...	Chtěl/Chtěla bych ... m/f	khtyel/khtye·luh bikh ...
audio set	audio guide	ow·di·o gaid
catalogue	katalog	kuh·tuh·log
guide	průvodce	proo·vod·tse
(in English)	(v angličtině)	(f uhn·glich·tyi·nye)
(local) map	mapu (okolí)	ma·pu (o·ko·lee)
Do you have information on ... sights?	Máte informace o ... pamětihod- nostech?	ma·te in·for·muh·tse o ... puh·mye·ti·hod· nos·tekh
cultural	kulturních	kul·tur·nyeekh
historical	historických	his·to·rits·keekh
religious	náboženských	na·bo·zhens·keekh

I'd like to see ...
*Chtěl/Chtěla bych
vidět ... m/f*
khtyel/khtye·luh bikh
vi·dyet ...

What's that?
Co je to?
tso ye to

Who built it?
Kdo to nechal postavit?
kdo to ne·khuhl pos·tuh·vit

Who made it?
Kdo to stvořil?
kdo to stvo·rzhil

How old is it?
Jak je to staré?
yuhk ye to stuh·rair

Could you take a photo of me/us?
Můžete mě/nás vyfotit? moo·zhe·te mye/nas vi·fo·tyit

Can I take a photo of this?
Mohu toto fotografovat? mo·hu to·to fo·to·gruh·fo·vuht

Can I take a photo of you?
Mohu si vás vyfotit? mo·hu si vas vi·fo·tyit

I'll send you the photo.
Pošlu vám fotografii. posh·lu vam fo·to·gruh·fi·i

getting in

navštěvování

What time does it open/close?
V kolik hodin otevírají/ f ko·lik ho·dyin o·te·vee·ruh·yee/
zavírají? zuh·vee·ruh·yee

What's the admission charge?
Kolik stojí vstupné? ko·lik sto·yee vstup·nair

Is there a discount	*Máte slevu*	ma·te sle·vu
for …?	*pro …?*	pro …
children	*děti*	dye·tyi
families	*rodiny*	ro·dyi·ni
groups	*skupiny*	sku·pi·ni
older people	*starší lidi*	stuhr·shee li·dyi
pensioners	*důchodce*	doo·khod·tse
students	*studenty*	stu·den·ti

tours

okružní jízdy

Can you recommend a sightseeing tour?
Můžete mi doporučit moo·zhe·te mi do·po·ru·chit
okružní jízdu po o·kruzh·nyee yeez·du po
pamětihodnostech? puh·mye·tyi·hod·nos·tekh

When's the	Kdy je	gdi ye
next …?	příští …?	przheesh·tyee …
boat trip	projížďka	pro·yeezhd'·kuh
	lodí	lo·dyee
day trip	celodenní	tse·lo·de·nyee
	výlet	vee·let
(sightseeing)	okružní	o·kruzh·nyee
tour	jízda (po	yeez·duh (po
	pamětihod-	puh·mye·tyi·hod·
	nostech)	nos·tekh)
Is … included?	Je zahrnuto/a …? n/f	ye zuh·hr·nu·to/uh …
accommodation	ubytování n	u·bi·to·va·nyee
admission	vstupné n	fstup·nair
food	strava f	struh·vuh
transport	doprava f	do·pruh·vuh

The guide will pay.
Průvodce zaplatí. proo·vod·tse zuh·pluh·tyee

The guide has paid.
Průvodce zaplatil. proo·vod·tse zuh·pluh·tyil

How long is the tour?
Jak dlouho bude yuhk dloh·ho bu·de
trvat tento zájezd? tr·vuht ten·to za·yezd

What time should we be back?
V kolik hodin se máme f ko·lik ho·dyin se ma·me
vrátit? vra·tyit

I'm with them.
Jsem s nimi. ysem s nyi·mi

I've lost my group.
Ztratil/Ztratila jsem se struh·tyil/struh·tyi·luh ysem se
mojí skupině. m/f mo·yee sku·pi·nye

signs

Informace	*in*·for·muh·tse	**Information**
Otevřeno	*o*·tev·rzhe·no	**Open**
Studené	*stu*·de·nair	**Cold**
Teplé	*tep*·lair	**Hot**
Toalety/WC	to·uh·*le*·ti/*vair*·tsair	**Toilet**
Dámy/Ženy	*da*·mi/*zhe*·ni	**Women**
Páni/Muži	*pa*·ni/*mu*·zhi	**Men**
Vjezd	vyezd	**Entrance**
Východ	*vee*·khod	**Exit**
Zákazáno	*za*·kuh·za·no	**Prohibited**
Zákaz	*za*·kuhz	**No Smoking**
kouření	*koh*·rzhe·nyee	
Zákaz	*za*·kuhz	**No Photography**
fotografování	fo·to·gruh·fo·va·nyee	
Zavřeno	*zuh*·vrzhe·no	**Closed**

doing business

I'm attending a ...	Jsem účastníkem ...	ysem oo·chuhst·nyee·kem ...
conference	konference	kon·fe·ren·tse
course	kursu	kur·su
meeting	schůze	skhoo·ze
trade fair	veletrhu	ve·le·tr·hu

I'm with ...	Jsem ...	ysem ...
my colleague	s kolegou	s ko·le·goh
my colleagues	s kolegi	s ko·le·gi
(Papírny Vetřní)	z (Papírny Vetřní)	z (puh·peer·ni vetrzh·nyee)
the others	s ostatními	s os·tuht·nyee·mi

I'm alone.
Jsem sám/sama. **m/f**   ysem sam/*suh*·muh

I have an appointment with ...
Mám schůzku s ...   mam *skhooz*·ku s ...

I'm staying at the (Hotel u Medvídků), room (205).
Jsem ubytovaný/á v (Hotelu u Medvídků), pokoj (dvěstě pět). **m/f**   ysem u·bi·to·vuh·nee/a v (ho·te·lu u med·veed·koo), po·koy (dvyes·tye pyet)

I'm here for (two) days/weeks.
Jsem zde na (dva) dny/týdny.   ysem zde nuh (dvuh) dni/teed·ni

Can I please have your business card?
Můžete mě prosím dát vaší vizitku?   moo·zhe·te mye pro·seem dat vuh·shee vi·zit·ku

Here's my business card.
Tady je má visitka.   tuh·di ye ma vi·sit·kuh

Here's my ...	*Zde je moje ...*	zde ye *mo*·ye ...
What's your ...?	*Jaké/Jaká je*	yuh·kair/yuh·ka ye
	vaše ...? n/f	*vuh*·she ...
(email) address	*(email)*	(*ee*·meyl)
	adresa f	*uh*·dre·suh
mobile/cell	*číslo mobilu* n	*chees*·lo *mo*·bi·lu
number		
fax number	*faxové*	*fuhk*·so·vair
	číslo n	*chees*·lo
phone number	*telefonní*	te·le·fo·nyee
	číslo n	*chees*·lo
work number	*číslo do*	*chees*·lo do
	kanceláře n	*kuhn*·tse·la·rzhe
Where's the ...?	*Kde je ...?*	gde ye ...
business centre	*kongresový sál*	*kon*·gre·so·vee sal
conference	*konference*	*kon*·fe·ren·tse
meeting	*schůze*	*skhoo*·ze
I need ...	*Potřebuji ...*	*pot*·rzhe·bu·yi ...
a computer	*počítač*	*po*·chee·tuhch
an Internet	*připojení*	*przhi*·po·ye·nyee
connection	*na internet*	nuh *in*·ter·net
an interpreter	*(anglicko)*	(*uhn*·glits·ko)
who speaks	*mluvícího*	mlu·vee·tsee·ho
(English)	*tlumočníka*	tlu·moch·nyee·kuh
more business	*více vizitek*	*vee*·tse *vi*·zi·tek
cards		
space to set up	*místo pro své*	*mees*·to pro svair
	věci	*vye*·tsi
to send a fax	*poslat fax*	*po*·sluht fuhks

That went very well.
To vyšlo výborně. to *vish*·lo *vee*·bor·nye

Thank you for your time.
Děkuji za vaší *dye*·ku·yi zuh *vuh*·shee
pozornost. *po*·zor·nost

Shall we go for a drink/meal?
Půjdem na skleničku/ *pooy*·dem nuh *skle*·nyich·ku/
jídlo? *yeed*·lo

looking for a job

Where are jobs advertised?

Kde jsou inzerce	gde ysoh *in·zer·tse*
zaměstnání?	*zuh·myest·na·nyee*

I'm enquiring about the position advertised.

Můžete mi dát	*moo·zhe·te mi dat*
informace o	*in·for·muh·tse o*
vámi inzerované práci?	*va·mi in·ze·ro·va·nair pra·tsi*

I'm looking for ... work.	*Hledám ....*	*hle·*dam ...
bar	*práci v baru*	*pra·*tsi f *buh·*ru
casual	*příležitostnou práci*	*przhee·*le·zhi·tost·noh *pra·*tsi
English-teaching	*prácl učitele angličtiny*	*pra·*tsi u·chi·te·le *uhn·*glich·tyi·ni
fruit-picking	*práci ve sběru ovoce*	*pra·*tsi ve *sbye·*ru o·vo·tse
full-time	*práci na plný úvazek*	*pra·*tsi nuh *pl·*nee oo·vuh·zek
labouring	*práci jako pomocný dělník*	*pra·*tsi *yuh·*ko po·mots·nce dyel·nyeek
office	*kancelářskou práci*	*kuhn·*tse·larzh·skoh *pra·*tsi
part-time	*práci na zkrácený úvazek*	*pra·*tsi nuh zkra·tse·nee oo·vuh·zek
waitering	*práci jako číšník*	*pra·*tsi *yuh·*ko cheesh·nyeek

Do I need (a) …? | *Potřebuji …?* | pot·rzhe·bu·yi …
- **contract** | *smlouvu* | smloh·vu
- **experience** | *praxi* | pruh·ksi
- **insurance** | *pojištění* | po·yish·tye·nyee
- **work permit** | *pracovní* | pruh·tsov·nyee
  | *povolení* | po·vo·le·nyee

I've had experience.
Měl/Měla jsem praxi. **m/f** | myel/*mye*·luh ysem pruh·ksi

What's the wage?
Jaká je mzda? | yuh·ka ye mzduh

Here are my bank account details.
Zde jsou podrobnosti | zde ysoh po·drob·nos·tyi
mého bankovního účtu. | mair·ho buhn·kov·nyee·ho ooch·tu

Here's my … | *Zde je …* | zde ye …
- **CV** | *můj životopis* | mooy zhi·vo·to·pis
- **visa** | *mé vísum* | mair vee·sum
- **work permit** | *mé pracovní* | mair pruh·tsov·nyee
  | *povolení* | po·vo·le·nyee

I can start … | *Mohu* | mo·hu
  | *nastoupit …* | nuh·stoh·pit …
- **at (eight) o'clock** | *v (osm) hodin* | f (o·sm) ho·dyin
- **today** | *dnes* | dnes
- **tomorrow** | *zítra* | zee·truh
- **next week** | *příští* | przheesh·tyee
  | *týden* | tee·den

What time do I …? | *V kolik hodin …?* | f ko·lik ho·dyin …
- **start** | *začínám* | zuh·chee·nam
- **have a break** | *mám přestávku* | mam przhes·taf·ku
- **finish** | *končím* | kon·cheem

I have a disability.
Jsem tělesně   ysem *tye*·les·nye
postižený/á. m/f   *pos*·tyi·zhe·nee/a

I need assistance.
Potřebuji pomoc.   *pot*·rze·bu·yi *po*·mots

I'm deaf.
Jsem hluchý/á. m/f   ysem *hlu*·khee/a

I have a hearing aid.
Mám naslouchátko.   mam *nuh*·sloh·khat·ko

My companion's blind.
Muj druh je slepý. m   muy drooh ye *sle*·pee
Moje družka je slepá. f   *mo*·ye *druzh*·kuh ye *sle*·pa

What services do you have for people with a disability?
Jaké služby poskytujete   yuh·kair *sluzh*·bi *pos*·ki·tu·ye·te
tělesně postiženým?   *tye*·les·nye *pos*·tyi·zhe·neem

Are guide dogs permitted?
Je vstup slepeckým   ye fstup *sle*·pets·keem
psům povolen?   psoom *po*·vo·len

Are there disabled parking spaces?
Jsou tam parkovací   ysoh tuhm *puhr*·ko·vuh·tsee
místa pro invalidy?   *mees*·tuh pro *in*·vuh·li·di

Is there wheelchair access?
Je tam přístup pro   ye tuhm *przhees*·tup pro
invalidní vozík?   *in*·vuh·lid·nyee *vo*·zeek

How wide is the entrance?
Jak široký je vchod?   yuhk *shi*·ro·kee ye fkhod

How many steps are there?
Kolik je zde schodů?   *ko*·lik ye zde *skho*·doo

Is there an elevator?
Je tam výtah?   ye tuhm *vee*·tah

Are there disabled toilets?

Jsou tam toalety pro   ysoh tuhm *to·*uh·le·ti pro
tělesně postižené?   *tye·*les·nye *pos·*tyi·zhe·nair

Are there rails in the bathroom?

Jsou v koupelně madla?   ysoh v *koh·*pel·nye *muhd·*luh

Is there somewhere I can sit down?

Je někde místo na   ye *nyek·*de *mees·*to nuh
sezení?   se·ze·nyee

Could you help me cross the street safely?

Můžete mě bezpečně   *moo·*zhe·te mye *bez·*pech·nye
převést přes ulici?   *przhe·*vairst przhes *u·*li·tsi

Could you call me a disabled taxi?

Můžete mi zavolat   *moo·*zhe·te mi *zuh·*vo·luht
taxi pro tělesně   *tuhk·*si pro *tye·*les·nye
postižené?   *pos·*tyi·zhe·nair

guide dog	*slepecký pes* m	*sle·*pets·kee pes
older person	*senior* m	*se·*nyi·or
person with	*člověk s*	*chlo·*vyek s
a disability	*tělesným*	*tye·*les·neem
	postiženým m	*pos·*tyi·zhe·neem
ramp	*rampa* f	*ruhm·*puh
walking frame	*chodítko* n	*kho·*dyeet·ko
walking stick	*hůl* f	hool
wheelchair	*invalidní vozík* m	*in·*vuh·lid·nyee *vo·*zeek

---

every day is a holiday

Czechs have a tradition of celebrating 'name days' (*svátek* *sva·*tek). They aren't birthdays (*narozeniny* nuh·ro·ze·nyi·ni), but celebrations for all people bearing the same name. Each day of the year has a name of a saint attached to it. The name day is an opportunity for friends and family to get together and celebrate, without having to deal with their age. The appropriate greeting is:

Happy name day!

Všechno nejlepší   *vshekh·*no ney·lep·shee
k svátku!   k *svat·*ku

travelling with children

cestování s dětmi

Is there a crèche?	Jsou zde jesle?	ysoh zde yes·le
Is there a …?	Máte …?	ma·te …
baby change room	zde přebalovací místnost pro děti	zde przhe·buh·lo·vuh·tsee meest·nost pro dye·tyi
child-minding service	zde službu pro hlídání dětí	zde sluzh·bu pro hlee·da·nyee dye·tyee
children's menu	dětský jídelníček	dyets·kee yee·del·nyee·chek
child's portion	dětské porce	dyets·kair por·tse
discount for children	slevy pro děti	sle·vi pro dye·tyi
family ticket	rodinné vstupné	ro·dyi·nair vstup·nair
I need a/an …	Potřebuji …	pot·rzhe·bu·yi …
baby seat (English-speaking)	auto sedačku (anglicko mluvící)	ow·to se·duhch·ku (uhn·glits·ko mlu·vee·tsee)
babysitter	chůvu	khoo·vu
booster seat	podsedák	pod·se·dak
highchair	dětskou stoličku	dyet·skoh sto·lich·ku
plastic bag	igelitovou tašku	i·ge·li·to·voh tuhsh·ku
plastic sheet	Igelltové prostěradlo	i·ge·li·to·vair pros·tye·ruhd·lo
potty	nočník	noch·nyeek
pram	kočárek	ko·cha·rek
sick bag	sáček při nevolnosti	sa·chek przhi ne·vol·nos·tyi

Do you sell …?	Prodáváte …?	pro·da·va·te …
baby wipes	dětské utěrky	dyets·kair u·tyer·ki
disposable nappies/ diapers	jednorázové pleny	yed·no·ra·zo·vair ple·ni
painkillers for infants	prášky proti bolesti u kojenců	prash·ki pro·tyi bo·les·tyi u ko·yen·tsoo
tissues	kosmetické kapesníky	kos·me·tits·kair kuh·pes·nyee·ki

Where's the nearest …?	Kde je nejbližší …?	gde ye ney·blizh·shee …
drinking fountain	fontánka s pitnou vodou	fon·tan·kuh s pit·noh vo·doh
park	park	puhrk
playground	hřiště	hrzhish·tye
swimming pool	bazén	buh·zairn
tap	kohoutek	ko·hoh·tek
theme park	zábavný park	za·buhv·nee puhrk
toyshop	hračkářství	hruhch·karzh·stvee

Are there any good places to take children around here?

Jsou v okolí nějaká zajímavá místa pro děti?

ysoh f o·ko·lee nye·yuh·ka zuh·yee·muh·va mees·tuh pro dye·tyi

Are children allowed?

Je povolen vstup dětem? ye po·vo·len vstup dye·tem

Is there space for a pram?

Je tam místo pro kočárek? ye tuhm mees·to pro ko·cha·rek

Where can I change a nappy/diaper?

Kde mohu vyměnit plenu? gde mo·hu vi·mye·nyit ple·nu

Do you mind if I breast-feed here?

Nebude vám vadit, když nakojím své dítě?

ne·bu·de vam vuh·dyit gdizh nuh·ko·yeem svair dyee·tye

Could I have some paper and pencils, please?

Můžete mi dát papír a tužky, prosím?

moo·zhe·te mi dat puh·peer uh tuzh·ki pro·seem

Is this suitable for (six)-year-old children?
Je to vhodné pro   ye to *vhod*·nair pro
(šesti)leté děti?   (*shes*·tyi·)*le*·tair *dye*·ti

Do you know a dentist/doctor who is good with children?
Znáte zubaře/lékaře   *zna*·te zu·buh·rzhe/*lair*·kuh·rzhe
který to umí s dětmi?   *kte*·ree to u·mee s *dyet*·mi

If your child is sick, see **health**, page 191.

talking with children

pohovor s dětmi

In this section, phrases are in the informal *ty* ti (you) form only.
See the box **all about you** on page 172 for more details.

What's your name?
Jak se jmenuješ?   yuhk se *yme*·nu·yesh

How old are you?
Kolik je ti let?   *ko*·lik ye tyi let

When's your birthday?
Kdy máš narozeniny?   gdi mash *nuh*·ro·ze·nyi·ni

Do you go to school/kindergarten?
Chodíš do školy/školky?   *kho*·dyeesh do *shko*·li/*shkol*·ki

What grade are you in?
Do jaké třídy chodíš?   do *yuh*·kair *trzhee*·di *kho*·dyeesh

Do you like …?	*Máš rád/*	mash rad/
	ráda …? m/f	*ra*·duh …
school	*školu*	*shko*·lu
sport	*sport*	sport
your teacher	*svého učitele* m	*svair*·ho u·chi·te·le
	svojí učitelku f	*svo*·yee u·chi·tel·ku

talking about children

When's the baby due?
Kdy očekáváte porod?   gdi o·che·ka·va·te po·rod

What are you going to call the baby?
Jaké jméno dáte   yuh·kair ymair·no da·te
miminku?   mi·min·ku

Is this your first child?
Je to vaše první dítě?   ye to vuh·she prv·nyee dyee·tye

How many children do you have?
Kolik máte dětí?   ko·lik ma·te dye·tyee

Is it a boy or a girl?
Je to kluk nebo holka?   ye to kluk ne·bo hol·kuh

How old is he/she?
Jak je starý/á?   yuhk ye stuh·ree/a

Does he/she go to school?
Chodí do školy?   kho·dyee do shko·li

What's his/her name?
Jaké je jeho/její jméno?   yuh·kair ye ye·ho/ye·yee ymair·no

What a beautiful child!
To je krásné dítě!   to ye kras·nair dyee·tye

He/She looks like you.
On/Ona se vám podobá.   on/o·nuh se vam po·do·ba

a guest appearance

If you're invited to someone's home for dinner, bring some flowers for the hostess, a bottle of wine for the host and chocolates for the children. Remember to give an odd number of flowers, as even numbers are placed on graves and are regarded as an insult if given to a living person. Take off the wrapping paper before you present the flowers.

When entering someone's home, take off your shoes or ask *Mám si zout boty?* mam si zoht bo·ti (Should I take off my shoes?). The hosts will normally offer a pair of slippers.

PRACTICAL

basics

Yes.	*Ano.*	uh·no
No.	*Ne.*	ne
Please.	*Prosím.*	pro·seem
Thank you (very much).	*(Mnohokrát) Děkuji.*	(mno·ho·krat) dye·ku·yi
You're welcome.	*Prosím.*	pro·seem
Excuse me. (attention/apology)	*Promiňte.*	pro·min'·te
Excuse me. (to get past)	*Pardon.*	puhr·don
Sorry.	*Promiňte.*	pro·min'·te

it's a yes

Even though it sounds much like the English 'no', remember that the Czech word *ano* uh·no is actually the affirmative – 'yes'. Don't be confused either if you hear people saying *jo* yo or *no* no while nodding in agreement – these are the more informal versions of *ano* (like the English 'yeah').

greetings & goodbyes

In the Czech Republic, it's very common for people – whether friends or strangers, male or female – to shake hands when they meet. Family members and friends give each other a kiss on the cheek, and sometimes they might also embrace. At social events, a man may kiss a woman's hand after being introduced.

Hello.	Ahoj.	*uh*·hoy
Hi.	Čau.	chow
Good afternoon.	Dobré odpoledne.	*dob*·rair ot·po·led·ne
Good day.	Dobrý den.	*dob*·ree den
Good evening.	Dobrý večer.	*dob*·ree *ve*·cher
Good morning.	Dobré ráno.	*dob*·rair *ra*·no

How are you?
  Jak se máte?   yuhk se *ma*·te

Fine. And you?
  Dobře. A vy?   *dob*·rzhe a vi

What's your name?
  Jak se jmenujete?   yuhk se *yme*·nu·ye·te

My name is …
  Jmenuji se …   *yme*·nu·yi se …

I'd like to introduce you to (Zdeněk).
  Mohu vás představit   *mo*·hu vas *przhed*·stuh·vit
  (Zdeňkovi).   (*zden'*·ko·vi)

I'm pleased to meet you.
  Těší mě.   *tye*·shee mye

This is my ...	*To je můj/*	to ye mooy/
	moje ... m/f	mo·ye ...
colleague	*kolega* m	ko·le·guh
	kolegyně f	ko·le·gi·nye
daughter	*dcera* f	dtse·ruh
friend	*přítel* m	przhee·tel
	přítelkyně f	przhee·tel·ki·nye
husband	*manžel* m	muhn·zhel
partner	*partner* m	puhrt·ner
(intimate)	*partnerka* f	puhrt·ner·kuh
son	*syn* m	sin
wife	*manželka* f	muhn·zhel·kuh

See you later.	*Na viděnou.*	nuh vi·dye·noh
Bye.	*Ahoj/Čau.*	uh·hoy/chow
Goodbye.	*Na shledanou.*	nuh·skhle·duh·noh
Good night.	*Dobrou noc.*	do·broh nots
Bon voyage!	*Šťastnou cestu!*	shtyuhst·noh tses·tu

addressing people

The following titles can be used with surnames or on their own:

Mr	*pan*	puhn
Mrs	*paní*	puh·nyee
Miss	*slečna*	slech·nuh

a few words between friends

There are several informal terms of address among friends. The most common one is *kamarád(ka)* kuh·muh·rad(·kuh) m/f (friend), which is often shortened to *kámoš* ka·mosh. The words *brácho* bra·kho (a variation of *bratr* bruh·tr – brother) and *chlape* khluh·pe (man) are used between male friends, just like the English 'mate' or 'buddy'. *Vole* vo·le (lit: ox) is another affectionate term used between both male and female friends, but it can also be used as an insult.

meeting people

making conversation

What a beautiful day!
To je krásný den! — to ye *kras*·nee den

Nice/Awful weather, isn't it?
Není krásně/ošklivo? — *ne*·nyi *kras*·nye/*osh*·kli·vo

What's happening?
Co se děje? — tso se *dye*·ye

Do you live here?
Bydlíte zde? — *bid*·lee·te zde

Where are you going?
Kam jdete? — kuhm *yde*·te

What are you doing?
Co děláte? — tso *dye*·la·te

in conversation

It's polite to maintain eye contact during a conversation. It's not polite, however, to interrupt someone speaking, keep your hands in your pockets, scratch yourself, blow your nose or smack your tongue!

Do you like it here?
Líbí se vám zde? — *lee*·bee se vam zde

I love it here.
Je to zde výborné. — ye to zde *vee*·bor·nair

What are your interests?
Jaké máte zájmy? — *yuh*·kair *ma*·te *zai*·mi

What's this called?
Jak se to jmenuje? — yuhk se to *yme*·nu·ye

That's (beautiful), isn't it!
To je (krásné), že! — to ye (*kras*·nair) zhe

Can I take a photo of this?
Mohu si toto vyfotit? — *mo*·hu si *to*·to *vi*·fo·tyit

Can I take a photo of you?
Mohu si vás vyfotit? — mo·hu si vas vi·fo·tyit

Can you take a photo of me/us?
Můžete mě/nás vyfotit? — moo·zhe·te mye/nas vi·fo·tyit

I'll send you the photo.
Pošlu vám fotku. — posh·lu vam fot·ku

How long are you here for?
Na jak dlouho jste zde? — nuh yuhk dloh·ho yste zde

I'm here for (four) weeks/days.
Jsem zde na (čtyři) týdny/dny. — ysem zde nuh (chti·rzhi) teed·ni/dni

Are you here on holiday?
Jste zde na dovolené? — yste zde nuh do·vo·le·nair

I'm here ...	*Jsem zde ...*	ysem zde ...
for a holiday	*na dovolené*	nuh do·vo·le·nair
on business	*služebně*	slu·zheb·nye
to study	*na studiích*	nuh stu·di·eekh

---

local talk

Hey!	*Hej!*	hey
Great!	*Skvělý!*	skvye·lee
Sure.	*Jistě.*	yis·tye
Maybe.	*Možná.*	mozh·na
No way!	*V žádném případě!*	v zhad·nairm przhee·puh·dye
Just a minute.	*Moment.*	mo·ment
Just joking.	*Jen žertuji.*	yen zher·tu·yi
It's OK.	*To je v pořádku.*	to ye v po·rzhad·ku
It's not worth it.	*Nestojí to za to.*	nes·to·yee to zuh to
Excellent!	*Výborný!*	vee·bor·nee
Superb!	*Super!*	su·per
No problem.	*Není problém.*	ne·ni prob·lairm

nationalities

Where are you from?
  Odkud jste?   ot·kud yste

I'm from ...   *Jsem z ...*   ysem s ...
  Australia   *Austrálie*   ow·stra·li·ye
  Canada   *Kanady*   kuh·nuh·di
  England   *Anglie*   uhn·gli·ye
  USA   *Ameriky*   uh·meh·ri·ki

age

How old ...?   *Kolik ...?*   ko·lik ...
  are you   *je vám let*   ye vam let
  is your   *let je vaší*   let ye *vuh*·shee
    daughter   *dceři*   dtse·rzhi
  is your son   *let je vašemu*   let ye *vuh*·she·mu
              synovi   si·no·vi

I'm ... years old.
  Je mi ... let.   ye mi ... let

He's ... years old.
  Je mu ... let.   ye mu ... let

She's ... years old.
  Jí je ... let.   yee ye ... let

Too old!
  Moc starý!   mots *stuh*·ree

I'm younger than I look.
  Jsem mladší než   ysem *mluhd*·shee nezh
  vypadám.   vi·puh·dam

occupations & studies

What's your occupation?
Jaké je vaše povolání? yuh·kair ye vuh·she po·vo·la·nyee

I work in administration.
Jsem zaměstnaný/á ysem zuh·myest·nuh·nee/a
v administrativě. m/f v uhd·mi·ni·struh·ti·vye

I work in health.
Jsem zaměstnaný/á ysem zuh·myest·nuh·nee/a
ve zdravotnictví. m/f ve zdruh·vot·nyits·tvee

I work in sales and marketing.
Jsem zaměstnaný/á v ysem zuh·myest·nuh·nee/a v
obchodu a marketingu. m/f op·kho·du uh muhr·ke·tin·gu

I'm a/an ...	*Jsem ...*	ysem ...
artist	*umělec* m	u·mye·lets
	umělkyně f	u·myel·ki·nye
businessperson	*obchodník* m&f	op·khod·nyeek
farmer	*zemědělec* m	ze·mye·dye·lets
	zemědělkyně f	ze·mye·dyel·ki·nye
labourer	*dělník* m	dyel·nyeek
	dělnice f	dyel·nyi·tse
office worker	*úředník* m	oo·rzhed·nyeek
	úřednice f	oo·rzhed·nyi·tse
scientist	*vědec* m	vye·dets
	vědkyně f	vyed·ki·nye
student	*student* m	stu·dent
	studentka f	stu·dent·kuh

I'm ...	*Jsem ...*	ysem ...
retired	*v důchodu*	v doo·kho·du
self-employed	*samostatně*	suh·mo·stuht·nye
	výdělečně	vee·dye·lech·nye
	činný	chi·nee
unemployed	*nezaměst-*	ne·zuh·myest·
	naný/á m/f	nuh·nee/a

What are you studying?
Co studujete?   tso *stu*·du·ye·te

I'm studying ...   *Studuji ...*   *stu*·du·yi ...
  Czech   *češtinu*   *chesh*·tyi·nu
  humanities   *humanitní*   *hu*·muh·nit·nyee
                 vědy   *vye*·di
  science   *vědu*   *vye*·du

family

Do you have a ...?   *Máte ...?*   *ma*·te ...
I (don't) have a ...   *(Ne)Mám ....*   (*ne*·)mam ...
  brother   *bratra*   *bruh*·truh
  daughter   *dceru*   *dtse*·ru
  husband   *manžela*   *muhn*·zhe·luh
  partner   *partnera* m   *puhrt*·ne·ruh
    (intimate)   *partnerku* f   *puhrt*·ner·ku
  sister   *sestru*   *ses*·tru
  son   *syna*   *si*·nuh
  wife   *manželku*   *muhn*·zhel·ku

Are you married?
Jste ženatý/vdaná? m/f   yste *zhe*·nuh·tee/*fduh*·na

I'm married.
Jsem ženatý/vdaná. m/f   ysem *zhe*·nuh·tee/*fduh*·na

I'm single.
Jsem svobodný/á. m/f   ysem *svo*·bod·nee/a

I live with someone.
Žiju s někým jiným.   *zhi*·yu s *nye*·keem *yi*·neem

I'm separated.
Žiju odděleně od   *zhi*·yu od·*dye*·le·nye od
manželky/manžela. m/f   *mun*·zhel·ki/*muhn*·zhe·luh

family talk

The family is very important to Czechs. When talking with friends and family members, they like to use diminutives (words that express the 'smallness' of something – like the word 'doggy' in English) to show affection. In Czech, diminutives are usually formed by adding the following endings to nouns: -ek -ek m, -ka -kuh f and -ko -ko n. In the examples below, diminutives are given after the 'neutral' kinship terms.

brother	*bratr/bratříček* m	*bruh*·tr/*bruht*·rzhee·chek
daughter	*dcera/dceruška* f	*dtse*·ruh/*dtse*·rush·kuh
grandfather	*děda/dědeček* m	*dye*·duh/*dye*·de·chek
grandmother	*babí/babička* f	*buh*·bee/*buh*·bich·kuh
sister	*sestra/sestřička* f	*ses*·truh/*sest*·rzhich·kuh
son	*syn/synáček* m	sin/*si*·na·chek

Teenage siblings also call each other *ségro* sair·gro (sister) and *brácho* bra·kho (brother). Furthermore, you might hear elderly people addressing boys as *chlapče* khluhp·che (boy) and girls as *děvče* dyev·che (girl).

farewells

loučení

Tomorrow is my last day here.
   Zítra jsem tady naposled.   zee·truh ysem *tuh*·di *nuh*·po·sled

If you come to (Scotland), you can stay with me.
   Až přijedete do (Skotska),   uhzh *przhi*·ye·de·te do (*skots*·kuh)
   můžete zůstat u mě.   moo·zhe·te *zoos*·tuht u mye

It's been great meeting you.
   Bylo skvělé že jsem se   *bi*·lo *skyve*·lair zhe ysem se
   s vámi setkal/setkala. m/f   s *va*·mi *set*·kuhl/*set*·kuh·luh

Keep in touch!
   Ozvěte se!   *oz*·vye·te se

What's your (email) address?
> *Jakou máte (email)*   *yuh·koh ma·te (ee·meyl)*
> *adresu?*   *uh·dre·su*

What's your phone number?
> *Jaké máte telefonní*   *yuh·kair ma·te te·le·fo·nyee*
> *číslo?*   *chees·lo*

Here's my ...	*Tady je moje ...*	*tuh·di ye mo·ye ...*
(email)	*(email)*	*(ee·meyl)*
address	*adresa*	*uh·dre·suh*
phone	*telefonní*	*te·le·fo·nyee*
number	*číslo*	*chees·lo*

well-wishing

Bless you!	*Na zdraví!*	nuh *zdruh·*vee
Congratulations!	*Blahopřeji!*	*bluh·*hop·rzhe·yi
Good luck!	*Mnoho štěstí!*	*mno·*ho *shtyes·*tyee

Happy birthday!
> *Všechno nejlepší k*   *vshekh·*no *ney·*lep·shee k
> *narozeninám!*   *nuh·*ro·ze·nyi·nam

Happy name day!
> *Všechno nejlepší*   *vshekh·*no *ney·*lep·shee
> *k svátku!*   k *svat·*ku

Happy Easter!
> *Veselé Velikonoce!*   *ve·*se·lair *ve·*li·ko·no·tse

Happy New Year!
> *Šťastný Nový rok!*   *shtyuhst·*nee *no·*vee rok

Merry Christmas!
> *Veselé Vánoce!*   *ve·*se·lair *va·*no·tse

common interests

What do you do in your spare time?

Jak trávíte svůj		yuhk *tra*·vee·te svooy
volný čas?		*vol*·nee chuhs

Do you like …?	*Máte rád/ráda …?* m/f	*ma*·te rad/*ra*·duh …
I like …	*Mám rád/ráda …* m/f	mam rad/*ra*·duh …
I don't like …	*Nemám rád/*	*ne*·mam rad/
	ráda … m/f	*ra*·duh …

art	*umění*	*u*·mye·nyee
cooking	*vaření*	*vuh*·rzhe·nyee
dancing	*tancování*	*tuhn*·tso·va·nyee
drawing	*kreslení*	*kre*·sle·nyee
films	*filmy*	*fil*·mi
hiking	*turistiku*	*tu*·ris·ti·ku
mushrooming	*sbírání hub*	*sbee*·ra·nyee hub
music	*hudbu*	*hud*·bu
painting	*malování*	*muh*·lo·va·nyee
painting	*malování*	*muh*·lo·va·nyee
Easter eggs	*kraslic*	*kruhs*·lits
photography	*fotografii*	*fo*·to·gruh·fi·i
reading	*čtení*	*chte*·nyee
socialising	*chození do*	*kho*·ze·nyee do
	společnosti	*spo*·lech·nos·tyi
sport	*sport*	sport
surfing the	*brouzdání po*	*brohz*·da·nyee po
Internet	*internetu*	*in*·ter·ne·tu
travelling	*cestování*	*tses*·to·va·nyee
watching TV	*dívání se*	*dyee*·va·nyee se
	na televizi	nuh *te*·le·vi·zi

For types of sport, see **sport**, page 145, and the **dictionary**.

music

Do you …?

dance	*Tancujete?*	*tuhn*·tsu·ye·te
go to concerts	*Chodíte na koncerty?*	*kho*·dyee·te nuh *kon*·tser·ti
listen to music	*Posloucháte hudbu?*	*po*·sloh·kha·te *hud*·bu
play an instrument	*Hrajete na hudební nástroj?*	*hruh*·ye·te nuh *hu*·deb·nyee *nas*·troy
sing	*Zpíváte?*	*spee*·va·te

Which … do you like? — *Libí se vám …?* — *lee*·bee se vam …

bands	*skupiny*	*sku*·pi·ni
music	*hudba*	*hud*·buh
performers	*umělci* m	*u*·myel·tsi
	umělkyně f	*u*·myel·ki·nye
singers	*zpěváci* m	*spye*·va·tsi
	zpěvačky f	*spye*·vuhch·ki

… music	… *hudba*	… *hud*·buh
classical	*klasická*	*kluh*·sits·ka
electronic	*elektronická*	*e*·lek·tro·nits·ka
folk	*lidová*	*li*·do·va
pop	*populární*	*po*·pu·lar·nyee
rock	*rocková*	*ro*·ko·va
traditional	*tradiční*	*truh*·dyich·nyee

Planning to go to a concert? See **tickets**, page 47, and **going out**, page 129.

cinema & theatre

I feel like going to a/an ...	Chtěl/Chtěla bych vidět ... m/f	khtyel/khtye·luh bikh vi·dyet ...
Did you like the ...?	Máte rád/ráda ...? m/f	ma·te rad/ra·duh ...
ballet	balet	buh·let
film	film	film
opera	operu	o·pe·ru
play	hru	hru
puppet show	loutkové představení	loht·ko·vair przhed·stuh·ve·nyee

What's showing at the cinema/theatre tonight?
Co dávají v kině/ divadle dnes večer? — tso da·vuh·yee f ki·nye/ dyi·vuhd·le dnes ve·cher

Is it in (English)?
Je to v (angličtině)? — ye to f (uhn·glich·tyi·nye)

Does it have (English) subtitles?
Je to s (anglickými) titulky? — ye to s (uhn·glits·kee·mi) ti·tul·ki

Is this seat available?
Je toto místo volné? — ye to·to mees·to vol·nair

Do you have tickets for ...?
Máte lístky na ...? — ma·te leest·ki nuh ...

Are there any extra tickets?
Máte více lístků? — ma·te vee·tse leest·koo

I'd like the cheap tickets.
Chtěl/Chtěla bych levné lístky. m/f — khtyel/khtye·luh bikh lev·nair leest·ki

I'd like the best tickets.
Chtěl/Chtěla bych nejlepší lístky. m/f — khtyel/khtye·luh bikh ney·lep·shee leest·ki

Is there a matinee show?
Hraje se odpolední představení? — hruh·ye se od·po·led·nyee przhed·stuh·ve·nyee

Have you seen (Želary)?
Viděli jste (Želary)?   *vi·dye·li yste (zhe·luh·ri)*

Who's in it?
Kdo v tom hraje?   *gdo f tom hruh·ye*

It stars (Aňa Gaislerová).
V hlavní roli hraje   *v hluhv·nyee ro·li hruh·ye*
(Aňa Gaislerová).   *(uh·nyuh gais·le·ro·va)*

I thought	*Myslel/Myslela*	*mis·lel/mis·le·luh*
it was …	*jsem že to*	*ysem zhe to*
	bylo … m/f	*bi·lo …*
excellent	*vynikající*	*vi·nyi·kuh·yee·tsee*
long	*dlouhé*	*dloh·hair*
OK	*fajn*	*fain*

I (don't) like …	*(Ne)Mám*	*(ne·)mam*
	rád/ráda … m/f	*rad/ra·duh …*
action movies	*akční filmy*	*uhk·chnyee fil·mi*
animated films	*animované*	*uh·ni·mo·vuh·nair*
	filmy	*fil·mi*
(Czech) cinema	*(českou)*	*(ches·koh)*
	kinematografii	*ki·ne·muh·to·gruh·fi·yi*
comedies	*komedie*	*ko·me·di·ye*
documentaries	*dokumentární*	*do·ku·men·tar·nyee*
	filmy	*fil·mi*
drama	*činohru*	*chi·no·hru*
horror movies	*horory*	*ho·ro·ri*
short films	*krátké filmy*	*krat·kair fil·mi*
thrillers	*napínavé*	*nuh·pee·nuh·vair*
	příběhy	*przhee·bye·hi*
war movies	*válečné filmy*	*va·lech·nair fil·mi*

turn on the black lights

A popular art form in the Czech Republic is the black-light theatre (*černé divadlo* *cher·nair dyi·vuhd·lo*) – a mixture of mime, drama and puppetry. Objects, puppets and live actors in fluorescent costumes are illuminated by ultraviolet lights, with the stage completely black in order to eliminate distractions.

feelings

pocity

Are you ...?	Jste ...?	yste ...
I'm/I'm not ...	Jsem/Nejsem ...	ysem/ney·sem ...
annoyed	mrzutý/á m/f	mr·zu·tee/a
disappointed	zklamaný/á m/f	skluh·muh·nee/a
happy	šťastný/á m/f	shtyuhst·nee/a
hungry	hladový/á m/f	hluh·do·vee/a
sad	smutný/á m/f	smut·nee/a
surprised	překvapený/á m/f	przhek·vuh·pe·nee/a
thirsty	žíznivý/á m/f	zheez·nyi·vee/a
tired	unavený/á m/f	u·nuh·ve·nee/a
well	zdravý/á m/f	zdruh·vee/a
worried	znepokojený/á m/f	zne·po·ko·ye·nee/a

gender issues

In Czech, gender differences affect not only the form of nouns and pronouns, but also the endings of adjectives and verbs. The most frequent endings, which tell you whether an adjective is in the masculine or feminine form, are -ý -ee and -á -a respectively. To show that you need to substitute one letter for another, we've used a slash – eg smutný/á m/f smut·nee/a (sad). On the other hand, in some verb tenses the masculine form normally ends in -l -l or another consonant, and the ending -a -uh is added for the feminine form. In this case, we've spelled out both forms of the verb in full.

I'd like to practise Czech.

Rád/Ráda bych si
procvičil/procvičila
češtinu. m/f

rad/ra·duh bikh si
prots·vi·chil/prots·vi·chi·luh
chesh·tyi·nu

mixed feelings

not at all	*vůbec ne*	voo·bets ne
I don't care at all.		
Mně na tom vůbec nezáleží.		mnye nuh tom *voo*·bets *ne*·za·le·zhee
a little	*trochu*	*tro*·khu
I'm a little sad.		
Jsem trochu smutný/á. **m/f**		ysem *tro*·khu *smut*·nee/a
very	*velmi*	*vel*·mi
I feel very lucky.		
Cítím se velmi šťastně.		tsee·tyeem se *vel*·mi *shtyuhst*·nye
extremely	*nesmírně*	*ne*·smeer·nye
I'm extremely sorry.		
Je mi to nesmírně líto		ye mi to *ne*·smeer·nye *lee*·to

Are you cold?	*Je vám zima?*	ye vam *zi*·muh
I'm cold.	*Je mi zima.*	ye mi *zi*·muh
I'm not cold.	*Není mi zima.*	*ne*·nyi mi *zi*·muh
Are you hot?	*Je vám horko?*	ye vam *hor*·ko
I'm hot.	*Je mi horko.*	ye mi *hor*·ko
I'm not hot.	*Není mi horko.*	*ne*·nyi mi *hor*·ko
Are you in a hurry?	*Spěcháte?*	*spye*·kha·te
I'm in a hurry.	*Spěchám.*	*spye*·kham
I'm not in a hurry.	*Nespěchám.*	nes·*pye*·kham

If you're not feeling well, see **health**, page 191.

SOCIAL

opinions

Czechs love to discuss politics and sport. Though they're generally very polite and peaceful, Czechs can get quite animated in political discussions. They're also passionately proud of Czech sporting heroes who have achieved victories at world level.

Did you like it?
| *Líbilo se vám to?* | *lee*·bi·lo se vam to |

What do you think of it?
| *Co si o tom myslíte?* | tso si o tom *mis*·lee·te |

I thought	*Myslel/Myslela jsem*	*mis*·lel/*mis*·le·luh ysem
it was …	*si že to bylo …* m/f	si zhe to *bi*·lo …
It's …	*Je to …*	ye to …
awful	*hrozné*	*hroz*·nair
beautiful	*krásné*	*kras*·nair
boring	*nudné*	*nud*·nair
great	*nezapome-nutelné*	*ne*·zuh·po·me·nu·tel·nair
interesting	*zajímavé*	*zuh*·yee·muh·vair
OK	*fajn*	fain
strange	*divné*	*dyiv*·nair
(too) expensive	*(moc) drahé*	(mots) *druh*·hair

---

hot topics

Some topics are best avoided, as they could arouse nationalistic reactions from many Czechs. You might be surprised to encounter racist attitudes towards the Roma (*Romové* ro·mo·vair), although these are generally not displayed openly and mostly appear to be just a reflection of what people have heard since childhood. The dislike of Russians (*Rusů* ru·soo) and Germans is a result of their communist legacy and the Nazi occupation respectively. A particularly touchy subject is the post-war expulsion of the Sudeten Germans (*Sudetští Němci* su·det·shtyee *nyem*·tsi) – a German minority that lived in the former Czechoslovakia.

politics & social issues

Who do you vote for?
Koho volíte?   *ko·ho vo·lee·te*

I support the (green) party.
Podporuji (zelenou)   *pod·po·ru·yi (ze·le·noh)*
stranu.   *struh·nu*

I'm a member	*Jsem členem*	ysem *chle·*nem
of the … party.	*… strany.*	*… struh·*ni
communist	*komunistické*	*ko·*mu·nis·tits·kair
conservative	*konzervativní*	*kon·*zer·vuh·tiv·nyee
democratic	*demokratické*	*de·*mo·kruh·tits·kair
green	*zelené*	*ze·*le·nair
liberal	*liberální*	*li·*be·ral·nyee
social	*sociálně*	*so·*tsi·al·nye
** democratic**	*demokratické*	*de·*mo·kruh·tits·kair
socialist	*socialistické*	*so·*tsi·uh·lis·tits·kair

party talk

These are the main political parties in the Czech Republic:

Česká strana sociálně demokratická
*ches·*ka *struh·*nuh   Czech Social
*so·*tsi·al·nye *de·*mo·kruh·tits·ka   Democratic Party

Komunistická strana Čech a Moravy
*ko·*mu·nis·tits·ka *struh·*nuh   Czech and Moravian
chekh uh *mo·*ruh·vi   Communist Party

Křesťansko demokratická unie – Česká strana lidová
*krzhes·*tyan·sko   Christian
*de·*mo·kruh·tits·ka *u·*ni·ye –   Democratic Union –
*ches·*ka *struh·*nuh *li·*do·va   Czech People's Party

Občanská demokratická strana
*ob·*chuhn·ska *de·*mo·kruh·tits·ka Civic Democratic
*struh·*nuh   Party

SOCIAL

Did you hear about …?
Slyšeli jste o …?   sli·she·li yste o …

Do you agree with it?
Souhlasíte s tím?   soh·hluh·see·te s tyeem

I agree/I don't agree with …
Souhlasím/   soh·hluh·seem/
Nesouhlasím s …   ne·soh·hluh·seem s …

How do people feel about …?
Co si lidé myslí o …?   tso si li·dair mis·lee o …

How can we protest against …?
Jak můžeme   yuhk moo·zhe·me
protestovat proti …?   pro·tes·to·vuht pro·tyi …

How can we support …?
Jak můžeme   yuhk moo·zhe·me
podpořit …?   pot·po·rzhit …

abortion	*potrat* m	po·truht
animal rights	*práva zvířat* f pl	pra·vuh zvee·rzhuht
communism	*komunismus* m	ko·mu·nis·mus
corruption	*korupce* f	ko·rup·tse
crime	*kriminalita* f	kri·mi·nuh·li·tuh
discrimination	*diskriminace* f	dis·kri·mi·nuh·tse
drugs	*drogy* f pl	dro·gi
the economy	*ekonomie* f	e·ko·no·mi·ye
education	*vzdělání* n	vzdye·la·nyee
the environment	*životní*	zhi·vot·nyee
	prostředí n	prost·rzhe·dyee
equal opportunity	*rovnoprávnost* f	rov·no·prav·nost
European Union	*Evropská unie* f	e·vrop·ska u·ni·ye
euthanasia	*euthanasie* f	eu·tuh·nuh·si·ye
globalisation	*globalizace* f	glo·buh·li·zuh·tse
human rights	*lidská práva* f pl	lid·ska pra·vuh
immigration	*imigrace* f	i·mi·gruh·tse
inequality	*nerovnoprávnost* f	ne·rov·no·prav·nost
nationalism	*nacionalismus* m	nuh·tsi·o·nuh·lis·mus
party politics	*stranická*	struh·nyits·ka
	politika f	po·li·ti·kuh

poverty	*chudoba* f	khu·do·buh
privatisation	*privatizace* f	pri·vuh·ti·zuh·tse
racism	*rasismus* m	ruh·sis·mus
sexism	*sexismus* m	sek·sis·mus
social welfare	*sociální*	so·tsi·al·nyee
	péče f	pair·che
terrorism	*terorismus* m	te·ro·ris·mus
unemployment	*nezaměstnanost* f	ne·zuh·myest·nuh·nost
the war in …	*válka v …* f	val·kuh v …
Is there help	*Jaké pomoci*	yuh·kair po·mo·tsi
for (the) …?	*se dostává …?*	se dos·ta·va …
aged	*starým lidém*	stuh·reem li·dem
beggars	*žebrákům*	zhe·bra·koom
disabled	*invalidům*	in·vuh·li·doom
homeless	*bezdomovcům*	bez·do·mof·tsoom
street kids	*bezprizorním*	bez·pri·zor·nyeem
	dětem	dye·tem

---

check your czech

The word 'Czech', in its one and only English form, can be used for a number of different notions, together with another word which clarifies what's meant. These various concepts are covered by separate words in the Czech language itself:

the Czech language	*čeština* f	chesh·tyi·nuh
a Czech woman	*Češka* f	chesh·kuh
a Czech man	*Čech* m	chekh
the Czech Republic	*Česká*	ches·ka
	republika f	re·pu·bli·kuh
Czech (adjective)	*český* m	ches·kee
	česká f	ches·ka
	české n	ches·kair

the environment

Is there a ... problem here?
Je zde problém s ...?   ye zde *pro*·blairm s ...

What should be done about ...?
Co se má dělat s ...?   tso se ma *dye*·luht s ...

acid rain	*kyselý déšť* m	*ki*·se·lee dairsht'
alternative	*alternativní*	*uhl*·ter·nuh·tiv·nyee
energy sources	*energetické*	e·ner·ge·tits·kair
	zdroje m pl	zdro·ye
animal rights	*práva zvířat* f pl	*pra*·vuh zvee·rzhuht
conservation	*ochrana*	*okh*·ruh·nuh
	přírody f	*przhee*·ro·di
deforestation	*odlesňování* n	od·les·nyo·va·nyee
drought	*období sucha* n	*ob*·do·bee *su*·khuh
ecosystem	*ekosystém* m	e·ko·sis·tairm
endangered	*ohrožené*	o·hro·zhe·nair
species	*druhy* m pl	*dru*·hi
the environment	*životní*	*zhi*·vot·nyee
	prostředí n	prost·rzhe·dyee
genetically	*geneticky*	*ge*·ne·tits·ki
modified food	*modifikované*	mo·di·fi·ko·vuh·nair
	potraviny f pl	*po*·truh·vi·ni
hunting	*lov* m	lof
hydroelectricity	*hydroelektřina* f	*hi*·dro·e·lek·trzhi·nuh
irrigation	*zavlažování* n	zuh·vluh·zho·va·nyee
nuclear energy	*jaderná energie* f	*yuh*·der·na e·ner·gi·e
ozone layer	*ozónová vrstva* f	o·zaw·no·va *vrst*·vuh
pesticides	*pesticidy* m pl	*pes*·ti·tsi·di
pollution	*znečistění*	zne·chis·tye·nyee
	životního	*zhi*·vot·nyee·ho
	prostředí n	prost·rzhe·dyee
recycling	*recyklace* f	*re*·tsi·kluh·tse
toxic waste	*toxický odpad* m	*tok*·sits·kee *od*·puhd
water supply	*zásobování*	za·so·bo·va·nyee
	vodou n	*vo*·doh

feelings & opinions

127

Is this a	Je tento …	ye *ten*·to …
protected …?	*chráněný?*	*khra*·nye·nee
forest	*les*	les
park	*park*	puhrk
species	*druh*	drukh

Here are some of the Czech views on life, courtesy of local sayings …

In the middle of nowhere.
Místo kde lišky davájí   mees·to gde *lish*·ki *duh*·va·yee
dobrou noc.   *do*·broh nots
(lit: place where foxes say good night)

Look before you leap.
Ráno moudřejší   *ra*·no mohd·rzhey·shee
večera.   ve·che·ruh
(lit: morning wiser than evening)

Out of the frying pan into the fire.
Dostat se z bláta do   dos·tuht se z *bla*·tuh do
louže.   loh·zhe
(lit: out of the mud into the puddle)

To have a chip on the shoulder.
Mít máslo na hlavě.   meet *mas*·lo nuh *hluh*·vye
(lit: to have butter on the head)

It's all Greek to him.
Je to pro něj španělská   ye to pro nyey *shpuh*·nyel·ska
vesnice.   ves·ni·tse
(lit: it's a Spanish village to him)

It's as old as the hills.
To je starý jak Praha.   to ye *stuh*·ree yuhk *pruh*·huh
(lit: it's as old as Prague)

Beer makes beautiful bodies.
Pivo dělá hezká těla.   pi·vo *dye*·la *hez*·ka *tye*·luh

In this chapter, phrases are in the informal *ty* ti (you) form. If you're not sure what this means, see the box **all about you** on page 172 for more details.

where to go

kam jít

What's there to do in the evenings?
Kam se dá večer jít?   kuhm se da *ve*·cher yeet

What's on …?	*Kde se … můžeme pobavit?*	gde se … *moo*·zhe·me *po*·buh·vit
locally	*v okolí*	f *o*·ko·lee
today	*dnes*	dnes
tonight	*večer*	*ve*·cher
this weekend	*tento víkend*	*ten*·to *vee*·kend

Where can I find …?	*Kde mohu najít …?*	gde *mo*·hu *nuh*·yeet …
cafés	*kavárny*	*kuh*·var·ni
clubs	*kluby*	*klu*·bi
gay/lesbian venues	*homosexuální/ lesbický zábavné podniky*	*ho*·mo·sek·su·al·nyee/ *les*·bits·kee *za*·buhv·nair pod·ni·ki
places to eat	*stravovací místa*	struh·vo·vuh·tsee *mees*·tuh
pubs	*hospody*	*hos*·po·di

Is there a local ... guide?	Existuje ...?	ek·sis·tu·ye ...
entertainment	přehled kulturních programů	przhe·hled kul·tur·nyeekh pro·gruh·moo
film	program kin	pro·gruhm kin
gay/lesbian entertainment	přehled kulturních programů pro homosexuály/ lesbičky	przhe·hled kul·tur·nyeekh pro·gruh·moo pro ho·mo·sek·su·a·li/ les·bich·ki
music	přehled hudebních programů	przhe·hled hu·deb·nyeekh pro·gruh·moo

I feel like going to a ...	Rád/Ráda bych šel/šla ... m/f	rad/ra·duh bikh shel/shluh ...
ballet	na balet	nuh buh·let
bar	do baru	do buh·ru
café	do kavárny	do kuh·var·ni
concert	na koncert	nuh kon·tsert
film	do kina	do ki·nuh
karaoke bar	do karaoke baru	do kuh·ruh·o·ke buh·ru
nightclub	do večerního klubu	do ve·cher·nyee·ho klu·bu
party	na mejdan/ večírek	nuh mey·duhn/ ve·chee·rek
performance	na představení	nuh przhed·stuh·ve·nyee
play	na hru	nuh hru
pub	do hospody	do hos·po·di
puppet show	na loutkové představeni	nuh loht·ko·vair przhed·stuh·ve·nyee
restaurant	do restaurace	do res·tow·ruh·tse

For more on bars, drinks and partying, see **romance**, page 135, and **eating out**, page 159.

In the Czech Republic, it's not only men who get a chance to politely say *Až po vás.* uzh po vas (lit: After you. **pol**). Of course, good old manners dictate that the man lets the woman enter first when going out to a nice, expensive restaurant. However, the man goes in first if it's a pub, bar or a cheap restaurant – so a girl can have her turn to casually offer *Po tobě.* po *to*·bye (lit: After you. **inf**).

invitations

What are you doing now?
  Co teď děláš?   tso teď *dye*·lash

What are you doing tonight?
  Co děláš dnes večer?   tso *dye*·lash dnes *ve*·cher

What are you doing this weekend?
  Co budeš dělat   tso *bu*·desh *dye*·luht
  tento víkend?   *ten*·to *vee*·kend

My round.
  To platím já.   to *pluh*·tyim ya

Would you like	*Chtěl/Chtěla*	khtyel/*khtye*·luh
to go (for a) …?	*bys jít …?* m/f	bis yeet …
I feel like going	*Rad bych šel …* m	rad bikh shel …
(for a) …	*Rada bych šla …* f	*ra*·duh bikh shluh …
dancing	*tancovat*	*tuhn*·tso·vuht
coffee	*na kafe*	nuh *kuh*·fe
drink	*na sklenku*	nuh *sklen*·ku
meal	*na jídlo*	nuh *yeed*·lo
walk	*na vycházku*	nuh *vi*·khaz·ku

party people

Different generations, different jargons – generally speaking, middle-aged and older Czechs say *večírek* ve·chee·rek when referring to a party, while *mejdan* mey·duhn is the word used by younger people. Of course, their ideas of a good party are probably quite different too …

Do you know a good restaurant?
Znáš dobrou restauraci? znash *dob*·roh *res*·tow·ruh·tsi

Do you want to come to the concert with me?
Chceš jít se mnou khtsesh yeet se mnoh
na koncert? nuh *kon*·tsert

We're having a party.
Pořádáme večírek/ *po*·rzha·da·me ve·chee·rek/
mejdan. mey·duhn

You should come.
Měl/Měla bys přijít. m/f myel/*mye*·luh bis *przhi*·yeet

responding to invitations

Sure!
Jistě! yis·tye

Yes, I'd love to.
Ano, velmi rád/ráda. m/f uh·no *vel*·mi rad/*ra*·duh

Where shall we go?
Kam půjdeme? kuhm *pooy*·de·me

No, I'm afraid I can't.
Ne, obávám se, že nemohu. ne o·ba·vam se zhe *ne*·mo·hu

Sorry, I can't sing/dance.
Promiň, nemohu *pro*·min' *ne*·mo·hu
zpívat/tančit. spee·vuht/*tuhn*·chit

What about tomorrow?
Co zítra? tso *zee*·truh

arranging to meet

What time will we meet?
V kolik hodin se setkáme?   f ko·lik ho·dyin se set·ka·me

Where will we meet?
Kde se setkáme?   gde se set·ka·me

Let's meet at ...   *Setkáme se ...*   set·ka·me se ...
  (eight) o'clock   *v (osm) hodin*   f (o·sm) ho·dyin
  the (entrance)   *u (vchodu)*   u (fkho·du)

lonely letters

The single consonants in our coloured pronunciation guides haven't been pushed out of an overcrowded Czech word by mistake. They're Czech versions of some common prepositions (eg 'with', 'in') and are usually joined in pronunciation with the following word. You'll see v or f for the sound of the letter *v*, k for *k* and s or z for the letters *s* and *z*. For more on prepositions, see the **phrasebuilder**, page 25.

OK!
Fajn!   fain

I'll pick you up.
Vyzvednu tě.   viz·ved·nu tye

Are you ready?
Jsi připravený/á? m/f   ysi przhi·pruh·ve·nee/a

I'm ready.
Jsem připravený/á. m/f   ysem przhi·pruh·ve·nee/a

I'll be coming later.
Přijdu později.   przhiy·du poz·dye·yi

Where will you be?
Kde budeš?   gde bu·desh

If I'm not there by (nine), don't wait for me.
Když tam nebudu do   gdizh tuhm ne·bu·du do
(devíti), nečekej na mě.   (de·vee·tyi) ne·che·key na mye

I'll see you then.
Uvidíme se pak.   u·vi·dyee·me se puhk

See you later.
Na shledanou.   nuh·skhle·duh·noh

See you tomorrow.
Na shledanou zítra.   nuh·skhle·duh·noh zee·truh

I'm looking forward to it.
Těším se na to.   tye·sheem se nuh to

Sorry I'm late.
Promiň jdu pozdě.   pro·min' ydu poz·dye

Never mind.
Nevadí.   ne·vuh·dyee

drugs

drogy

I don't take drugs.
Neberu drogy.   ne·be·ru dro·gi

I take ... occasionally.
Příležitostně si   przhee·le·zhi·tost·nye si
vezmu ...   vez·mu ...

Do you want to have a smoke?
Chceš si zakouřit?   khtsesh si zuh·koh·rzhit

Do you have a light?
Můžu si zapálit?   moo·zhu si zuh·pa·lit

I'm high.
Jsem zfetovaný/á. m/f   ysem zfe·to·vuh·nee/a

If the police are talking to you about drugs, see **police**, page 188, for useful phrases.

---

why, oh why

Remember that the apostrophe ' in the pronunciation guide is said as a slight 'y' sound after a consonant while the y (eg *jsem* ysem) is always pronounced like the 'y' in 'yes'.

In this chapter, phrases are in the informal *ty* ti (you) form. If you're not sure what this means, see the box **all about you** on page 172 for more details.

asking someone out

pozvat někoho na rande

Where would you like to go (tonight)?
Kam bys chtěl/chtěla kuhm bis khtyel/*khtye*·luh
jít (dnes večer)? m/f yeet (dnes *ve*·cher)

Would you like to do something (tomorrow)?
Chtěl/Chtěla bys něco khtyel/*khtye*·luh bis *nye*·tso
(zítra) podniknout? m/f (*zee*·truh) *pod*·nyik·noht

Yes, I'd love to.
Ano, rád/ráda. m/f uh·no rad/*ra*·duh

Sorry, I can't.
Promiň, nemohu. *pro*·min' *ne*·mo·hu

local talk		
He's a babe.	On je frajer.	on ye *fruh*·yer
She's a babe.	Ona je kočka.	o·nuh ye *koch*·kuh
She's hot.	Ona je rajcovní	o·nuh ye *rai*·tsov·nyee
	ženská.	zhen·ska
He's a bastard.	On je parchant.	on ye *puhr*·khuhnt
She's a bitch.	Ona je mrcha.	o·nuh ye *mr*·khuh
He's a lout.	On je grázl.	on ye *gra*·zl
He gets around.	On je děvkař.	on ye *dyef*·kuhrzh
She gets around.	Ona je děvka.	o·nuh ye *dyef*·kuh

pick-up lines

Would you like a drink?
Mohu tě pozvat — mo·hu tye *poz*·vuht
na sklenku? — nuh *sklen*·ku

You look like someone I know.
Vypadáš, jako někdo — vi·puh·dash yuh·ko nyek·do
koho znám. — ko·ho znam

You're a fantastic dancer.
Jsi výtečný tanečník. m — ysi vee·tech·nee tuh·nech·nyeek

You're a fantastic dancer.
Jsi výtečná tanečnice. f — ysi vee·tech·na tuh·nech·nyi·tse

Can I …?	*Mohu …?*	mo·hu …
dance with you	*si s tebou*	si s te·boh
	zatančit	zuh·tuhn·chit
sit here	*si k tobě*	si k to·bye
	přisednout	przhi·sed·noht
take you home	*tě pozvat k*	tye poz·vuht k
	sobě domů	so·bye do·mu

rejections

I'm here with my girlfriend.
Jsem zde s mojí — ysem zde s mo·yee
přítelkyní. — przhee·tel·ki·nyee

I'm here with my boyfriend.
Jsem zde s mým — ysem zde s meem
přítelem. — przhee·te·lem

I'd rather not.
Raději ne. — ruh·dye·yi ne

No, thank you.
Ne, děkuji. — ne dye·ku·yi

Excuse me, I have to go now.
  Promiň, ale musím   pro·min' uh·le mu·seem
  teď jít.   ted' yeet

Pity, but I'm doing something else.
  Škoda, ale mám   shko·duh uh·le mam
  jiný program.   yi·nee pro·gruhm

Thank you, but I'm not interested.
  Děkuji, ale nemám zájem.   dye·ku·yi uh·le ne·mam za·yem

---

local talk

Leave me alone!
  Nech mě na pokoji!   nekh mye nuh po·ko·yi

Don't bother me!
  Neobtěžuj mě!   ne·ob·tye·zhuy mye

Don't touch me!
  Nedotíkej se mě!   ne·do·tee·key se mye

Take a hike!	*Běž k šípku!*	byezh k sheep·ku
Piss off!	*Odprejskni!*	od·preysk·nyi
Get stuffed!	*Jdi se vycpat!*	ydyi se vits·puht

---

getting closer

sbližování

I really like you. (man speaking)
  Mám tě moc rád.   mam tye mots rad

I really like you. (woman speaking)
  Mám tě moc ráda.   mam tye mots ra·duh

You're great.
  Jsi báječný/á. m/f   ysi ba·yech·nee/a

Can I kiss you?
  Mohu tě políbit?   mo·hu tye po·lee·bit

Do you want to come inside for a while?
  Chceš jít na chvíli ke mě?   khtsesh yeet nuh khvi·li ke mye

Do you want a massage?
Chceš udělat masáž?   khtsesh u·dye·luht *muh*·sazh

Would you like to stay over?
Chceš u mě přespat?   khtsesh u mye *przhes*·puht

Can I stay over?
Mohu zde přespat?   *mo*·hu zde *przhes*·puht

sex

Kiss me.   *Polib mě.*   *po*·lib mye
I want you.   *Chci tě.*   khtsi tye
Let's go to bed.   *Pojďme do*   *poyd'*·me do
                       postele.   *pos*·te·le
Touch me here.   *Dotkni se mě.*   *dot*·knyi se mye
Do you like this? *Líbí se ti to?*   *lee*·bee se tyi to

I like that.
Mám to rád/ráda. m/f   mam to rad/*ra*·duh

I don't like that.
Nemám to rád/ráda. m/f   ne·mam to rad/*ra*·duh

I think we should stop now.
Myslím si, že by jsme   *mis*·leem si zhe bi ysme
měli přestat.   *mye*·li *przhes*·tuht

Do you have a (condom)?
Máš (prezervativ)?   mash (*pre*·zer·vuh·tif)

Let's use a (condom).
Použijeme (prezervativ).   po·u·zhi·ye·me (*pre*·zer·vuh·tif)

I won't do it without protection.
Nebudu to dělat   ne·bu·du to *dye*·luht
bez ochrany.   bez o·khruh·ni

It's my first time.
Pro mě je to poprvé.   pro mye ye to *po*·pr·vair

Don't worry, I'll do it myself.
Neboj se, udělám to   ne·boy se u·dye·lam to
sám/sama. m/f   sam/*suh*·muh

Oh my god!	*Ó muj bože!*	oo muy *bo*·zhe
That's great.	*To je skvělé.*	to ye *skve*·lair
Easy tiger!	*Zpomal divochu/ divoško!* m/f	*spo*·muhl *dyi*·vo·khu/ *dyi*·vosh·ko
faster	*rychleji*	*ri*·khle·yi
harder	*tvrději*	*tvr*·dye·yi
slower	*pomaleji*	*po*·muh·le·yi
softer	*jemněji*	*yem*·nye·yi
That was …	*To bylo …*	to *bi*·lo …
amazing	*báječný*	*ba*·yech·nee
romantic	*romantický*	*ro*·muhn·tits·kee
wild	*divoký*	*dyi*·vo·kee

sweet talk

my bottom	*prdelko*	*pr*·del·ko
my darling	*můj miláčku*	mooy *mi*·lach·ku
my gold	*zlatíčko*	*zluh*·tyeech·ko
my sweetheart	*srdíčko*	*sr*·dyeech·ko
sweetie	*drahoušku*	*druh*·hohsh·ku

love

láska

I think we're good together.
Myslím, že patříme k sobě.
mis·leem zhe *puht*·rzhee·me k *so*·bye

Will you go out with me?
Budeš se mnou chodit?
bu·desh se mnoh *kho*·dyit

I love you.
Miluji tě.
mi·lu·yi tye

Will you meet my parents?
Chceš se seznámit s mými rodiči?
khtsesh se *sez*·na·mit s *mee*·mi *ro*·dyi·chi

Will you marry me?
Vezmeš si mě?
vez·mesh si mye

problems

I don't think it's working out.
Myslím, že nám to　　　*mis*·leem zhe nam to
nefunguje.　　　　　　　*ne*·fun·gu·ye

Are you seeing someone else?
Chodíš s někým jiným?　*kho*·dyeesh s *nye*·keem *yi*·neem

He's just a friend.
On je jenom kamarád.　　on ye *ye*·nom *kuh*·muh·rad

She's just a friend.
Ona je jenom kamarádka.　*o*·nuh ye *ye*·nom *kuh*·muh·rad·kuh

You're just using me for sex.
Jen mně zneužíváš　　　yen mnye *zne*·u·zhee·vash
pro sex.　　　　　　　　pro seks

I never want to see you again.
Už tě nikdy nechci vidět.　uzh tye *nyik*·di *nekh*·tsi *vi*·dyet

We'll work it out.
Vyřešíme to.　　　　　*vi*·rzhe·shee·me to

leaving

I have to leave (tomorrow).
(Zítra) Odcházím.　　　(*zeet*·ruh) *od*·kha·zeem

I'll keep in touch.
Chci udržovat kontakt.　*khtsi* u·dr·zho·vuht *kon*·tuhkt

I'll miss you.
Budeš mi chybět.　　　*bu*·desh mye *khi*·byet

I'll visit you.
Navštívím tě.　　　　　*nuhf*·shtyee·veem tye

beliefs & cultural differences
náboženské víry & kulturní rozdíly

religion

Although religion plays little part in urban Czechs' lives (especially in Prague and other major cities), certain rural parts of the country, particularly in the east, are fairly religious.

What's your religion?
Jaká je vaše víra? yuh·ka ye *vuh*·she *vee*·ruh

I'm not religious.
Jsem bez vyznání. ysem bez *viz*·na·nyee

I'm (a) ...	*Jsem ...*	ysem ...
agnostic	*agnostik* m	*uhg*·nos·tik
	agnostička f	*uhg*·nos·tich·kuh
Buddhist	*buddhista* m	*bud*·his·tuh
	buddhistka f	*bud*·hist·kuh
Catholic	*katolík* m	*kuh*·to·leek
	katolička f	*kuh*·to·lich·kuh
Christian	*křesťan* m	*krzhes*·tyuhn
	křesťanka f	*krzhes*·tyuhn·kuh
Hindu	*hind/hindka* m/f	hind/*hind*·kuh
Jewish	*žid/židovka* m/f	zhid/*zhi*·dof·kuh
Muslim	*muslim* m	*mus*·lim
	muslimka f	*mus*·lim·kuh
Protestant	*protestant* m	*pro*·tes·tuhnt
	protestantka f	*pro*·tes·tuhnt·kuh

I believe in ...	*Věřím v ...*	*vye*·rzheem f ...
I don't believe in ...	*Nevěřím v ...*	*ne*·vye·rzheem f ...
astrology	*astrologii*	*uhs*·tro·lo·gi·yi
fate	*osud*	*o*·sud
God	*Boha*	*bo*·huh

Can I ... here?	Mohu se zde ...?	mo·hu se zde ...
Where can I ...?	Kde se mohu ...?	gde se mo·hu ...
attend a	účastnit	oo·chuhst·nyit
service	bohoslužby	bo·ho·sluzh·bi
attend mass	účastnit mše	oo·chuhst·nyit mshe
pray	modlit	mod·lit

Can I worship here?
Mohu zde uctívat?   mo·hu zde uts·tyee·vuht

Where can I worship?
Kde mohu uctívat?   gde mo·hu uts·tyee·vuht

cultural differences

kulturní rozdíly

Is this a local or national custom?
Je to místní nebo   ye to meest·nyee ne·bo
národní zvyk?   na·rod·nyee zvik

I don't want to offend you.
Nechci vás urazit.   nekh·tsi vas u·ruh·zit

I'm not used to this.
Nejsem na to zvyklí/á. m/f   ney·sem nuh to zvi·klee/a

I'd rather not join in.
Radši se nepřipojím.   ruhd·shi se nep·rzhi·po·yeem

I'll try it.
Zkusím to.   sku·seem to

I'm sorry, it's	Promiňte, je to	pro·min'·te ye to
against my ...	proti ...	pro·tyi ...
beliefs	mojí víře	mo·yee vee·rzhe
religion	mému	mair·mu
	náboženství	na·bo·zhen·stvee

This is ...	Toto je ...	to·to ye ...
different	jiné	yi·nair
fun	legrace	le·gruh·tse
interesting	zajímavé	zuh·yee·muh·vair

When's the gallery/museum open?
V kolik hodin otevírá galerie/museum? — f ko·lik ho·dyin o·te·vee·ra guh·le·ri·e/mu·ze·um

What kind of art are you interested in?
O jaký druh umění máte zájem? — o yuh·kee drooh u·mye·nyee ma·te za·yem

What's in the collection?
Co je ve sbírce? — tso ye ve zbeer·tse

It's an exhibition of …
To je výstava … — to ye vees·tuh·vuh …

What do you think of …?
Co si myslíte o …? — tso si mis·lee·te o …

I'm interested in …
Mám zájem o … — mam zuh·yem o …

I like the works of …
Mám rád/ráda dílo od … m/f — mam rad/ra·duh dyee·lo od …

It reminds me of …
Připomíná mi to … — przhi·po·mee·na mi to …

Art Nouveau a	*secesní*	se·tses·nyee
baroque a	*barokní*	buh·rok·nyee
cubist a	*kubistický*	ku·bis·tits·kee
Gothic a	*gotický*	go·tits·kee
graphic a	*grafický*	gruh·fits·kee
impressionist a	*impresionistický*	im·pre·si·o·nis·tits·kee
medieval	*středověký*	strzhe·do·vye·kee
modern	*moderní*	mo·der·nyee
performance a	*představení*	przhed·stuh·ve·nyee
Renaissance a	*renesanční*	re·ne·zuhn·chnyee
rococo a	*rokokový*	ro·ko·ko·vee
Romanesque	*románský*	ro·man·skee
Socialist a	*socialistický*	so·tsi·uh·lis·tits·kee

architecture	*architektura* f	*uhr·khi·tek·tu·ruh*
art	*umění* n	*u·mye·nyee*
artwork	*umělecké dílo* n	*u·mye·lets·kair dyee·lo*
curator	*kustod* m	*kus·tod*
design	*vzor* m	*vzor*
etching	*lept* m	*lept*
exhibit	*exponát* m	*eks·po·nat*
exhibition hall	*výstavní hala* f	*vees·tuhv·nyee huh·luh*
installation	*instalace* f	*in·stuh·luh·tse*
opening	*vernisáž* f	*ver·nyi·sazh*
painter	*malíř* m	*muh·leerzh*
painting (artwork)	*obraz* m	*o·bruhz*
painting (technique)	*malování* n	*muh·lo·va·nyee*
period	*období* n	*ob·do·bee*
permanent collection	*stálá sbírka* f	*sta·la sbeer·kuh*
print	*reprodukce* f	*re·pro·duk·tse*
sculptor	*sochař* m	*so·khuhrzh*
sculpture	*sochařství* n	*so·khuhrzh·stvee*
statue	*socha* f	*so·khuh*
studio	*ateliér* m	*uh·te·li·er*
style	*sloh* m	*slokh*
technique	*metoda* f	*me·to·duh*

name your castle

Various types of beautiful castles around the Czech Republic are usually called by one of the following two names – *hrad* hruhd, which refers to a medieval defensive structure, or *zámek* za·mek, which is something like a Renaissance or Imperial chateau – a grand manor house.

SOCIAL

sporting interests

Czechs use both the 'international' names for basketball and volleyball (given in the list below) and the Czech words *košíková* ko·shee·ko·va and *odbíjená* od·bee·ye·na respectively. For more information on the use of the term 'hockey', see the box on page 153.

What sport do you …?	Jaký sport …?	yuh·kee sport …
follow	sledujete	sle·du·ye·te
play	hrajete	hruh·ye·te

I play/do …	Hraji …	hruh·yi …
I follow …	Sleduji …	sle·du·yi …
athletics	atletiku	uht·le·ti·ku
basketball	basketbal	buhs·ket·buhl
football (soccer)	fotbal	fot·buhl
handball	házenou	ha·ze·noh
(ice) hockey	(lední) hokej	(led·nyee) ho·key
karate	karate	kuh·ruh·te
tennis	tenis	te·nis
volleyball	volejbal	vo·ley·buhl

I cycle.	Jezdím na kole.	yez·deem nuh ko·le
I go canoeing.	Jezdím na kánoi.	yez·deem nuh ka·no·i
I go kayaking.	Jezdím na kajaku.	yez·deem nuh kuh·yuh·ku
I run.	Běhám.	bye·ham
I ski.	Lyžuji.	li·zhu·yi
I snowboard.	Snowborduji.	snoh·bor·du·yi
I walk.	Chodím.	kho·dyeem

For more sports, see the **dictionary**.

Do you like (tennis)?
Máte rád/ráda (tenis)? m/f · *ma*·te rad/*ra*·duh (*te*·nis)

Yes, very much.
Ano, velmi. · *uh*·no *vel*·mi

Not really.
Moc ne. · mots ne

I like watching it.
Rád/Ráda se na to · rad/*ra*·duh se nuh to
dívám. m/f · *dyee*·vam

Who's your favourite sportsperson?
Kdo je váš · gdo ye vash
nejoblíbenější · *ney*·o·blee·be·nyey·shee
sportovec/sportovkyně? m/f · *spor*·to·vets/*spor*·tof·ki·nye

What's your favourite team?
Které je vaše · *kte*·rair ye vuh·she
nejoblíbenější · *ney*·o·blee·be·nyey·shee
mužstvo? · *muzh*·stvo

going to a game

jde se na zápas

Would you like to go to a game?
Chcete jít na zápas? · *khtse*·te yeet nuh *za*·puhs

Who are you supporting?
Komu fandíte? · *ko*·mu *fuhn*·dyee·te

Who's playing/winning?
Kdo hraje/vyhrává · gdo *hruh*·ye/*vi*·hra·va

scoring		
What's the score?	*Kolik je to?*	*ko*·lik ye to
draw/even	*nerozhodně/*	*ne*·roz·hod·nye/
	remíza	*re*·mee·zuh
love/nil (zero)	*nula*	*nu*·luh
match-point	*mečbol*	*mech*·bol

What a …!	To je …!	to ye …
goal	gól	gawl
hit	trefa	tre·fuh
kick	střela	strzhe·luh
pass	přihrávka	przhi·hraf·kuh
performance	výkon	vee·kon

That was a … game!	To byl … zápas!	to bil … za·puhs
bad	špatný	shpuht·nee
boring	nudný	nud·nee
great	výborný	vee·bor·nee

playing sport

sportování

Do you want to play?
Chcete hrát?   khtse·te hrat

Can I join in?
Mohu se přidat?   mo·hu se przhi·duht

That would be great.
To je skvělé.   to ye skvye·lair

I can't.
Nemohu.   ne·mo·hu

I have an injury.
Jsem zraněný/á. m/f   ysem zruh·nye·nee/a

Your/My point.
Váš/Můj bod.   vash/mooy bod

Kick/Pass it to me!
Kopni/Přihraj mi to! inf   kop·ni/przhi·hrai mi to

You're a good player.
Jste dobrý hráč.   yste dob·ree hrach

Thanks for the game.
Děkuji za hru.   dye·ku·yi zuh hru

sport

147

Where's a good place to …?	Kde je dobré místo …?	gde ye *dob*·rair *mees*·to …
fish	na rybaření	nuh ri·buh·rzhe·nyee
go horse riding	pro jízdu na koni	pro *yeez*·du nuh *ko*·nyi
run	na běhání	nuh *bye*·ha·nyee
ski	na lyžování	nuh *li*·zho·va·nyee

Where's the nearest …?	Kde je nejbližší …?	gde ye *ney*·blizh·shee …
golf course	golfové hřiště	*gol*·fo·vair hrzhish·tye
gym	posilovna	*po*·si·lov·nuh
swimming pool	bazén	*buh*·zairn
tennis court	tenisový kurt	*te*·ni·so·vee kurt

What's the charge per …?	Kolik stojí …?	*ko*·lik *sto*·yee …
day	den	den
game	hra	hruh
hour	hodina	*ho*·dyi·nuh
visit	návštěva	naf·shtye·vuh

Can I hire a …?	Mohu si půjčit …?	*mo*·hu si *pooy*·chit …
ball	míč	meech
bicycle	kolo	*ko*·lo
court	kurt	kurt
racquet	pálku	*pal*·ku

Do I have to be a member to attend?

Musím být členem abych se mohl/mohla zúčastnit? m/f	*mus*·eem beet *chle*·nem uh·bikh se *mo*·hl/*mo*·hluh zoo·chuhst·nyit

Is there a women-only session?

Je to někdy vyhrazeno jen pro ženy?	ye to *nyek*·di *vi*·hruh·ze·no yen pro *zhe*·ni

Where are the changing rooms?

Kde jsou šatny?	gde ysoh *shuht*·ni

horse riding

How much is a (one)-hour ride?
*Kolik stojí (jedna)-
hodinová jízda?*
ko·lik *sto*·yee (*yed*·nuh)·
ho·dyi·no·va *yeez*·duh

How long is the ride?
Jak dlouho trvá jízda?
yuhk *dloh*·ho *tr*·va *yeez*·duh

I'm an experienced rider.
*Jsem zkušený/á
jezdec/jezdkyně.* **m/f**
ysem *sku*·she·nee/a
yez·dets/*yezd*·ki·nye

I'm not an experienced rider.
*Jsem nezkušený/á
jezdec/jezdkyně.* **m/f**
ysem *ne*·sku·she·nee/a
yez·dets/*yezd*·ki·nye

Can I rent a hat and boots?
*Mohu si půjčit čepici
a boty?*
mo·hu si *pooy*·chit *che*·pi·tsi
uh *bo*·ti

bit	*udidlo* n	*u*·dyi·dlo
bridle	*uzda* f	*uz*·duh
canter v	*lehce cválat*	*lekh*·tse *tsva*·luht
crop n	*bičík* m	*bi*·cheek
gallop v	*cválat*	*tsva*·luht
gelding	*valach* m	*vuh*·luhkh
groom v	*hřebelcovat*	*hrzhe*·bel·tso·vuht
horse	*kůň* m	koon'
pony	*poník* m	*po*·nyeek
reins	*otěže* f pl	*o*·tye·zhe
saddle	*sedlo* n	*sed*·lo
stable	*stáj* m	stai
stallion	*hřebec* m	*hrzhe*·bets
stirrup	*třmen* m	*trzh*·men
trot v	*klusat*	*klu*·suht
walk v	*chodit*	*kho*·dyit

skiing

I'd like to hire (a) ...	Chtěl/Chtěla bych si půjčit ... m/f	khtyel/khtye·luh bikh si pooy·chit ...
boots	přeskáče	przhes·ka·che
gloves	rukavice	ru·kuh·vi·tse
goggles	brýle	bree·le
poles	hůlky	hool·ki
skis	lyže	li·zhe
ski suit	lyžařskou kombinézu	li·zhuhrzh·skoh kom·bi·nair·zu

How much is a pass?
Kolik stojí pernamentka?   ko·lik sto·yee per·nuh·ment·kuh

Can I take lessons?
Mohu si vzít lekce lyžování?   mo·hu si vzeet lek·tse li·zho·va·nyee

What level is that slope?
    Jakou obtížnost má   *yuh*·koh *ob*·tyeezh·nost ma
    tato sjezdovka?   *tuh*·to *syez*·dof·kuh

Which are the   *Které svahy*   *kte*·rair *svuh*·hi
... slopes?   *jsou pro ...?*   ysoh pro ...
  beginner   *začátečníky*   *zuh*·cha·tech·nyee·ki
  intermediate   *pokročilé*   *po*·kro·chi·lair
  advanced   *dobré lyžaře*   *dob*·rair li·zha·rzhe

What are the   *Jaké jsou*   *yuh*·kair ysoh
conditions   *lyžařské*   *li*·zharzh·skair
like ...?   *podmínky ...?*   *pod*·meen·ki ...
  at (Špindlerův   *ve (Špindlerově*   ve (*shpind*·le·ro·vye
    Mlýn)   *Mlýně)*   *mlee*·nye)
  higher up   *výš*   veesh
  on that run   *na této*   nuh *tair*·to
    sjezdovce   *syez*·dov·tse

Is it possible   *Je zde*   ye zde
to go ...?   *možné ...?*   *mozh*·nair ...
  Alpine skiing   *sjezdové*   *syez*·do·vair
    lyžování   li·zho·va·nyee
  cross-country   *lyžovat na*   *li*·zho·vuht nuh
    skiing   *běžkách*   *byezh*·kakh
  snowboarding   *snowbordovat*   *snoh*·bor·do·vuht
  tobogganing   *sáňkovat*   *san'*·ko·vuht

cable car   *lanovka* f   *luh*·nof·kuh
chairlift   *sedačková*   *se*·duhch·ko·va
    lanovka f   *luh*·nof·kuh
instructor   *instruktor* m   *in*·struk·tor
resort   *lyžařské*   *li*·zharzh·skair
    středisko n   *strzhe*·dyis·ko
ski lift   *lyžařský vlek* m   *li*·zharzh·skee vlek
sled   *sáně* f   *sa*·nye

soccer/football

Who plays for (Slavia)?
Kdo hraje za (Slavii)?   gdo *hruh*·ye zuh (*sluh*·vi·yi)

He's a great (player).
Je výborný (hráč).   ye *vee*·bor·nee (hrach)

He played brilliantly in the match against (Italy).
Hrál brilantně v zápase   hral *bri*·luhnt·nye v *za*·puh·se
proti (Itálii).   *pro*·tyi (*i*·ta·li·yi)

Which team is at the top of the league?
Které mužstvo je   kte·rair *muzh*·stvo ye
první v lize?   *prv*·nyee v *li*·ze

What a great/terrible team!
To je výborné/hrozné   to ye *vee*·bor·nair/*hroz*·nair
mužstvo!   *muzh*·stvo

ball	*míč* m	meech
coach	*trenér* m	*tre*·nair
corner (kick)	*rohový kop* m	*ro*·ho·vee kop
expulsion	*vyloučení* n	*vi*·loh·che·nye
fan	*fanoušek* m	*fuh*·noh·shek
foul n	*faul* m	fowl
free kick	*volný kop* m	*vol*·nee kop
goal (structure)	*branka* f	*bruhn*·kuh
goalkeeper	*brankář* m	*bruhn*·karzh
manager	*manažer* m	*muh*·nuh·zher
offside	*ofsajd* m	*of*·said
penalty	*penalta* f	*pe*·nuhl·tuh
player	*hráč* m	hrach
red card	*červená karta* f	*cher*·ve·na *kuhr*·tuh
referee	*rozhodčí* m	*roz*·hod·chee
striker	*útočník* m	*oo*·toch·nyeek
throw in v	*vhazovat míč*	*vhuh*·zo·vuht meech
yellow card	*žlutá karta* f	*zhlu*·ta *kuhr*·tuh

Off to see a match? Check out **going to a game**, page 146.

The ice hockey tradition among Czechs goes back to the start of the 20th century. These days they boast one of the world's best national teams, with 17 European titles, 11 world titles and one Olympic Games title in their possession. The Czech ice hockey season runs from September to April.

Just like Canadians and Americans, Czechs refer to ice hockey as simply 'hockey' (*hokej* ho·key), but you can also use the more specific phrase *lední hokej* led·nyee ho·key (ice hockey). If they talk about field hockey, they use the term *pozemní hokej* po·zem·nyee ho·key. Here's some more hockey terminology:

blue-line offside	*postavení*	*pos*·tuh·ve·nyee
	mimo hru na	*mi*·mo hru nuh
	modré čáře n	*mo*·drair *cha*·rzhe
defender	*obránce* m	*o*·bran·tse
dropping the puck	*vhazování* n	*vhuh*·zo·va·nyee
forward	*útočník* m	*oo*·toch·nyeek
hockey stick	*hokejka* f	*ho*·key·kuh
penalty	*vyloučení* n	*vi*·loh·che·nyee
puck	*puk* m	puk
red-line offside	*zakázané*	*zuh*·ka·zuh·nair
	uvolnění n	*u*·vol·nye·nyee

tennis & table tennis

tenis & stolní tenis

I'd like to ...	*Chtěl/Chtěla*	khtyel/*khtye*·luh
	bych si ... m/f	bikh si ...
book a time	*rezervovat*	*re*·zer·vo·vuht
to play	*hodinu*	*ho*·dyi·nu
play (table)	*zahrát (stolní)*	*zuh*·hrat (*stol*·nyee)
tennis	*tenis*	*te*·nis

Can we play at night?
  Můžem hrát v noci? moo·zhem hrat v no·tsi

I need my racquet restrung.
  Potřebuji vyplést pot·rzhe·bu·yi vi·plairst
  moji raketu. mo·yi ruh·ke·tu

ace	*eso* n	e·so
advantage	*výhoda* f	vee·ho·duh
bat (table tennis)	*pálka* f	pal·kuh
clay	*antuka* f	uhn·tu·kuh
fault	*chybné podání* n	khib·nair po·da·nyee
game, set, match	*hra, sada,*	hruh suh·duh
	zápas	za·puhs
grass	*tráva* f	tra·vuh
hard court	*tvrdý dvorec* m	tvr·dee dvo·rets
net	*síť* f	seet'
ping-pong ball	*ping-pongový*	ping·pon·go·vee
	míček m	mee·chek
play doubles v	*hrát čtyřhru*	hrat chtirzh·hru
racquet	*raketa* f	ruh·ke·tuh
serve n	*podání* n	po·da·nyee
serve v	*podávat*	po·da·vuht
set	*sada* f	suh·duh
tennis ball	*tenisový míč* m	te·ni·so·vee meech
table-tennis	*ping-pongový*	ping·pon·go·vee
table	*stůl* m	stool

hiking

Where can I …?	Kde mohu …?	gde mo·hu …
buy supplies	koupit zásoby	koh·pit za·so·bi
find someone	najít někoho,	nuh·yeet nye·ko·ho
who knows	kdo zná tuto	gdo zna tu·to
the area	oblast	o·bluhst
get a map	dostat mapu	dos·tuht muh·pu
hire hiking	půjčit horskou	pooy·chit hors·koh
gear	výbavu	vee·buh·vu

Do we need a guide?
Potřebujeme průvodce? pot·rzhe·bu·ye·me proo·vod·tse

Are there guided treks?
Jsou túry s průvodcem? ysoh too·ri s proo·vod·tsem

Is it safe?
Je to bezpečné? ye to bez·pech·nair

Is there a hut?
Je tam chata? ye tuhm khuh·tuh

When does it get dark?
V kolik se stmívá? f ko·lik se stmee·va

How high is the climb?
Jaké je převýšení yuh·kair ye przhe·vee·she·nyee
výstupu? vees·tu·pu

How long is the trail?
Jak dlouhá je stezka? yuhk dloh·ha ye stez·kuh

Do we need to take ...?	Musíme si vzít ...?	mu·see·me si vzeet ...
bedding	ložní prádlo	lozh·nyee prad·lo
food	jídlo	yeed·lo
water	vodu	vo·du

Is the track ...?	Je stezka ...?	ye stez·kuh ...
(well-)marked	(dobře)	(dob·rzhe)
	značená	znuh·che·na
open	otevřená	o·tev·rzhe·na
scenic	malebná	muh·leb·na

Which is the ... route?	Která trasa je ...?	kte·ra truh·suh ye ...
easiest	nejlehčí	ney·leh·chee
most interesting	nejzají- mavější	ney·za·yee· muh·vyey·shee
shortest	nejkratší	ney·kruht·shee

Where can I find the ...?	Kde mohu najít ... ?	gde mo·hu nuh·yeet ...
camping ground	stanový tábor	stuh·no·vee ta·bor
nearest	nejbližší	ney·blizh·shee
village	vesnici	ves·nyi·tsi
showers	sprchy	spr·khi
toilets	toalety	to·uh·le·ti

Where have you come from?
Odkud jste přišli? od·kud yste przhi·shli

How long did it take?
Jak to dlouho trvalo? yuhk to dloh·ho tr·vuh·lo

Does this path go to (Labská Bouda)?
Vede tato stezka k (Labské Boudě)? ve·de tuh·to stez·kuh k (luhp·skair boh·dye)

Can I go through here?
Mohu zde projít? mo·hu zde pro·yeet

Is the water OK to drink?
Je ta voda pitná? ye tuh vo·duh pit·na

weather

What's the weather like?
Jaké je počasí? yuh·kair ye po·chuh·see

What will the weather be like tomorrow?
Jaké bude zítra počasí? yuh·kair bu·de zee·truh po·chuh·see

It's …
cloudy	*Je zataženo.*	ye zuh·tuh·zhe·no
cold	*Je chladno.*	ye khluhd·no
fine	*Je krásně.*	ye kras·nye
freezing	*Mrzne.*	mrz·ne
hot	*Je horko.*	ye hor·ko
raining	*Prší.*	pr·shee
snowing	*Sněží.*	snye·zhee
sunny	*Je slunečno.*	ye slu·nech·no
warm	*Je teplo.*	ye tep·lo
windy	*Je větrno.*	ye vye·tr·no

Where can I buy a/an …?	*Kde mohu koupit …?*	gde mo·hu koh·pit …
rain jacket	*pláštěnku*	plash·tyen·ku
umbrella	*deštník*	desht·nyeek

flora & fauna

flóra & fauna

What … is that?	*Co je to za …?*	tso ye to zuh …
animal	*zvíře*	zvee·rzhe
flower	*květinu*	kvye·tyi·nu
plant	*rostlinu*	rost·li·nu
tree	*strom*	strom

outdoors

157

What's it used for?
Na co se to používá?   nuh tso se to *po*·u·zhee·va

Can you eat the fruit?
Může se toto ovoce jíst?   moo·zhe se *to*·to *o*·vo·tse yeest

Is it …?	*Je to … ?*	ye to …
common	*obecný*	o·bets·nee
dangerous	*nebezpečný*	*ne*·bez·pech·nee
endangered	*ohrožený*	o·hro·zhe·nee
poisonous	*jedovatý*	ye·do·vuh·tee
protected	*chráněný*	khra·nye·nee

local animals & plants

adder	*zmije* f	*zmi*·ye
badger	*jezevec* m	*ye*·ze·vets
bear	*medvěd* m	*med*·vyed
deer	*jelen* m	*ye*·len
duck	*kachna* f	*kuhkh*·nuh
eagle	*orel* m	*o*·rel
lynx	*rys* m	ris
marmot	*svišť* m	svisht'
marten	*kuna* f	*ku*·nuh
mink	*norek* m	*no*·rek
otter	*vydra* f	*vid*·ruh
pheasant	*bažant* m	*buh*·zhuhnt
roe deer	*srnka* f	*srn*·kuh
wolf	*vlk* m	vlk
beech	*buk* m	buk
birch	*bříza* f	*brzhee*·zuh
linden	*lípa* f	*lee*·puh
oak	*dub* m	dub
spruce	*smrk* m	smrk

For geographical and agricultural terms, and more names of animals and plants, see the **dictionary**.

SOCIAL

basics

breakfast	*snídaně* f	snee·duh·nye
lunch	*oběd* m	o·byed
dinner	*večeře* f	ve·che·rzhe
snack	*občerstvení* n	ob·cherst·ve·nyee
eat v	*jíst*	yeest
drink v	*pít*	peet
I'd like …	*Chtěl/Chtěla bych …* m/f	khtyel/khtye·luh bikh …
I'm starving!	*Jsem vyhladovělý/á.* m/f	ysem vi·hluh·do·vye·lee/a

food glorious food

A Czech breakfast typically consists of a cup of tea or coffee followed by bread or bread rolls with ham, salami, cheese or jam. However, cereals or muesli have also become popular.

No Czech would start lunch without having soup first – for example *drštková polévka* drsht'·ko·va po·lairf·kuh (tripe soup) or *česnečková polévka* ches·nech·ko·va po·lairf·kuh (garlic soup). This is generally followed by delicacies such as *knedlo* kned·lo (bread dumplings), *zelo* ze·lo (sauerkraut) and *vepřo* vep·rzho (roasted pork).

Most families have dinner at home – usually bread or bread rolls with various types of cold sausage meats, fish or cheese. If they're going to a restaurant or a pub, dinner can mean anything from grilled meats and fish to pasta, pizzas or salads.

Last but not least, open sandwiches (*obložené chlebíčky* o·blo·zhe·nair khle·beech·ki) are a popular snack. There's a wide variety of toppings for these, such as mayonnaise-based salads with vegetables, sausage meats or fish salads.

finding a place to eat

Can you recommend a ...?	*Můžete doporučit ...?*	moo·zhe·te do·po·ru·chit ...
café	*kavárnu*	kuh·var·nu
pub	*hospodu*	hos·po·du
restaurant	*restauraci*	res·tow·ruh·tsi

Where would you go for ...?	*Kam byste doporučil/ doporučila jít na ...?* m/f	kuhm bis·te do·po·ru·chil/ do·po·ru·chi·luh yeet nuh ...
a celebration	*oslavu*	os·luh·vu
a cheap meal	*laciné jídlo*	luh·tsi·nair yeed·lo
local specialities	*místní speciality*	meest·nyee spe·tsi·a·li·ti

I'd like to reserve a table for ...	*Chtěl/Chtěla bych rezervovat stůl ...* m/f	khtyel/khtye·luh bikh re·zer·vo·vuht stool ...
(two) people	*pro (dvě) osoby*	pro (dvye) o·so·bi
(eight) o'clock	*na (osmou) hodinu*	nuh (os·moh) ho·dyi·nu

---

czech eateries

bageteria f   buh·ge·te·ri·yuh
sells mainly baguette-style sandwiches

bufet m   bu·fet
mostly stand-up cheap eatery which serves hot and cold food, alcoholic and nonalcoholic drinks

jídelna f   yee·del·nuh
basic and cheap eatery offering hot and cold food, alcoholic and nonalcoholic drinks

lahůdky f pl   luh·hood·ki
sells open-bread and other sandwiches, sweets and drinks

Are you still serving food?
Podáváte ještě jídlo?   po·da·va·te yesh·tye yeed·lo

How long is the wait?
Jak dlouho budu čekat?   yuhk dloh·ho bu·du che·kuht

listen for ...		
Máme zavřeno.	ma·me zuhv·rzhe·no	**We're closed.**
Máme plno.	ma·me pl·no	**We're full.**
Moment.	mo·ment	**One moment.**

at the restaurant

v restauraci

Before Czechs start eating, they say *Dobrou chuť!* do·broh khut' (Bon appétit!), and before having a drink they toast with *Na zdraví!* nuh zdruh·vee (Cheers!). When making a toast, always look into the other person's eyes.

What would you recommend?
Co byste doporučil/   tso bis·te do·po·ru·chil/
doporučila? m/f   do·po·ru·chi·luh

What's in that dish?
Co je v tom pokrmu?   tso ye f tom po·kr·mu

What's that called?
Jak se toto jmenuje?   yuhk se to·to yme·nu·ye

I'll have that.
Dám si tohle.   dam sI to·hle

Does it take long to prepare?
Jak dlouho to trvá   yuhk dloh·ho to tr·va
připravit?   przhi·pruh·vit

Is it self-serve?
Obsloužíme se samy?   ob·sloh·zhee·me se sa·mi

Is service included in the bill?
Je to včetně obsluhy?   ye to vchet·nye op·slu·hi

Kam si chcete sednout?	kuhm si *khtse*·te *sed*·noht	**Where would you like to sit?**
Co vám mohu přinést?	tso vam *mo*·hu *przhi*·nairst	**What can I get for you?**
Tady to máte!	*tuh*·di to *ma*·te	**Here you go!**
Nechte si chutnat.	*nekh*·te si *khut*·nuht	**Enjoy your meal.**
Přejete si …?	*przhe*·ye·te si …	**Do you like …?**
Mohu doporučit …	*mo*·hu *do*·po·ru·chit …	**I suggest the …**
Jak byste to chtěl/chtěla uvařit? **m/f**	yuhk *bis*·te to khtyel/ *khtye*·luh *u*·vuh·rzhit	**How would you like that cooked?**

Is there a cover/service charge?
Účtujete couvert/ *přirážku za obsluhu?*
ooch·tu·ye·te *ku*·vert/ *przhi*·razh·ku zuh *op*·slu·hu

Are these complimentary?
Je toto zdarma?
ye *to*·to *zduhr*·muh

Could I please see the wine list?
Můžete mi dát *vinný lístek?*
moo·zhe·te mi dat *vi*·nee *lees*·tek

Can you recommend a good local wine?
Můžete mi doporučit *dobré místní víno?*
moo·zhe·te mi *do*·po·ru·chit *do*·brair *meest*·nyee *vee*·no

I'd like (a/the) ...,	Chtěl/Chtěla bych	khtyel/khtye·luh bikh
please.	..., prosím. m/f	... pro·seem
children's	dětský	dyets·kee
menu	jídelníček	yee·del·nyee·chek
drink list	nápojový	na·po·yo·vee
	lístek	lees·tek
half portion	poloviční	po·lo·vich·nyee
	porci	por·tsi
local speciality	místní	meest·nyee
	specialitu	spe·tsi·uh·li·tu
meal fit for	královskou	kra·lovs·koh
a king	hostinu	hos·tyi·nu
menu	jídelníček	yee·del·nyee·chek
(in English)	(v angličtině)	(f uhn·glich·tyi·nye)
nonsmoking	nekuřáckou	ne·ku·rzhats·koh
section	místnost	meest·nost
smoking	kuřáckou	ku·rzhats·koh
section	místnost	meest·nost
table for (five)	stůl pro (pět)	stool pro (pyet)
that dish	ten pokrm	ten po·krm

on the menu

The main courses on the menu in inexpensive or ordinary restaurants serving Czech food are often divided into two sections.

Hotová jídla ho·to·va yeed·luh (ready-to-serve dishes) are precooked in the morning and served from 11am until sold out that day. *Jídla na objednávku* yeed·luh nuh o·byed·naf·ku (à la carte dishes) are cooked to order – for example, various meats, steaks and fish.

You might also come across the phrase *Bez masá jídla* bez muh·sa yeed·luh (dishes without meat). Beware – contrary to what the phrase suggests, these aren't always vegetarian dishes. Some of them may include bacon or are cooked in animal fat, such as *knedlíky s vejci* kned·lee·ki s vey·tsi (fried dumplings with eggs) or *omeleta se sýrem a bramborem* o·me·le·tuh se see·rem uh bruhm·bo·rem (omelette with cheese and potato).

I'd like it with ...	Chtěl/Chtěla bych to ... m/f	khtyel/khtye·luh bikh to ...
cheese	se sýrem	se see·rem
chilli	s pfeferonkou	s fe·fe·ron·koh
chilli sauce	s pfeferonkovou omáčkou	s fe·fe·ron·ko·voh o·mach·koh
garlic	s česnekem	s ches·ne·kem
ketchup	s kečupem	s ke·chu·pem
nuts	s ořechy	s o·rzhe·khi
oil	s olejem	s o·le·yem
pepper	s pepřem	s pep·rzhem
salt	se solí	se so·lee
tomato sauce	s rajskou omáčkou	s rais·koh o·mach·koh
vinegar	s octem	s ots·tem

I'd like it without ...	Chtěl/Chtěla bych to bez ... m/f	khtyel/khtye·luh bikh to bez ...
cheese	sýru	see·ru
chilli	pfeferonky	fe·fe·ron·ki
chilli sauce	pfeferonkové omáčky	fe·fe·ron·ko·vair o·mach·ki
garlic	česneku	ches·ne·ku
ketchup	kečupu	ke·chu·pu
nuts	ořechů	o·rzhe·khoo
oil	oleje	o·le·ye
pepper	pepře	pep·rzhe
salt	sole	so·le
tomato sauce	rajské omáčky	rais·kair o·mach·ki
vinegar	octu	ots·tu

For other specific meal requests, see **vegetarian & special meals**, page 177.

FOOD

164

Chuťovky	chu·tyof·ki	Appetisers
Polévky	po·lairf·ki	Soups
Studené předkrmy	stu·de·nair przhed·kr·mi	Cold Entrees
Teplé předkrmy	te·plair przhed·kr·mi	Warm Entrees
Saláty	suh·la·ti	Salads
Hlavní jídla	hluhv·nyee yeed·luh	Main Courses
Přílohy	przhee·lo·hi	Side Dishes
Moučníky	mohch·nyee·ki	Desserts
Aperitivy	uh·pe·ri·ti·vi	Apéritifs
Nápoje	na·po·ye	Drinks
Nealkoholické nápoje	ne·uhl·ko·ho·lits·kair na·po·ye	Soft Drinks
Lihoviny	li·ho·vi·ni	Spirits
Piva	pi·vuh	Beers
Šumivá vína	shu·mi·va vee·nuh	Sparkling Wines
Bílá vína	bee·la vee·na	White Wines
Červená vína	cher·ve·na vee·nuh	Red Wines
Dezertní vína	de·zert·nyee vee·nuh	Dessert Wines
Zažívací likéry	zuh·zhee·vuh·tsee li·kair·ri	Digestifs

For additional items, see the **culinary reader**, page 179.

at the table

u stolu

Please bring a/the ...	Prosím přineste ...	pro·seem przhi·nes·te ...
bill	účet	oo·chet
cutlery	příbor	przhee·bor
(wine)glass	skleničku (na víno)	skle·nyich·ku (nuh vee·no)
serviette	ubrousek	u·broh·sek
tablecloth	ubrus	u·brus

I didn't order this.
Toto jsem si neobjednal/ to·to ysem si *ne*·ob·yed·nuhl/
neobjednala. m/f ne·ob·yed·nuh·la

There's a mistake in the bill.
Na účtu je chyba. nuh *ooch*·tu ye *khl*·buh

talking food

I love this dish.
Mám rád/ráda toto jídlo. m/f mam rad/*ra*·duh to·to *yeed*·lo

I love the local cuisine.
Mám rád/ráda místní mam rad/*ra*·duh
kuchyň. m/f ku·khin'

That was delicious!
To bylo lahodné! to *bi*·lo luh·hod·nair

My compliments to the chef.
Poklonu šéfkuchaři. pok·lo·nu *shairf*·ku·khuh·rzhi

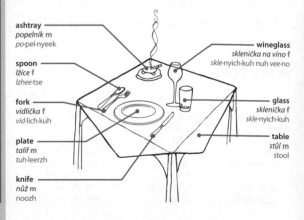

ashtray
popelník m
po·pel·nyeek

spoon
lžíce f
lzhee·tse

fork
vidlička f
vid·lich·kuh

plate
talíř m
tuh·leerzh

knife
nůž m
noozh

wineglass
sklenička na víno f
skle·nyich·kuh nuh *vee*·no

glass
sklenička f
skle·nyich·kuh

table
stůl m
stool

I'm full.	Jsem najedený/á. **m/f**	ysem nuh·ye·de·nee/a
This is …	Toto je …	to·to ye …
burnt	spálené	spa·le·nair
(too) cold	(moc) studené	(mots) stu·de·nair
(too) spicy	(moc) pálivé	(mots) pa·li·vair
stale	okoralé	o·ko·ruh·lair
superb	výtečné	vee·tech·nair

methods of preparation

postupy příprav jídla

I'd like it …	Chtěl/Chtěla bych … **m/f**	khtyel/khtye·luh bikh …
I don't want it …	Nechtěl/Nechtěla bych … **m/f**	nekh·tyel/nekh·tye·luh bikh …
boiled	vařené	vuh·rzhe·nair
broiled	grilovaný	gri·lo·vuh·nee
deep-fried	fritovaný	fri·to·vuh·nee
fried	smažený	smuh·zhe·nee
grilled	grilovaný	gri·lo·vuh·nee
mashed	rozmačkané	roz·muhch·ka·nair
medium	středně	strzhed·nyc
	propečený	pro·pe·che·nee
rare	krvavý	kr·vuh·vee
reheated	ohřátý	o·hrzha·tee
steamed	dušený	du·she·nee
well-done	propečený	pro·pe·che·nee
without …	bez …	bez …
with the dressing on the side	nálev jako přílohu	na·lev yuh·ko przhee·lo·hu

bramborová placka f	*bruhm·bo·ro·va pluhts·kuh*	potato cake
hamburger m	*huhm·bur·ger*	hamburger
hranolky m	*hruh·nol·ki*	chips
klobása f	*klo·ba·suh*	sausage
párek v rohlíku m	*pa·rek v ro·hlee·ku*	hot dog
smažák m	*smuh·zhak*	fried cheese
smažený sýr m	*smuh·zhe·nee seer*	fried cheese
zmrzlina f	*zmr·zli·nuh*	ice cream

nonalcoholic drinks

nealkoholické nápoje

(cup of) coffee ...	*(šálek) kávy ...*	*(sha·lek) ka·vi ...*
(cup of) tea ...	*(šálek) čaje ...*	*(sha·lek) chuh·ye ...*
with (milk)	*s (mlékem)*	s *(mlair·kem)*
without (sugar)	*bez (cukru)*	bez *(tsu·kru)*
... mineral water	*... minerální voda*	*... mi·ne·ral·nyee vo·duh*
sparkling	*perlivá*	*per·li·va*
still	*neperlivá*	*ne·per·li·va*
(hot) water	*(horká) voda* f	*(hor·ka) vo·duh*
orange juice	*pomerančový džus* m	*po·me·ruhn·cho·vee dzhus*
soft drink	*nealkoholický nápoj* m	*ne·uhl·ko·ho·lits·kee na·poy*

black	*černá*	*cher·na*
iced	*ledová*	*le·do·va*
strong	*silná*	*sil·na*
weak	*slabá*	*sluh·ba*
white	*bílá*	*bee·la*

FOOD

168

alcoholic drinks

beer	*pivo* n	*pi*·vo
brandy	*brandy* f	*bruhn*·di
champagne	*šampaňské* n	*shuhm*·puhn'·skair
cocktail	*koktejl* m	*kok*·teyl

a shot of ...	*panák* ...	*puh*·nak ...
gin	*ginu*	*dzhi*·nu
rum	*rumu*	*ru*·mu
tequila	*tequily*	*te*·ki·li
vodka	*vodky*	*vod*·ki
whisky	*whisky*	*vis*·ki

a bottle/glass	*láhev/skleničku*	*la*·hef/*skle*·nyich·ku
of ... wine	... *vína*	... *vee*·nuh
dessert	*dezertního*	*de*·zert·nyee·ho
red	*červeného*	*cher*·ve·nair·ho
rosé	*růžového*	*roo*·zho·vair·ho
sparkling	*šumivého*	*shu*·mi·vair·ho
white	*bílého*	*bee*·lair·ho

a ... of beer	... *piva*	... *pi*·vuh
glass	*sklenička*	*skle*·nyich·kuh
jug	*džbán*	dzhban
large bottle	*velká láhev*	*vel*·ka *la*·hef
small bottle	*malá láhev*	*muh*·la *la*·hef

how much beer can you drink?

There's no equivalent to a pint in Czech, as metric units are used, not imperial. People don't ask for a glass of beer either: just ask for *pivo* pi·vo (a beer) and you'll get a half-litre glass or mug of the amber liquid. If you're not such a big drinker and want to order less than this, ask for *malé pivo* muh·lair pi·vo and you'll get a small glass (roughly 300ml). Among Czech beer drinkers, it's a no-no to pour the remainder of beer from the old glass into a fresh glass of beer.

absinth m	*uhb*·sint	absinthe
Becherovka f	*be*·khe·rof·kuh	herb schnapps
borovička f	*bo*·ro·vich·kuh	juniper berry liquor
griotka f	*gri*·ot·kuh	cherry liqueur
meruňkovice f	*me*·run'·ko·vi·tse	apricot liquor
slivovice f	*sli*·vo·vi·tse	plum brandy

For additional items, see the **culinary reader**, page 179, and the **dictionary**.

in the bar

v baru

In a bar or pub, before you take a seat ask *Je tu volno?* ye tu *vol*·no (Is the seat free?). Normally, you don't pay straight away for drinks – a tab is run for you on a slip of paper placed on the table next to your drink. The tipping is the same as in a restaurant – the final sum is rounded up to the next whole number to about 5 to 10%.

Excuse me!
Promiňte!   pro·min'·te

I'm next.
Teď jsem na řadě já.   ted' ysem nuh *rzhuh*·dye ya

I'll have a (Becherovka).
Dám si (Becherovku).   dam si (be·khe·rof·ku)

Same again, please.
To samé, prosím.   to *suh*·mair *pro*·seem

No ice, thanks.
Bez ledu, děkuji.   bez *le*·du *dye*·ku·yi

I'll buy you a drink.
Zvu vás na sklenku.   zvu vas nuh *sklen*·ku

What would you like?
Co byste si přál/přála? m/f   tso *bis*·te si przhal/*przha*·la

I don't drink alcohol.
   Nepiji alkohol.   ne·pi·yi *uhl*·ko·hol

It's my round.
   To je moje runda.   to ye *mo*·ye *run*·duh

How much is that?
   Kolik to stojí?   *ko*·lik to *sto*·yee

Do you serve meals here?
   Podáváte zde jídlo?   po·da·va·te zde *yeed*·lo

drinking up

když se pije

In the Czech Republic, you can go for a drink at either a *pivnice* piv·ni·tse (a pub or beer hall that doesn't serve food), or a *vinárna* vi·nar·nuh (a wine bar). If you want something to take away, note that all food shops and supermarkets sell alcohol. There's also a store which sells only wine – *vinotéka* vi·no·tair·kuh.

Cheers!
   Na zdraví!   nuh *zdruh*·vee

This is hitting the spot.
   To mi bodlo.   to mi *bod*·lo

I feel fantastic!
   Cítím se fantasticky!   *tsee*·tyeem se *fuhn*·tuhs·tits·ki

---

listen for ...

Co si dáte?
   tso si *da*·te   **What are you having?**

Myslím že jste měl/měla dost. **m/f**
   mis·leem zhe yste   **I think you've had enough.**
   myel/*mye*·luh dost

Poslední objednávky.
   pos·led·nyee ob·yed·naf·ki   **Last orders.**

I think I've had one too many.
Myslím si, že mám dost.   mis·leem si zhe mam dost

I'm feeling drunk.
Cítím se opilý/á. **m/f**   tsee·tyeem se o·pi·lee/a

I'm pissed.
Jsem ožralý/á. **m/f**   ysem ozh·ruh·lee/a

I feel ill.
Je mi zle.   ye mi zle

Where's the toilet?
Kde je toaleta?   gde ye to·uh·le·tuh

I'm tired, I'd better go home.
Jsem unavený/á,   ysem u·nuh·ve·nee/a
měl/měla bych jít   myel/mye·luh bikh yeet
domů. **m/f**   do·moo

Can you call a taxi for me?
Můžete mi zavolat   moo·zhe·te mi zuh·vo·luht
taxi?   tuhk·si

I don't think you should drive.
Myslím, že byste neměl/   mis·leem zhe bis·te ne·myel/
neměla řídit. **m/f**   ne·mye·luh rzhee·dyit

---

all about you

In Czech, there are two forms of the singular 'you', the informal *ty* ti and the polite *vy* vi. They're often omitted though, because the verb endings (singular and plural respectively) already indicate which form is intended.

Czechs address their friends, family and children with the informal *ty*, while strangers, older people and people in authority are always addressed with the formal *vy*. It's very important to use *vy* with a stranger, as the use of *ty* is considered rude and disrespectful.

Czechs will generally offer to use the familiar instead of the respectful form of speech by saying something like *Můžeme si tykat* moo·zhe·me si ti·kuht (We can use the informal speech). Throughout this phrasebook, the polite form has normally been used unless marked otherwise.

buying food

nakupování jídla

What's the local speciality?
Co je místní specialita? tso ye *meest*·nyee spe·tsi·uh·li·tuh

What's that?
Co to je? tso to ye

Can I taste it?
Mohu to ochutnat? *mo*·hu to *o*·khut·nuht

Can I have a bag, please?
Můžete mi dát *moo*·zhe·te mi dat
tašku, prosím? *tuhsh*·ku *pro*·seem

I don't need a bag, thanks.
Nepotřebuji tašku, ne·pot·rzhe·bu·yi *tuhsh*·ku
děkuji. dye·ku·yi

How much is (500 grams of cheese)?
Kolik stojí (padesát ko·lik sto·yee (puh·de·sat
deka sýra)? de·kuh see·ruh)

underweight

When you go food shopping in the Czech Republic, you'll notice that prices are calculated according to weight. However, Czechs use decagrams (*deka* de·kuh), not grams, for food – for example, 100 grams equals 10 decagrams, or *deset deka* de·set de·kuh in Czech.

I'd like …	Chtěl/Chtěla bych … m/f	khtyel/khtye·luh bikh …
200 grams	dvacet deka	dvuh·tset de·kuh
half a dozen	půl tuctu	pool tuts·tu
a dozen	tucet	tu·tset
half a kilo	půl kila	pool ki·luh
a kilo	kilo	ki·lo
(two) kilos	(dvě) kila	(dvye) ki·luh
a bottle	láhev	la·hef
a jar	sklenici	skle·nyi·tsi
a packet	sáček	sa·chek
a piece	kus	kus
(three) pieces	(tři) kusy	(trzhi) ku·si
a slice	krajíc	kruh·yeets
(six) slices	(šest) krajíců	(shest) kruh·yee·tsoo
a tin	plechovku	ple·khof·ku
(just) a little	(jen) trochu	(yen) tro·khu
more	více	vee·tse
some	několik	nye·ko·lik
that one	tamten	tuhm·ten
this one	tento	ten·to

food stuff

cooked	uvařený	u·vuh·rzhe·nee
cured	naložený	nuh·lo·zhe·nee
dried	sušený	su·she·nee
fresh	čerstvý	cherst·vee
frozen	mražený	mruh·zhe·nee
raw (uncooked)	syrový	si·ro·vee
raw (unprocessed)	surový	su·ro·vee
smoked	uzený	u·ze·nee

slice it up

The Czech word *krajíc* kruh·yeets (slice) is only used to refer to a slice of bread. A slice of salami or lemon is called *kolečko* ko·lech·ko, and a 'piece of cake' is *kus dortu* kus dor·tu.

Less.	*Méně.*	*mair*·nye
A bit more.	*Trochu více.*	*tro*·khu *vee*·tse
Enough.	*Stačí.*	*stuh*·chee

Do you have …?	*Máte …?*	*ma*·te …
anything	*něco*	*nye*·tso
cheaper	*levnějšího*	*lev*·nyey·shee·ho
other kinds	*jiné druhy*	*yi*·nair *dru*·hi

Where can I find the … section?	*Kde mohu najít regál s …?*	gde *mo*·hu *nuh*·yeet *re*·gal s …
dairy	*mléčnými produkty*	*mlairch*·nee·mi *pro*·duk·ti
fish	*rybami*	*ri*·buh·mi
frozen goods	*mraženým zbožím*	*mruh*·zhe·neem *zbo*·zheem
fruit and vegetable	*ovocem a zeleninou*	*o*·vo·tsem uh *ze*·le·nyi·noh
meat	*masem*	*muh*·sem
poultry	*drůbeží*	*droo*·be·zhee

For food items, see the **culinary reader**, page 179, and the **dictionary**.

listen for …

Mohu vám pomoci? *mo*·hu vam *po*·mo·tsi	**Can I help you?**
Přejete si něco? *przhe*·ye·te si *nye*·tso	**What would you like?**
Přejete si ještě něco? *przhe*·ye·te si *yesh*·tye *nye*·tso	**Anything else?**
Žádný nemáme. *zhad*·nee *ne*·ma·me	**There isn't any.**

self-catering

175

cooking utensils

Could I please	*Mohu si prosím*	mo·hu si pro·seem
borrow a ...?	*půjčit ...?*	pooy·chit ...
I need a ...	*Potřebuji ...*	pot·rzhe·bu·yi ...
chopping board	*prkýnko*	pr·keen·ko
frying pan	*pánev*	pa·nef
knife	*nůž*	noozh
saucepan	*kastrol*	kuhs·trol

For more cooking implements, see the **dictionary**.

---

festival flavour

The festivities that accompany the two main religious holidays in the Czech Republic have a specific local flavour:

Velikonoce   ve·li·ko·no·tse   Easter
In villages, a figure made of sticks and cloth symbolising death is thrown into a river to drown. This ritual, called 'carrying of death' (*vynášení smrti* vi·na·she·nyee smr·tyi), is a symbolic cleansing act at the start of spring. The rite of *pomlázka* pom·las·kuh (lit: rejuvenation), which was originally meant to rid women of evil spirits, is still popular on Easter Monday. Men splash women with water and lightly whip them around the ankles with willow branches. Women give painted eggs (*kraslice* kruh·sli·tse) in return.

Vánoce   va·no·tse   Christmas
One of the most common Christmas rituals is the slicing of the apple. If the core is in the shape of a star (*hvězda* hvyez·duh), the whole family will be present next year, but if it's in the form of a cross (*kříž* krzheezh), there might be a death in the family. Pouring molten lead into a bowl of water is an old way of telling the future for the following year. The shape of a ball (*kulička* ku·lich·kuh) means a long journey, a cylinder (*ovál* o·val) brings friendship, and a jug (*džbán* dzhban) shape indicates a wedding.

ordering food

Do you have … food?	Máte … jídla?	ma·te … yeed·luh
halal	halal	huh·luhl
kosher	košer	ko·sher
vegetarian	vegetariánská	ve·ge·tuh·ri·ans·ka

I don't eat …	Nejím …	ne·yeem …
butter	máslo	mas·lo
eggs	vejce	vey·tse
fish	ryby	ri·bi
fish stock	rybí vývar	ri·bee vee·vuhr
meat stock	bujón	bu·yawn
oil	olej	o·ley
pork	vepřové	vep·rzho·vair
poultry	drůbež	droo·bezh
red meat	tmavé maso	tmuh·vair muh·so

Is this …?	Je to …?	ye to …
decaffeinated	bez kofeinu	bez ko·fey·nu
free of animal produce	bez zvířecích produktů	bez zvee·rzhe·tseekh pro·duk·too
free-range	z volného výběhu	z vol·nair·ho vee·bye·hu
genetically modified	geneticky modifikované	ge·ne·tits·ki mo·di·fi·ko·va·nair
gluten-free	bez glutenu	bez glu·te·nu
low-fat	nizkotučné	nyees·ko·tuch·nair
low in sugar	s omezeným cukrem	s o·me·ze·neem tsu·krem
organic	organické	or·guh·nits·kair
salt-free	bez soli	bez so·li

special diets & allergies

I'm on a special diet.
Držím speciální dietu.   dr·zheem spe·tsi·al·nyee di·ye·tu

I'm a vegan.
Jsem vegan/veganka. m/f   ysem ve·guhn/ve·guhn·kuh

I'm a vegetarian.
Jsem vegetarián/   ysem ve·ge·tuh·ri·an/
vegetariánka. m/f   ve·ge·tuh·ri·an·ka

Could you prepare a meal without ...?
Mohl/Mohla by jste   mo·hl/mo·hluh bi yste
připravit jídlo bez ...? m/f   przhi·pruh·vit yeed·lo bez ...

I'm allergic to ...	*Mám alergii na ...*	mam uh·ler·gi·yi nuh ...
dairy	*mléčné*	*mlair·chnair*
produce	*výrobky*	*vee·rob·ki*
eggs	*vejce*	*vey·tse*
gelatine	*želatinu*	*zhe·luh·ti·nu*
gluten	*lepek*	*le·pek*
honey	*med*	med
MSG	*glutaman*	*glu·tuh·muhn*
	sodný	*sod·nee*
nuts	*ořechy*	*o·rzhe·khi*
peanuts	*arašídy*	*uh·ruh·shee·di*
seafood	*plody moře*	*plo·di mo·rzhe*
shellfish	*korýše a*	*ko·ree·she uh*
	měkkýše	*mye·kee·she*

To explain your dietary restrictions with reference to religious beliefs, see **beliefs & cultural differences**, page 141.

culinary reader
kulinářská čítanka

This guide to Czech cuisine is in Czech alphabetical order (shown below). It's designed to help you find your way around Czech menus and markets. Czech nouns have their gender marked as ⓜ masculine, ⓕ feminine or ⓝ neuter. If it's a plural noun, you'll also see pl. Adjectives are given in the masculine form only – for more information on gender, see the **phrasebuilder**, page 20.

alphabet											
Aa Áá Bb Cc Čč Dd Ďď Ee Éé Ěě Ff Gg Hh Chch											
Ii Íí Jj Kk Ll Mm Nn Ňň Oo Óó Pp Qq Rr Řř											
Ss Šš Tt Ťť Uu Úú Ůů Vv Ww Xx Yy Ýý Zz Žž											

A

absinth ⓜ *uhb*·sint *absinthe*
ananas ⓜ *uh*·nuh·nuhs *pineapple*
angrešt ⓜ *uhn*·gresht *gooseberry*
arašídy ⓜ pl *uh*·ruh·shee·di *peanuts*
avokádo ⓝ *uh*·vo·ka·do *avocado*

B

baklažán ⓜ *buh*·kluh·zhan
  aubergine (eggplant)
banán ⓜ *buh*·nan *banana*
bažant ⓜ *buh*·zhuhnt *pheasant*
Becherovka ⓕ *be*·khe·rof·kuh
  herb schnapps
bez kofeinu bez ko·fey·nu *decaffeinated*
bez ledu bez *le*·du *without ice*
bez masá jídla ⓝ pl bez muh·sa *yeed*·luh
  dishes without meat
biftek ⓜ *bif*·tek *beef steak*
bílá káva ⓕ *bee*·la *ka*·vuh *white coffee*
bílé víno ⓝ *bee*·lair vee·no *white wine*
borovička ⓕ *bo*·ro·vich·kuh
  juniper berry liquor
boršč ⓜ borshch *beetroot soup*
borůvky ⓕ pl *bo*·roof·ki *blueberries*

borůvkové knedlíky ⓜ pl *bo*·roof·ko·vair
  kned·lee·ki *blueberry dumplings*
brambor ⓕ *bruhm*·bor *potato*
bramboračka ⓕ *bruhm*·bo·ruhch·kuh
  thick soup of potatoes & mushrooms
bramborák ⓜ *bruhm*·bo·rak *potato cake*
bramborová kaše ⓕ *bruhm*·bo·ro·va
  kuh·she *mashed potatoes often served
  with diced onions fried in butter*
bramborová placka ⓕ
  bruhm·bo·ro·va *pluhts*·kuh *potato cake*
bramborová polévka ⓕ
  bruhm·bo·ro·va *po*·lairf·kuh *potato soup*
bramborové knedlíky ⓜ pl
  bruhm·bo·ro·vair *kned*·lee·ki
  potato dumplings
bramborový salát ⓜ *bruhm*·bo·ro·vee
  suh·lat *potato salad – mayonnaise-
  based with yogurt, diced potatoes,
  carrots, peas, dill pickles, onions & corn*
brokolice ⓕ *bro*·ko·li·tse *broccoli*
broskev ⓕ *bros*·kef *peach*
bujón ⓜ *bu*·yawn *broth with egg*
burčák ⓜ *bur*·chak *young & sweet wine*
bylinkový čaj ⓜ *bi*·lin·ko·vee *chai
  herbal tea*

C

celer ⓜ *tse*-ler *celery*
celozrný chléb ⓜ *tse*-lo-zr-nee khlairb
  wholemeal bread
cereálie ⓕ *tse*-re-a-li-ye *cereal (breakfast)*
cibulačka ⓕ *tsi*-bu-luhch-kuh *onion soup*
cibule ⓕ *tsi*-bu-le *onion*
císařský lusk ⓜ *tsee*-suhrzh-skee lusk
  snow pea
citrón ⓜ *tsi*-trawn *lemon*
cizrna ⓕ *tsi*-zr-nuh *chickpea*
cuketa ⓕ *tsu*-ke-tuh *zucchini (courgette)*
cukr ⓜ *tsu*-kr *sugar*
cukroví ⓝ pl *tsu*-kro-vee *sweet biscuits*

Č

čaj ⓜ chai *tea*
čaj s citrónem ⓜ chai s *tsi*-traw-nem
  tea with lemon
čaj s mlékem ⓜ chai s *mlair*-kem
  tea with milk
černá káva ⓕ *cher*-na *ka*-vuh *black coffee*
černé pivo ⓝ *cher*-nair *pi*-vo *dark beer*
čerstvý *cherst*-vee *fresh*
červená řepa ⓕ *cher*-ve-na *rzhe*-puh
  beetroot
červené víno ⓝ *cher*-ve-nair *vee*-no
  red wine
česnek ⓜ *ches*-nek *garlic*
česnečková polévka ⓕ
  ches-nech-ko-va po-lairf-kuh *garlic soup*
čevapčiči ⓝ *che*-vuhp-chi-chi
  fried or grilled minced veal, pork &
  mutton made into cone-like shapes
čočka ⓕ *choch*-kuh *lentil*
čočková polévka ⓕ
  choch-ko-va po-lairf-kuh *lentil soup*
čokoláda ⓕ *cho*-ko-la-duh *chocolate*

D

ďábelská topinka ⓕ
  dya-bel-ska *to*-pin-kuh
  a piquant toast with meat & cheese
datl ⓜ *duh*-tl *date*
dezertní víno ⓝ *de*-zert-nyee *vee*-no
  dessert wine

divoký *dyi*-vo-kee *wild*
domácí *do*-ma-tsee *homemade*
dort ⓜ dort *cake*
dortík ⓜ *dor*-tyeek *tart*
dršťková polévka ⓕ
  drsht'-ko-va po-lairf-kuh *spicy tripe soup*
dršťky ⓕ *drsht*-ki *sliced tripe*
dušená mrkev ⓕ *du*-she-na *mr*-kev
  stewed carrots
dušená roštěnka ⓕ
  du-she-na *rosh*-tyen-kuh
  braised beef slices in sauce
dušené fazole ⓕ pl *du*-she-nair *fuh*-zo-le
  stewed beans
dušený *du*-she-nee *steamed · stewed*
dýně ⓕ *dee*-nye *pumpkin*
džem ⓜ dzhem *jam*
džin ⓜ dzhin *gin*

F

fazole ⓝ *fuh*-zo-le *bean*
fazolová polévka ⓕ
  fuh-zo-lo-va po-lairf-kuh *bean soup*
fazolové klíčky ⓜ pl
  fuh-zo-lo-vair kleech-ki *bean sprouts*
fazolové lusky ⓜ pl *fuh*-zo-lo-vair *lus*-ki
  beans
fazolový salát ⓜ *fuh*-zo-lo-vee *suh*-lat
  bean salad
fík ⓜ feek *fig*
filé ⓝ *fi*-lair *fillet*
fritovaný *fri*-to-vuh-nee *deep-fried*

G

grilovaný *gri*-lo-vuh-nee *broiled · grilled*
  or on the spit
griotka ⓕ *gri*-ot-kuh *cherry liqueur*
guláš ⓜ *gu*-lash *thick, spicy stew, usually*
  made with beef & potatoes, sometimes
  with venison or mushrooms
gulášová polévka ⓕ *gu*-la-sho-va
  po-lairf-kuh *beef goulash soup*

H

hlávkový salát ⓜ *hlaf*-ko-vee *suh*-lat
  green salad in vinegar · lettuce

hlavní jídla ⓝ pl *hluhv·nyee yeed·luh*
main courses

hodně vypečený *hod·nye vi·pe·che·nee*
well-done (of meat)

horký *hor·kee* hot

hořčice ⓕ *horzh·chi·tse* mustard

hotová jídla ⓝ pl *ho·to·va yeed·luh*
ready-to-serve dishes

houba ⓕ *hoh·buh* mushroom

houbová polévka ⓕ
hoh·bo·va po·lairf·kuh mushroom soup

houska ⓕ *hohs·kuh* oval bread roll

houskové knedlíky ⓜ pl
hohs·ko·vair kned·lee·ki bread dumplings

hovězí (maso) ⓝ *ho·vye·zee (muh·so)*
beef

hovězí guláš ⓝ *ho·vye·zee gu·lash* beef
stew, sometimes served with dumplings

hovězí vývar s játrovými knedlíčky ⓜ
*ho·vye·zee vee·vuhr s ya·tro·vee·mi
kned·leech·ki* beef broth with little
dumplings of seasoned liver

hrách ⓜ hrakh dried peas

hrachová polévka ⓕ *hra·kho·va
po·lairf·kuh* thick pea soup with bacon

hrachová polévka s uzeným ⓕ
hra·kho·va po·lairf·kuh s u·ze·nyeem
pea soup with smoked pork

hranolky ⓕ pl *hruh·nol·ki* French fries

hrášek ⓜ *hra·shek* peas

hrozny ⓜ pl *hroz·ni* grapes

hruška ⓕ *hrush·kuh* pear

humr ⓜ *hu·mr* lobster

husa ⓕ *hu·suh* goose

Ch

chléb ⓜ khlairb bread

chřest ⓜ khrzhest asparagus

J

jablečný džus ⓜ *yuh·blech·nee dzhus*
apple juice

jablečný závin ⓜ *yuh·blech·nee za·vin*
apple strudel

jablko ⓝ *yuh·bl·ko* apple

jahoda ⓝ *yuh·ho·duh* strawberry

játra ⓝ *yat·ruh* liver

jehněčí (maso) ⓝ *yeh·nye·chee (muh·so)*
lamb

jelení (maso) ⓜ *ye·le·nyee (muh·so)*
venison

jelito ⓝ *ye·li·to* black pudding

jídla na objednávku ⓝ pl
yeed·luh nuh o·byed·naf·ku
à la carte dishes (cooked as ordered)

jitrnice ⓕ *yi·tr·nyi·tse* white pudding

jogurt ⓜ *yo·gurt* yogurt

K

kachna ⓕ *kuhkh·nuh* duck

kakao ⓝ *kuh·kuh·o* hot chocolate (drink)

kanec ⓜ *kuh·nets* boar

kantalup ⓜ *kuhn·tuh·lup* cantaloupe

kapr ⓜ *kuh·pr* carp

kapučíno ⓝ *kuh·pu·chee·no* cappuccino

kapusta ⓕ *kuh·pus·tuh* cabbage

karbanátek ⓜ *kuhr·buh·na·tek*
hamburger with breadcrumbs, egg,
diced white bread roll & onions

kari ⓝ *kuh·ri* curry

kaštan ⓜ *kuhsh·tuhn* chestnut

káva ⓕ *ka·vuh* coffee

káva bez kofeinu ⓕ *ka·vuh bez
ko·fey·nu* decaffeinated coffee

káva se smetanou ⓕ *ka·vuh se
sme·tuh·noh* coffee with cream

kaviár ⓜ *kuh·vi·ar* caviar

kečup ⓜ *ke·chup* ketchup

kedluben ⓜ *ked·lu·ben* kohlrabi

kešů ⓝ *ke·shoo* cashew

klobása ⓕ *klo·ba·suh* thick sausage

kmín ⓜ kmeen caraway

knedlíky ⓜ pl *kned·lee·ki* dumplings

knedlíky s vejci ⓜ pl *kned·lee·ki s vey·tsi*
fried dumplings with eggs

kobliha ⓕ *kob·li·huh* doughnut

kokos ⓜ *ko·kos* coconut

koláč ⓜ *ko·lach*
pastry (with various toppings)

koňak ⓜ *ko·nyuhk* brandy

kopr ⓜ *ko·pr* dill

koprová polévka ⓕ *kop·ro·va
po·lairf·kuh* dill & sour cream soup

kotleta ⓕ *kot·le·tuh* chop · cutlet

krajíc ⓜ *kruh·yeets* slice of bread

králík @ *kra*·leek rabbit
krevety ① pl *kre*·ve·ti prawns (shrimps)
krokety ① pl *kro*·ke·ti
 deep-fried mashed potato balls
krvavý *kr*·vuh·vee rare (of meat)
krůta ① *kroo*·tuh turkey
křen @ *krzhen* horseradish
křenová rolka ① *krzhe*·no·va *rol*·kuh
 ham & horseradish roll
kukuřice ① *ku*·ku·rzhi·tse corn
kukuřičné lupínky @ pl
 ku·ku·rzhich·nair *lu*·peen·ki cornflakes
kuře @ *ku*·rzhe chicken
kuřecí polévka s nudlemi ①
 ku·rzhe·tsee po·lairf·kuh s *nud*·le·mi
 chicken noodle soup
kuře na paprice @ *ku*·rzhe nuh
 puh·*pri*·tse chicken boiled in spicy
 paprika cream sauce
kuskus @ *kus*·kus couscous
květák @ *kvye*·tak cauliflower
kyselá smetana ① *ki*·se·la *sme*·tuh·nuh
 sour cream

L

lečo @ *le*·cho stewed onions, capsicums,
 tomatoes, eggs & sausage
led @ *led* ice
ledová káva ① *le*·do·va *ka*·vuh iced coffee
ledový čaj @ *le*·do·vee chai iced tea
ležák @ *le*·zhak lager
lilek @ *li*·lek aubergine • eggplant
limeta ① *li*·me·tuh lime
limonáda ① *li*·mo·na·duh
 lemonade • soft drink
lískový oříšek @ *lees*·ko·vee o·rzhee·shek
 hazelnut
losos @ *lo*·sos salmon
luštěnina ① *lush*·tye·nyi·nuh legume

M

majonéza ① *muh*·yo·nair·zuh mayonnaise
makový koláč @ *muh*·ko·vee ko·lach
 poppy seed pastry
makrela ① *muh*·kre·luh mackerel

malina ① *muh*·li·nuh raspberry
mandarinka ① *muhn*·duh·rin·kuh
 mandarin
mandle ① *muhnd*·le almond
mango @ *muhn*·go mango
margarín @ *muhr*·guh·reen margarine
máslo @ *mas*·lo butter
maso @ *muh*·so meat
med @ *med* honey
meloun @ *me*·lohn
 melon • watermelon
meruňka ① *me*·run'·kuh apricot
meruňkovice ① *me*·run'·ko·vi·tse
 apricot liquor
míchaná vejce ① pl *mee*·khuh·na *vey*·tse
 scrambled eggs
míchaná vejce s klobásou ① pl
 mee·khuh·na *vey*·tse s *klo*·ba·soh
 scrambled eggs with sausage
míchaný *mee*·khuh·nee mixed
minerálka ① *mi*·ne·ral·kuh mineral water
mléko @ *mlair*·ko milk
mleté maso @ *mle*·tair muh·so
 minced meat
moučník @ *mohch*·nyeek dessert
mouka ① *moh*·kuh flour
mrkev ① *mr*·kev carrot
mrkvový salát @ *mrk*·vo·vee *suh*·lat
 carrot salad

N

nadívaný *nuh*·dyee·vuh·nee stuffed
nakládaná okurka ①
 nuh·kla·duh·na o·kur·kuh dill pickle
nakládaná zelenina ①
 nuh·kla·duh·na ze·le·nyi·nuh pickles
nápoj @ *na*·poy drink
na roštu nuh rosh·tu grilled
natvrdo uvařený *nuht*·vr·do
 u·vuh·rzhe·nee hard-boiled (egg)
nealkoholický nápoj @
 ne·uhl·ko·ho·lits·kee *na*·poy soft drink
nektarínka ① *nek*·tuh·reen·kuh nectarine
neperlivá minerálka ① *ne*·per·li·va
 mi·ne·ral·kuh still mineral water
nudle ① pl *nud*·le noodles

nudlová polévka ① nud·lo·va
po·lairf·kuh *noodle soup made from
chicken broth with vegetables*

O

obložené chlebíčky ⑩ pl o·blo·zhe·nair
khle·beech·ki *open sandwiches on
French bread, with cold meat, eggs,
cheese and/or mayonnaise-based salads
such as lobster, fish, potatoes or ham*
ocet ⑩ o·tset *vinegar*
odstředěné mléko ⑩
od·strzhe·dye·nair mlair·ko *skim milk*
okurka ① o·kur·kuh
cucumber or dill pickle
okurkový salát ⑩ o·kur·ko·vee suh·lat
cucumber salad
olej ⑩ o·ley *oil*
oliva ① o·li·vuh *olive*
olivový olej ⑩ o·li·vo·vee o·ley *olive oil*
omáčka ① o·mach·kuh *sauce*
omeleta ① o·me·le·tuh *omelette*
omeleta se sýrem a bramborem ①
o·me·le·tuh se see·rem uh
bruhm·bo·rem *cheese & potato omelette*
opékané brambory ① pl o·pair·kuh·nair
bruhm·bo·ri *roasted potatoes*
oplatka ① o·pluht·kuh
large paper-thin waffle
ořechy ⑩ pl o·rzhe·khi *nuts*
oříšek ⑩ o·rzhe·shek *nut*
oves ① o·ves *oats*
ovoce ⑩ o·vo·tse *fruit*
ovocná šťáva ① o·vots·na shtya·vuh
fruit juice
ovocné knedlíky ⑩ pl
o·vots·nair kned·lee·ki *fruit dumplings
(the dough has a potato, cottage cheese
or yeast flour base & the fillings are
usually plums, apricots, strawberries or
blueberries)*
ovocný čaj ⑩ o·vots·nee chai *fruit tea*

P

palačinka ① puh·luh·chin·kuh
crepe • pancake
pálivý pa·li·vee *spicy*

paprika ① puh·pri·kuh
capsicum (bell pepper)
párek ⑩ pa·rek *thin sausage*
párek v rohlíku ⑩ pa·rek v ro·hlee·ku
hot dog
pasiflora ① puh·si·flo·ruh *passionfruit*
paštika ① puhsh·tyi·kuh *paté*
pečená husa ① pe·che·na hu·suh
roast goose
pečená kachna ① pe·che·na kuhkh·nuh
*roast duck (often served with cabbage or
sauerkraut & dumplings)*
pečená šunka s vejci ① pe·che·na
shun·kuh s vey·tsi *fried ham with eggs*
pečený pe·che·nee *baked • roasted*
pečivo ⑩ pe·chi·vo *bread rolls*
pepř ⑩ pe·przh *black pepper*
perlivá minerálka ① per·li·va
mi·ne·ral·kuh *carbonated mineral water*
perlivý per·li·vee *carbonated*
perník ⑩ per·nyek *gingerbread*
pfeferon ⑩ fe·fe·ron *chilli*
pfeferonová omáčka ①
fe·fe·ro·no·va o·mach·kuh *chilli sauce*
piroh ⑩ pi·roh *pastry (with a filling)*
pistácie ① pis·ta·tsi·ye *pistachio*
pivo ⑩ pi·vo *beer*
plněná paprika ① pl·nye·na puh·pri·kuh
*capsicum stuffed with minced meat &
rice, served with tomato sauce*
plody moře ⑩ pl plo·di mo·rzhe *seafood*
podzemnice olejná ①
pod·zem·nyi·tse o·ley·na *groundnut*
polévka ① po·lairf·kuh *soup*
pomeranč ⑩ po·me·ruhnch *orange*
pomerančový džus ⑩
po·me·ruhn·cho·vee dzhus *orange juice*
pórek ⑩ paw·rek *leek*
povidla ⑩ po·vid·luh *plum purée*
povidlový koláč ⑩ po·vid·lo·vee ko·lach
plum purée pastry
Pražská šunka ① pruhzh·ska shun·kuh
*Prague ham – ham pickled in brine &
spices & smoked over a beechwood fire*
Pražská šunka s okurkou ①
pruhzh·ska shun·kuh s o·kur·koh
Prague ham with gherkins

předkrmy ⓜ pl *przhed·kr·mi entrées*

přílohy ⓕ pl *przhee·lo·hi side dishes*

přírodně sycená minerálka ⓕ
*przhee·rod·nye si·tse·na mi·ne·ral·kuh
still mineral water*

přírodní řízek ⓜ *przhee·rod·nyee
rzhee·zek pork or veal schnitzel without
breadcrumbs*

propečený *pro·pe·che·nee
well-done (of meat)*

pstruh ⓜ *pstrooh trout*

pstruh na másle ⓜ *pstrooh nuh mas·le
grilled trout with butter*

pudink ⓜ *pu·dink custard*

R

rajčatový protlak ⓜ
rai·chuh·to·vee prot·luhk tomato purée

rajčatový salát ⓜ *rai·chuh·to·vee suh·lat
tomato salad with onions*

rajče ⓝ *rai·che tomato*

rajská omáčka ⓕ *rais·ka o·mach·kuh
tomato sauce – a sweeter version of the
original Italian sauce, served with meat
& rice or noodles*

rajské jablko ⓝ *rais·kair yuh·bl·ko
tomato*

rakvička ⓕ *ruhk·vich·kuh 'coffin' –
meringues topped with whipped cream*

rizoto ⓝ *ri·zo·to
a mixture of pork, onions, peas & rice*

rohlík ⓜ *roh·leek long bread roll*

roštěný *rosh·tye·nee broiled*

rozinky ⓕ pl *ro·zin·ki raisins · sultanas*

rozmačkané *roz·muhch·ka·nair mashed*

ruské vejce ⓝ *rus·kair vey·tse
hard-boiled eggs & ham, covered with
mayonnaise & topped with caviar*

růžové víno ⓝ *roo·zho·vair vee·no
rosé (wine)*

ryba ⓕ *ri·buh fish*

rybí filé ⓝ *ri·bee fi·lair fish fillet*

rybí polévka ⓕ *ri·bee po·lairf·kuh
fish soup usually made with carp & some
carrots, potatoes & peas*

rýže ⓕ *ree·zhe rice*

Ř

ředkvička ⓕ *rzhed·kvich·kuh radish*

S

salám ⓜ *suh·lam salami*

salát ⓜ *suh·lat salad*

salát z červené řepy ⓜ *suh·lat s
cher·ve·nair rzhe·pi beetroot salad*

sardinka ⓕ *suhr·din·kuh sardine*

segedínský guláš ⓜ *se·ge·deens·kee
gu·lash goulash with beef, pork, lamb &
sauerkraut in a paprika cream sauce,
served with dumplings*

sekaná ⓕ *se·kuh·na meatloaf*

sendvič ⓜ *send·vich sandwich*

skopové (maso) ⓝ *sko·po·vair (muh·so)
mutton*

sladký ⓜ *sluhd·kee sweet*

slanina ⓕ *sluh·nyi·nuh bacon*

slávka jedlá ⓕ *slaf·kuh yed·la mussels*

sleď ⓜ *sled' herring*

slivovice ⓕ *sli·vo·vi·tse plum brandy*

smažené žampiony ⓜ pl *smuh·zhe·nair
zhuhm·pi·yo·ni fried mushrooms often
mixed with onions & eggs*

smažený kapr ⓜ *smuh·zhe·nee kuh·pr
pieces of carp fried in breadcrumbs*

smažený květák ⓜ *smuh·zhe·nee kvye·tak
fried cauliflower in breadcrumbs*

smažený květák s bramborem ⓜ
*smuh·zhe·nee kvye·tak s bruhm·bo·rem
vegetarian dish of cauliflower florets
fried in breadcrumbs & served with
boiled potatoes & tartar sauce*

smažený sýr ⓜ *smuh·zhe·nee seer
fried cheese in breadcrumbs*

smažená vejce ⓝ pl
smuh·zhe·na vey·tse fried eggs

smažený vepřový řízek ⓜ
*smuh·zhe·nee ve·przho·vee rzhee·zek
schnitzel with potatoes or potato
salad*

smetana ⓕ *sme·tuh·nuh cream*

sójová omáčka ⓕ *saw·yo·va o·mach·kuh
soy sauce*

FOOD

sójové mléko ⓝ *saw·yo·vair mlair·ko*
soy milk

sójový tvaroh ⓜ *saw·yo·vee tvuh·rawh*
tofu

sterilizované zelí ⓝ *ste·re·li·zo·vuh·nair*
ze·lee pickled cabbage

středně propečený *strzhed·nye*
pro·pe·che·nee medium rare (of meat)

studený *stu·de·nee cold*

sůl ⓕ *sool salt*

sušené ovoce ⓝ *su·she·nair o·vo·tse*
dried fruit

svíčková ⓕ *sveech·ko·va sirloin*

svíčková na smetaně ⓕ
sveech·ko·va nuh sme·ta·nye
roast beef in carrot cream sauce with
dumplings, topped with lemon,
cranberries & whipped cream

sýr ⓜ *seer cheese*

syrový *si·ro·vee raw*

sýrový nářez ⓜ *see·ro·vee na·rzhez*
cheeseboard

Š

šampaňské ⓝ *shuhm·puhn'·skair*
champagne

šlehačka ⓕ *shle·huhch·kuh*
whipped cream

šopský salát ⓜ *shop·skee suh·lat*
lettuce, tomato, onion & cheese salad

španělský ptáček ⓜ *shpuh·nyel·skee*
pta·chek slice of beef rolled up & filled
with onions, capsicums, dill pickle,
bacon & sausage – cooked in beef sauce
& served with rice

špenát ⓜ *shpe·nat spinach*

(se) špenátem ⓜ *(se) shpe·na·tem*
finely chopped spinach, cooked with
onions, garlic & cream (often served with
potato dumplings & meat)

šťáva ⓕ *shtya·vuh juice*

šumivé víno ⓝ *shu·mi·vair vee·no*
sparkling wine

šumivý *shu·mi·vee carbonated*

šunka ⓕ *shun·kuh ham*

šunka lesnická ⓕ *shun·kuh les·nits·ka*
Prague ham cooked with red wine,
tomatoes, mushrooms, bacon & butter

šunka v aspiku ⓕ *shun·kuh f uhs·pi·ku*
ham in aspic

šunkové závitky s pórem ⓜ
shun·ko·vair za·vit·ki s paw·rem
rolled ham with cheese & leek

švestka ⓕ *shvest·kuh plum*

švestkové knedlíky ⓕ pl *shvest·ko·vair*
kned·lee·ki sweet dumplings filled with
fresh plums & sprinkled with poppy
seeds, sugar & melted butter

T

tatarská omáčka ⓕ *tuh·tuhrs·ka*
o·mach·kuh a mayonnaise-based tartar
sauce with diced onions & spices

tatarský biftek ⓜ *tuh·tuhrs·kee bif·tek*
raw steak

telecí (maso) ⓝ *te·le·tsee (muh·so) veal*

telecí kotleta ⓕ *te·le·tsee kot·le·tuh*
veal cutlet

telecí pečeně ⓕ *te·le·tsee pe·che·nye*
roast veal

teplý *tep·lee warm*

těstovina ⓕ *tyes·to·vi·na pasta*

tlačenka ⓕ *tluh·chen·kuh jellied meat*
loaf – pieces of pork pressed together
with additional ingredients

tlačenka s octem a cibulí ⓕ
tluh·chen·kuh s ots·tem a tsi·bu·lee
jellied meat loaf, served with vinegar &
brown onions

treska ⓕ *tres·kuh cod*

třešně ⓕ pl *trzhesh·nye cherries*

tuňák ⓜ *tu·nyak tuna*

tvaroh ⓜ *tvuh·rawkh cottage cheese*

tvarohový koláč ⓜ
tvuh·ro·ho·vee ko·lach
pastry with cottage cheese & raisins

U

uherský salám s okurkou ⓜ
u·hers·kee suh·lam s o·kur·koh
Hungarian salami with gherkins

ústřice ⓕ *oost·rzhi·tse oyster*

utopenci ⓜ *u·to·pen·tsi*
'the drowned one' – sliced pickled pork
sausage with onions & capsicums

culinary reader

185

uzené koleno ⓝ *u-ze-nair ko-le-no*
  smoked hock
uzené se zelím a knedlíky ⓝ *u-ze-nair*
  se ze-leem uh kned-lee-ki smoked pork
  with cooked sauerkraut & dumplings
uzený *u-ze-nee* smoked
uzený jazyk ⓜ *u-ze-nee yuh-zik*
  smoked tongue

V

vajíčko ⓝ *vuh-yeech-ko* egg
vanilka ⓕ *vuh-nil-kuh* vanilla
vařené brambory ⓕ pl *vuh-rzhe-nair*
  bruhm-bo-ri boiled potatoes
vařené vejce ⓕ pl *vuh-rzhe-nair vey-tse*
  boiled eggs
vařený *vuh-rzhe-nee* boiled
vařit ve skle *vuh-rzhit ve skle*
  poached (egg)
vejce ⓝ pl *vey-tse* eggs
vejce na měkko ⓝ pl *vey-tse nuh mye-ko*
  soft-boiled eggs
vejce se slaninou ⓝ pl
  vey-tse se sluh-nyi-noh bacon & eggs
vejce se šunkou ⓝ pl *vey-tse se shun-koh*
  ham & eggs
veka ⓕ *ve-kuh* French bread stick
vepřová játra ⓕ *vep-rzho-va yat-ruh*
  pork liver fried with onions
vepřová pečeně ⓕ
  vep-rzho-va pe-che-nye
  roast pork with caraway seeds
vepřová pečeně s knedlíky a zelím ⓕ
  vep-rzho-va pe-che-nye s kned-lee-ki uh
  ze-leem roast pork with dumplings &
  cooked sauerkraut
vepřové (maso) ⓝ *vep-rzho-vair (muh-so)*
  pork
víno ⓝ *vee-no* wine
víno rozlévané ⓝ *vee-no roz-lair-vuh-nair*
  wine by the glass

višně ⓕ pl *vish-nye* sour cherries
vlašský salát ⓜ *vluhsh-skee suh-lat*
  mayonnaise salad with ham, dill pickles,
  celery, peas, carrots & potatoes
voda ⓕ *vo-duh* water
voda s ledem ⓕ *vo-duh s le-dem*
  water with ice cubes
vuřt ⓜ *vurzht* pork sausage

Z

zajíc ⓜ *zuh-yeets* hare
zajíc na smetaně ⓜ *zuh-yeets nuh*
  sme-tuh-nye hare in cream sauce
zažívací likéry ⓕ pl
  zuh-zhee-vuh-tsee li-kair-ri digestifs
zapečená šunka plněná chřestem ⓕ
  zuh-pe-che-na shun-kuh pl-nye-na
  khrzhes-tem Prague ham baked with
  asparagus, breadcrumbs & cheese
zavináč ⓜ *zuh-vi-nach*
  rolled pickled herring fillets
zelenina ⓕ *ze-le-nyi-nuh* vegetables
zeleninová polévka ⓕ *ze-le-nyi-no-va*
  po-lairf-kuh vegetable soup
zeleninový míchaný salát ⓜ
  ze-le-nyi-no-vee mee-khuh-nee suh-lat
  mixed vegetable salad
zelí ⓝ *ze-lee* sauerkraut
zelňačka ⓕ *zel-nyuch-kuh*
  thick sauerkraut, potatoes & cream soup
zmrzlí *zmrz-lee* frozen
zmrzlina ⓕ *zmrz-li-nuh* ice cream
zmrzlinový pohár ⓜ
  zmrz-li-no-vee po-har ice cream sundae
znojemská pečeně ⓕ *zno-yem-ska*
  pe-che-nye sliced roast beef in gherkin
  sauce, often served with rice
zvěřinový guláš ⓕ *zvye-rzhi-no-vee*
  gu-lash goulash made from any game
  meat or any combination of game
  meats

emergencies

nouzové situace

Help!	*Pomoc!*	*po·mots*
Stop!	*Zastav!*	*zuhs·tuhf*
Go away!	*Běžte pryč!*	*byezh·te prich*
Thief!	*Zloděj!*	*zlo·dyey*
Fire!	*Hoří!*	*ho·rzhee*
Watch out!	*Pozor!*	*po·zor*

signs

Nemocnice	*ne·mots·nyi·tse*	**Hospital**
Policie	*po·li·tsi·ye*	**Police**
Pohotovostní	*po·ho·to·vost·nyee*	**Emergency**
oddělení	*od·dye·le·nyee*	**Department**

Call …!	*Zavolejte …!*	*zuh·vo·ley·te …*
a doctor	*lékaře*	*lair·kuh·rzhe*
an ambulance	*sanitku*	*suh·nit·ku*
the police	*policii*	*po·li·tsi·yi*

It's an emergency.
To je naléhavý případ. to ye *nuh·lair·huh·vee przhee·puhd*

There's been an accident.
Došlo k nehodě. *dosh·lo k ne·ho·dye*

Could you please help?
Můžete prosím pomoci?   moo·zhe·te *pro*·seem po·mo·tsi

Can I use your phone?
Mohu si zatelefonovat?   mo·hu si zuh·te·le·fo·no·vuht

I'm going to call the police.
Jdu zavolat policii.   ydu zuh·vo·luht po·li·tsi·yi

I'm lost.
Zabloudil/Zabloudila   zuh·bloh·dyil/zuh·bloh·dyi·luh
jsem. m/f   ysem

Where are the toilets?
Kde jsou toalety?   gde ysoh to·uh·le·ti

Is it safe at night?
Je to v noci bezpečné?   ye to v no·tsi bez·pech·nair

Is it safe …?	*Je to bezpečné pro …?*	ye to bez·pech·nair pro …
for gay people	*teplý*	tep·lee
for travellers	*cestovatele*	tses·to·vuh·te·le
for women	*ženy*	zhe·ni
on your own	*samotnou osobu*	suh·mot·noh o·so·bu

police

policie

Where's the police station?
Kde je policejní   gde ye po·li·tsey·nyee
stanice?   stuh·nyi·tse

Please telephone the Tourist Police.
Prosím zavolejte   pro·seem zuh·vo·ley·te
turistickou policii.   tu·ris·tits·koh po·li·tsi·yi

I want to report an offence.
Chci nahlásit trestný čin.   khtsi nuh·hla·sit trest·nee chin

It was him/her.
To byl on/ona.   to bil on/o·nuh

I've been ...	... mě.	... mye
assaulted	Přepadli	przhe·puhd·li
raped	Znásilnili	zna·sil·nyi·li
robbed	Okradli	o·kruhd·li

My ... was/ were stolen.	Ukradli mě ...	u·kruhd·li mye ...
I've lost my ...	Ztratil/Ztratila jsem ... m/f	ztruh·tyil/ztruh·tyi·luh ysem ...
backpack	batoh	buh·tawh
bag	zavazadlo	zuh·vuh·zuhd·lo
credit card	kreditní kartu	kre·dit·nyee kuhr·tu
handbag	kabelku	kuh·bel·ku
jewellery	šperky	shper·ki
money	peníze	pe·nyee·ze
papers	doklady	dok·luh·di
passport	pas	puhs
travellers cheques	cestovní šeky	tses·tov·nyee she·ki
wallet	peněženku	pe·nye·zhen·ku

I want to contact my ...	Potřebuji se obrátit na ...	pot·rzhe·bu·yi se o·bra·tyit nuh ...
consulate	můj konzulát	mooy kon·zu·lat mair
embassy	mé velvyslanectví	vel·vi·sluh·nets·tvee

I have insurance.
Jsem pojištěný/á. m/f ysem po·yish·tye·nee/a

What am I accused of?
Z čeho jsem obžalován/ obžalována? m/f z che·ho ysem ob·zhuh·lo·van/ ob·zhuh·lo·va·nuh

I didn't do it.
Neudělal/Neudělala jsem to. m/f ne·u·dye·luhl/ne·u·dye·luh·luh ysem to

Can I pay an on-the-spot fine?
Mohu zaplatit pokutu na místě? mo·hu zuh·pluh·tyit po·ku·tu nuh mees·tye

Can I make a phone call?
Mohu si zavolat? mo·hu si zuh·vo·luht

Can I have an English interpreter?

Můžete mi poskytnout   *moo·zhe·te mi pos·kit·noht*
tlumočníka   *tlu·moch·nyee·ka*
angličtiny?   *uhn·glich·tyi·ni*

Can I have a lawyer (who speaks English)?

Můžete mi poskytnout   *moo·zhe·te mi pos·kit·noht*
(anglickomluvícího)   *(uhn·glits·kom·lu·vee·tsee·ho)*
právníka?   *prav·nyee·kuh*

This drug is for personal use.

Tyto léky jsou pro mé   *ti·to lair·ki ysoh pro mair*
vlastní použití.   *vluhst·nyee po·u·zhi·tyee*

I have a prescription for this drug.

Mám lékařský   *mam lair·kuhrzh·skee*
předpis pro tento lék.   *przhed·pis pro ten·to lairk*

the police may say ...

Jste obžalován/	*yste ob·zhuh·lo·van/*	**You're charged**
obžalována	*ob·zhuh·lo·vuh·nuh*	**with ...**
z ... m/f	*z ...*	
krádeže v	*kra·de·zhe v*	**shoplifting**
obchodě	*ob·kho·dye*	
napadení	*nuh·puh·de·nyee*	**assault**
nelegálního	*ne·le·gal·nyee·ho*	**overstaying**
prodloužení	*pro·dloh·zhe·nyee*	**a visa**
pobytu	*po·bi·tu*	
nelegálního	*ne·le·gal·nyee·ho*	**not having**
vstupu	*fstu·pu*	**a visa**
nezákoné	*ne·za·ko·nair*	**possession**
držení	*dr·zhe·nyee*	**(of illegal**
(omamných	*(o·mam·neekh*	**substances)**
látek)	*la·tek)*	
porušování	*po·ru·sho·va·nyee*	**disturbing**
klidu	*kli·du*	**the peace**
To je pokuta za ...	*to ye po·ku·tuh zuh ...*	**It's a ... fine.**
parkování	*puhr·ko·va·nye*	**parking**
překročení	*przhe·kro·che·nyee*	**speeding**
povolené	*po·vo·le·nair*	
rychlosti	*rikh·los·tyi*	

doctor

lékař

Male and female doctors are addressed as *pane doktore* puh·ne *dok·to·re* (Mr Doctor) and *pani doktorko* puh·nyi *dok·tor·ko* (Mrs Doctor) respectively. These forms are also used for dentists.

Where's the nearest ...?	*Kde je nejbližší ...?*	gde ye *ney·blizh·shee ...*
dentist	*zubař*	*zu·*buhrzh
doctor	*lékař*	*lair·*kuhrzh
emergency department	*pohotovost*	po·ho·to·vost
hospital	*nemocnice*	ne·mots·nyi·tse
optometrist	*optik*	op·tik
(night)	*(non-stop)*	*(non·*stop)
pharmacist	*lékárník*	*lair·*kar·nyeek

I need a doctor (who speaks English).
Potřebuji *pot·*rzhe·bu·yi
(anglickomluvícího) *(uhn·*glits·kom·lu·vee·tsee·ho)
doktora. *dok·*to·ruh

Could I see a female doctor?
Mohla bych být *mo·*hluh bikh beet
vyšetřená lékařkou? *vi·*shet·rzhe·na *lair·*kuhrzh·koh

Could the doctor come here?
Může lékař přijít *moo·*zhe *lair·*kuhrzh *przhi·*yeet
k nám? k nam

Jaký máte problém?
yuh·kee ma·te pro·blairm — **What's the problem?**

Kde to bolí?
gde to bo·lee — **Where does it hurt?**

Máte teplotu?
ma·te tep·lo·tu — **Do you have a temperature?**

Jak dlouho již máte tyto příznaky?
yuhk dloh·ho yizh ma·te
ti·to przheez·nuh·ki — **How long have you been like this?**

Už jste měl/měla někdy něco podobného? **m/f**
uzh yste myel/mye·luh
nyek·di nye·tso po·dob·nair·ho — **Have you had this before?**

Jaký je váš intimní život?
yuh·kee ye vash
in·tim·nyee zhi·vot — **Are you sexually active?**

Měl/Měla jste nechráněný pohlavní styk? **m/f**
myel/mye·luh yste
ne·khra·nye·nee
po·hluhv·nyee stik — **Have you had unprotected sex?**

Pijete alkoholické nápoje?
pi·ye·te uhl·ko·ho·lits·kair
na·po·ye — **Do you drink?**

Kouříte?
koh·rzhee·te — **Do you smoke?**

Užíváte nějaké návykové látky?
u·zhee·va·te nye·yuh·kair
na·vi·ko·vair lat·ki — **Do you take drugs?**

Jste na něco alergický?
yste nuh nye·tso
uh·ler·gits·kee — **Are you allergic to anything?**

Berete nějaké léky?
be·re·te nye·yuh·kair lair·ki — **Are you on medication?**

Jak dlouho cestujete?
yuhk dloh·ho tses·tu·ye·te — **How long are you travelling for?**

the doctor may say ...

Potřebujete být hospitalizován.
pot·rzhe·bu·ye·te beet
hos·pi·tuh·li·zo·van

You need to be admitted to hospital.

Po návratu domu byste si měl/měla zajít na kontrolu. m/f
po *na*·vruh·tu *do*·mu *bis*·te
si myel/*mye*·luh *zuh*·yeet
nuh *kon*·tro·lu

You should have it checked when you go home.

Váš zdravotní stav vyžaduje léčení ve vaší zemi.
vash *zdruh*·vot·nyee stuhv
vi·zhuh·du·ye *lair*·che·nyee
ve *vuh*·shee ze·mi

You should return home for treatment.

Jste hypochondr.
yste *hi*·po·khon·dr

You're a hypochondriac.

Is there an after-hours emergency number?
Máte non-stop
pohotovostní
telefonní číslo?
ma·te *non*·stop
po·ho·to·vost·nyee
te·le·fo·nyee chees·lo

I've run out of my medication.
Došly mi léky.
dosh·li mi *lair*·ki

This is my usual medicine.
Toto jsou mé obvyklé léky.
to·to ysoh mair ob·vik·lair *lair*·ki

My child weighs (20 kilos).
Mé dítě váží
(dvacet kilo).
mair *dyee*·tye *va*·zhee
(*dvuh*·tset *ki*·lo)

What's the correct dosage?
Jaká je přesná dávka?
yuh·ka ye *przhes*·na *daf*·kuh

I don't want a blood transfusion.
Nechci transfůzi krve.　　nekh·tsi truhns·foo·zi kr·ve

Please use a new syringe.
Prosím použijte　　pro·seem po·u·zhiy·te
novou stříkačku.　　no·voh strzhee·kuhch·ku

I have my own syringe.
Mám svojí stříkačku.　　mam svo·yee strzhee·kuhch·ku

My prescription is …
Můj lékařský　　mooy lair·kuhrzh·skee
předpis je …　　przhed·pis ye …

Can I have a receipt for my insurance?
Můžete mi dát účtenku　　moo·zhe·te mi dat ooch·ten·ku
pro moji pojišťovnu?　　pro mo·yi po·yish·tyov·nu

I've been	*Byl/Byla jsem*	bil/*bi*·luh ysem
vaccinated	*očkovaný/á*	*och*·ko·vuh·nee/a
against …	*proti … m/f*	*pro*·tyi …
hepatitis	*žloutence*	*zhloh*·ten·tse
A/B/C	*A/B/C*	a/bair/tsair
lyme disease	*lymské*	*lim*·skair
	borelióze	bo·re·li·aw·ze
rabies	*vzteklině*	*vzte*·kli·nye
tetanus	*tetanusu*	*te*·tuh·nu·su
tick-borne	*meningo-*	*me*·nin·go·
encephalitis	*kokové*	ko·ko·vair
	encefalitidě	*en*·tse·fuh·li·ti·dye
typhoid	*tyfu*	*ti*·fu
I need new …	*Potřebuji …*	pot·rzhe·bu·yi …
contact lenses	*kontaktní*	*kon*·tuhkt·nyee
	čočky	*choch*·ki
glasses	*brýle*	*bree*·le

symptoms & conditions

I'm sick.
Jsem nemocný/á. m/f   ysem *ne*·mots·nee/a

My child is sick.
Moje dítě je nemocné.   mo·ye *dyee*·tye ye *ne*·mots·nair

I've been injured.
Byl/Byla jsem zraněný/á. m/f   bil/*bi*·luh ysem zruh·nye·nee/a

I've been vomiting.
Zvracel/Zvracela jsem. m/f   zvruh·tsel/zvruh·tse·luh ysem

He/She has been ...	*Byl/Byla ...* m/f	bil/*bi*·luh ...
injured	*zraněný/á* m/f	zruh·nye·nee/a
vomiting	*zvracel* m	*zvruh*·tsel
	zvracela f	*zvruh*·tse·luh

He/She is having a/an ...	*On/Ona má ...*	on/o·nuh ma ...
allergic reaction	*alergickou reakci*	uh·ler·gits·koh re·uhk·tsi
asthma attack	*astmatický záchvat*	uhst·muh·tits·kee zakh·vuht
epileptic fit	*epileptický záchvat*	e·pi·lep·tits·kee zakh·vuht
heart attack	*infarkt*	in·fuhrkt

I feel ...		
anxious	*Pociťuji úzkost.*	po·tsi·tyu·yi oos·kost
better	*Cítím se lépe.*	tsee·tyeem se lair·pe
depressed	*Mám depresi.*	mam de·pre·si
dizzy	*Mám závratě.*	mam za·vruh·tye
hot and cold	*Polévá mě horko a zima.*	po·lair·va mye hor·ko uh zi·muh
nauseous	*Je mi nevolno.*	ye mi ne·vol·no
shivery	*Třesu se.*	trzhe·su se
strange	*Je mi divně.*	ye mi dyiv·nye
weak	*Jsem slabý/á.* m/f	ysem sluh·bee/a
worse	*Cítím se hůř.*	tsee·tyeem se hoorzh

It hurts here.
Tady to bolí. tuh·di to bo·lee

I'm dehydrated.
Jsem dehydratovaný/á. m/f ysem de·hid·ruh·to·vuh·nee/a

I can't sleep.
Nemohu spát. ne·mo·hu spat

I'm on medication for …
Užívám léky na … u·zhee·vam lair·ki nuh …

He/She is on medication for …
On/Ona užívá on/o·nuh u·zhee·va
léky na … lair·ki nuh …

I have (a/an) …
Mám … mam …

He/She has (a/an) …
On/Ona má … on/o·nuh ma …

I've recently had (a/an) …
Nedávno jsem ne·dav·no ysem
měl/měla … m/f myel/mye·luh …

He/She has recently had (a/an) …
Nedávno měl/měla … m/f ne·dav·no myel/mye·luh …

asthma	*astma* n	uhst·muh
cold n	*nachlazení* n	nuh·khluh·ze·nyee
constipation	*zácpa* f	zats·puh
cough n	*kašel* m	kuh·shel
diabetes	*cukrovka* f	tsu·krof·kuh
diarrhoea	*průjem* m	proo·yem
fever	*horečka* f	ho·rech·kuh
headache	*bolesti hlavy* f	bo·les·tyi hluh·vi
nausea	*nevolnost* f	ne·vol·nost
pain n	*bolest* f	bo·lest
sore throat	*bolest v krku* f	bo·lest f kr·ku

women's health

(I think) I'm pregnant.
(Myslím že) Jsem těhotná. (mis·leem zhe) ysem *tye*·hot·na

I'm on the pill.
Užívám u·zhee·vam
antikoncepční pilulky. uhn·ti·kon·tsep·chnyee *pi*·lul·ki

I haven't had my period for (six) weeks.
Moje poslední mo·ye pos·led·nye
menstruace byla mens·tru·uh·tse *bi*·luh
před (šesti) týdny. przhed (shes·tyi) teed·ni

I've noticed a lump here.
Nahmatala jsem si bulku. nuh·hmuh·tuh·luh ysem si *bul*·ku

Do you have something for (period pain)?
Máte něco na ma·te *nye*·tso nuh
(menstruační bolesti)? (men·stru·uhch·nye bo·les·tyi)

I have a ...	*Mám ...*	mam ...
urinary tract	*infekci*	*in*·fek·tsi
infection	*močových cest*	mo·cho·veech tsest
yeast infection	*kvasinkovou*	*kvuh*·sin·ko·voh
	infekci	*in*·fek·tsi

---

the doctor may say ...

Užíváte antikoncepci?	
u·zhee·va·te	**Are you using**
uhn·ti·kon·tsep·tsi	**contraception?**
Máte právě menstruaci?	
ma·te prav·ye mens·tru·uh·tsi	**Are you menstruating?**
Jste těhotná?	
yste *tye*·hot·na	**Are you pregnant?**
Kdy jste naposledy měla menstruaci?	
gdi yste nuh·pos·le·di	**When did you last**
mye·luh mens·tru·uh·tsi	**have your period?**
Jste těhotná.	
yste *tye*·hot·na	**You're pregnant.**

I need (a/the) ...	Potřebuji ...	pot·rzhe·bu·yi ...
contraception	antikoncepční prostředek	uhn·ti·kon·tsep·chnyee pros·trzhe·dek
morning-after pill	postinor	pos·ti·nor
pregnancy test	těhotenský test	tye·ho·tens·kee test

allergies

alergie

I have a skin allergy.
Mám kožní alergii.   mam *kozh*·nyee *uh*·ler·gi·yi

I'm allergic to ...	Jsem alergický/á na ... m/f	ysem uh·ler·gits·kee/a nuh ...
He/She is allergic to ...	Je alergický/á na ... m/f	ye uh·ler·gits·kee/a nuh ...
antibiotics	antibiotika	uhn·ti·bi·o·ti·kuh
antiinflammatories	protizánětlivé léky	pro·tyi·za·nyet·li·vair lair·ki
aspirin	aspirin	uhs·pi·rin
bees	včely	fche·li
codeine	kodein	ko·deyn
penicillin	penicilin	pe·ni·tsi·lin
pollen	pyl	pil
sulphur-based drugs	léky obsahující síru	lair·ki ob·suh·hu·yee·tsee see·ru

antihistamines	antihistaminikum m	uhn·ti·his·tuh·mi·ni·kum
inhaler	inhalátor m	in·huh·la·tor
injection	injekce f	in·yek·tse

For food-related allergies, see **special diets & allergies**, page 178.

parts of the body

My ... hurts.
Bolí mě ...   bo·lee mye ...

I can't move my ...
Nemohu hýbat s ...   ne·mo·hu hee·but s ...

I have a cramp in my ...
Mám křeč v ...   mam krzhech v ...

My ... is swollen.
Mám oteklý ...   mam o·tek·lee ...

For other parts of the body, see the **dictionary**.

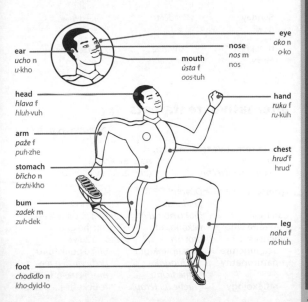

eye
oko n
o·ko

nose
nos m
nos

ear
ucho n
u·kho

mouth
ústa f
oos·tuh

head
hlava f
hluh·vuh

hand
ruku f
ru·kuh

arm
paže f
puh·zhe

chest
hruď f
hrud'

stomach
břicho n
brzhi·kho

bum
zadek m
zuh·dek

leg
noha f
no·huh

foot
chodidlo n
kho·dyid·lo

SAFE TRAVEL

soft talk

You'll notice from our coloured pronunciation guides that the Czech consonants *d*, *n* and *t*, when followed in writing by the vowels *ě*, *i* or *í*, are pronounced softly, with a slight 'y' sound after them – just like the letters *ď*, *ň* and *ť* are always pronounced, regardless of the letter following them. You don't need to think about this in most cases, as we've used the symbol y to help you pronounce these sounds naturally. However, to avoid mispronunciation (ie reading it as an ee after the consonant) when it appears at the end of a syllable or a word, we've used an apostrophe (') instead of the y symbol. For example:

thousand	tisíc	tyi·seets
rain	déšť	dairsht'
Sunday	neděle	ne·dye·le
now	teď	ted'
breakfast	snídaně	snee·duh·nye
Sorry.	Promiňte.	pro·min'·te

alternative treatments

alternativní léčbu

I use (alternative treatments).

Používám		po·u·zhee·vam
(alternativní léčbu).		(uhl·ter·na·tiv·nyee lairch·bu)

I prefer ...	Dávám	da·vam
	přednost ...	przhed·nost ...
Can I see	Mohu navštívit	mo·hu nav·shtyee·vit
someone who	někoho, kdo	nye·ko·ho gdo
practises ...?	provozuje ...?	pro·vo·zu·ye ...
acupuncture	akupunkturu	uh·ku·punk·tu·ru
naturopathy	přírodní	przhee·rod·nyee
	medicínu	me·di·tsee·nu
reflexology	reflexní terapii	re·fleks·nee te·ruh·pi·i

pharmacist

I need something for (a headache).
Potřebuji něco na   pot·rzhe·bu·yi nye·tso nuh
(bolest hlavy).   (bo·lest hluh·vi)

Do I need a prescription for (antihistamines)?
Potřebuji předpis na   pot·rzhe·bu·yi przhed·pis nuh
(antihistaminikum)?   (uhn·ti·his·tuh·mi·ni·kum)

I have a prescription.
Mám recept.   mam re·tsept

How many times a day?
Kolikrát denně?   ko·li·krat de·nye

Will it make me drowsy?
Budu potom ospalý/á? m/f   bu·du po·tom os·puh·lee/a

antiseptic	*antiseptický*	uhn·ti·sep·tits·kee
	prostředek m	prost·rzhe·dek
contraceptives	*antikoncepce* f	uhn·ti·kon·tsep·tse
painkillers	*prášky proti*	prash·ki pro·tyi
	bolesti m pl	bo·les·tyi
rehydration salts	*iontový nápoj* m	yon·to·vee na·poy
thermometer	*teploměr* m	te·plo·myer

the pharmacist may say ...

Dvakrát/Třikrát denně.
   dvuh·krat/trzhi·krat de·nye   **Twice/Three times a day.**

Před jídlem/Při jídle/Po jídle.
   przhed yeed·lem/   **Before/With/After food.**
   przhi yeed·le/po yeed·le

Užívali jste tento lék?
   u·zhee·va·li yste ten·to lairk   **Have you taken this before?**

Musíte využívat celé balení.
   mu·see·te vi·u·zhee·vuht   **You must complete the**
   tse·lair buh·le·nye   **course.**

For more pharmaceutical items, see the **dictionary**.

dentist

I have a ...	Mám ...	mam ...
broken tooth	*zlomený zub*	*zlo*·me·nee zub
cavity	*kaz*	kuhz
toothache	*bolavý zub*	*bo*·luh·vee zub

I've lost a filling.
Vypadla mi plomba.   *vi*·puhd·luh mi *plom*·buh

My dentures are broken.
Zubní protéza se mi   *zub*·nyee *pro*·tair·zuh se mi
rozbila.   *roz*·bi·luh

My gums hurt.
Bolí mě dásně.   *bo*·lee mye *das*·nye

I don't want it extracted.
Nechci to vytrhnout.   *nekh*·tsi to *vi*·trh·noht

I need a/an ...	Potřebuji ...	pot·rzhe·bu·yi ...
anaesthetic	*znecitlivění*	*zne*·tsit·li·vye·nyee
filling	*plombu*	*plom*·bu

---

the dentist may say ...

Hodně otevřete ústa.
   hod·nye o·tev·rzhe·te oos·tuh   **Open wide.**

Nebude to vůbec bolet.
   ne·bu·de to voo·bets bo·let   **This won't hurt a bit.**

Skousněte.
   skohs·nye·te   **Bite down on this.**

Nehýbejte se.
   ne·hee·bey·te se   **Don't move.**

Vypláchněte si.
   vi·plakh·nye·te si   **Rinse.**

Vraťte se, neskončil/neskončila jsem. **m/f**
   vruht'·te se nes·kon·chil/   **Come back, I haven't**
   nes·kon·chi·luh ysem   **finished.**

Czech nouns in the **dictionary** have their gender indicated by ⓜ (masculine), ⓕ (feminine) or ⓝ (neuter). If it's a plural noun, you'll also see pl. When a word that could be either a noun or a verb has no gender indicated, it's a verb. For added clarity, certain words are marked as adjectives a or verbs v. Adjectives, however, are given in the masculine form only. Both nouns and adjectives are provided in the nominative case only. For information on case and gender, refer to the **phrasebuilder**.

A

aboard *na palubě* nuh puh·lu·bye
abortion *potrat* ⓜ po·truht
about *o* o
above *nad* nuhd
abroad *v cizině* v tsi·zi·nye
accident *nehoda* ⓕ ne·ho·duh
accommodation *ubytování* ⓝ u·bi·to·va·nyee
account (bill) *účet* ⓜ oo·chet
acid rain *kyselý déšť* ⓜ ki·se·lee desht'
across *přes* przhez
activist *aktivista/aktivistka* ⓜ/ⓕ uhk·ti·vis·tuh/uhk·ti·vist·kuh
actor *herec/herečka* ⓜ/ⓕ he·rets/he·rech·kuh
acupuncture *akupunktura* ⓕ uh·ku·punk·tu·ruh
adaptor *adaptor* ⓜ uh·duhp·tor
addiction *závislost* ⓕ za·vis·lost
address *adresa* ⓕ uh·dre·suh
administration *správa* ⓕ spra·vuh
administrator *správce* ⓜ spraf·tse
admission (price) *vstupné* ⓝ fstup·nair
admit (let in) *vpustit* fpus·tyit
adult *dospělý/á* ⓜ/ⓕ dos·pye·lee/a
advertisement *inzerát* ⓜ in·ze·rat
advice *rada* ⓕ ruh·duh
aerobics *aerobik* ⓜ uh·e·ro·bik
aeroplane *letadlo* ⓝ le·tuhd·lo
Africa *Afrika* ⓕ uh·fri·kuh
after *po* po
afternoon *odpoledne* ⓝ ot·po·led·ne
aftershave *voda po holení* ⓕ vo·duh po ho·le·nyee
again *znovu* zno·vu
age *věk* ⓜ vyek

(three days) ago *před (třemi dny)* przhed (trzhe·mi dni)
agree *souhlasit* soh·hluh·sit
agriculture *zemědělství* ⓝ ze·mye·dyels·tvee
ahead *vpředu* fprzhe·du
AIDS *AIDS* ⓜ eyds
air *vzduch* ⓜ vzdukh
air-conditioned *klimatizovaný* kli·muh·ti·zo·vuh·nee
air conditioning *klimatizace* ⓕ kli·muh·ti·zuh·tse
airline *aerolinie* ⓕ uh·e·ro·li·ni·ye
airmail *letecká pošta* ⓕ le·tets·ka posh·tuh
airplane *letadlo* ⓝ le·tuhd·lo
airport *letiště* ⓝ le·tyish·tye
airport tax *letištní poplatek* ⓜ le·tyisht·nyee po·pluh·tek
aisle (on plane) *ulička* ⓕ u·lich·kuh
alarm clock *budík* ⓜ bu·dyeek
alcohol *alkohol* ⓜ uhl·ko·hol
all *všichni* vshikh·nyi
allergy *alergie* ⓕ uh·ler·gi·ye
almond *mandle* ⓕ muhn·dle
almost *skoro* sko·ro
alone *sám* sam
already *již* yizh
also *také* tuh·kair
altar *oltář* ⓜ ol·tarzh
altitude *nadmořská výška* ⓕ nuhd·morzh·ska veesh·kuh
always *vždy* vzhdi
ambassador *velvyslanec/velvyslankyně* ⓜ/ⓕ vel·vis·luh·nets/vel·vis·luhn·ki·nye
ambulance *ambulance* ⓕ uhm·bu·luhn·tse
American football *americký fotbal* ⓜ uh·me·rits·kee fot·buhl

anaemia *chudokrevnost* ① khu·do·kref·nost
anarchist *anarchista/anarchistka* ⑩/① uh·nuhr·khis·tuh/uh·nuhr·khist·kuh
ancient *starodávný* stuh·ro·dav·nee
and *a* uh
angry *rozhněvaný* rož·hnye·vuh·nee
animal *zvíře* ⑩ zvee·rzhe
ankle *kotník* ⑩ kot·nyeek
another *další* duhl·shee
answer *odpověď* ① ot·po·vyed'
answer v *odpovědět* ot·po·vye·dyet
ant *mravenec* ⑩ mruh·ve·nets
antibiotics *antibiotika* ⑩ pl uhn·ti·bi·o·ti·kuh
antinuclear *protiatomový* pro·tyi·uh·to·mo·vee
antique *starožitnost* ① stuh·ro·zhit·nost
antiseptic *antiseptikum* ⑩ uhn·ti·sep·ti·kum
any *nějaký* nye·yuh·kee
apartment *byt* ⑩ bit
appendix (body) *slepé střevo* ⑩ sle·pair strzhe·vo
apple *jablko* ⑩ yuh·bl·ko
appointment *schůzka* ① skhooz·kuh
apricot *meruňka* ① me·run'·kuh
April *duben* ⑩ du·ben
archaeological *archeologický* uhr·khe·o·lo·gits·kee
architect *architekt/architektka* ⑩/① uhr·khi·tekt/uhr·khi·tet·kuh
architecture *architektura* ① uhr·khi·tek·tu·ruh
argue *hádat se* ha·duht se
arm (body) *paže* ① puh·zhe
aromatherapy *aromaterapie* ① uh·ro·muh·te·ruh·pi·ye
arrest v *zatknout* zuht·knoht
arrivals *příjezd* ⑩ przhee·yezd
arrive *přijít* przhi·yeet
art *umění* ⑩ u·mye·nyee
art gallery *galerie* ① guh·le·ri·ye
artist *umělec/umělkyně* ⑩/① u·mye·lets/u·myel·ki·nye
ashtray *popelník* ⑩ po·pel·nyeek
Asia *Asie* ① a·si·ye
ask (a question) *ptát se* ptat se
ask (for something) *požádat po-* zha·duht
asparagus *chřest* ⑩ khrzhest
aspirin *aspirin* ⑩ uhs·pi·rin
asthma *astma* ⑩ uhst·muh
at *na* nuh

athletics *lehká atletika* ① leh·ka uht·le·ti·kuh
atmosphere *atmosféra* ① uht·mos·fair·ruh
aubergine *lilek* ⑩ li·lek
August *srpen* ⑩ sr·pen
aunt *teta* ① te·tuh
Australia *Austrálie* ① ow·stra·li·ye
Austria *Rakousko* ① ruh·kohs·ko
automated teller machine (ATM) *bankomat* ⑩ buhn·ko·muht
autumn *podzim* ⑩ pod·zim
avenue *třída* ① trzhee·duh
avocado *avokádo* ⑩ uh·vo·ka·do
awful *hrozný* hroz·nee

B

B&W (film) *černobílý* cher·no·bee·lee
baby *nemluvně* ⑩ nem·luv·nye
baby food *dětská výživa* ① dyets·ka vee·zhi·vuh
baby powder *dětský pudr* ⑩ dyets·kee pu·dr
babysitter *chůva* ① khoo·vuh
back (body) *záda* ① za·duh
back (position) *opěradlo* ⑩ o·pye·ruhd·lo
backpack *batoh* ⑩ buh·tawh
bacon *slanina* ① sluh·nyi·nuh
bad *špatný* shpuht·nee
bag *taška* ① tuhsh·kuh
baggage *zavazadlo* ⑩ zuh·vuh·zuhd·lo
baggage allowance *povolená váha zavazadel* ① po·vo·le·na va·huh zuh·vuh·zuh·del
baggage claim *výdej zavazadel* ⑩ vee·dey zuh·vuh·zuh·del
bakery *pekárna* ① pe·kar·nuh
balance (account) *zůstatek* ⑩ zoo·stuh·tek
balcony *balkón* ⑩ buhl·kawn
ball (sport) *míč* ⑩ meech
ballet *balet* ⑩ buh·let
banana *banán* ⑩ buh·nan
band (music) *skupina* ① sku·pi·nuh
bandage *obvaz* ⑩ ob·vuhz
Band-Aid *leukoplast* ① le·u·ko·pluhst
bank *banka* ① buhn·kuh
bank account *bankovní účet* ⑩ buhn·kov·nyee oo·chet
banknote *bankovka* ① buhn·kof·kuh
baptism *křest* krzhest
bar *bar* buhr
barber *holič* ⑩ ho·lich

bar work práce v baru ① pra·tse f buh·ru
baseball baseball ⑩ beys·bawl
basket koš ⑩ kosh
basketball košíková ① ko·shee·ko·va
bath koupel ① koh·pel
bathing suit plavky ① pluhf·ki
bathroom koupelna ① koh·pel·nuh
battery baterie ① buh·te·ri·ye
be být beet
beach pláž ① plazh
beach volleyball plážový volejbal ⑩
pla·zho·vee vo·ley·buhl
bean fazole ① fuh·zo·le
bean sprouts fazolové klíčky ⑩ pl
fuh·zo·lo·vair kleech·ki
beautician kosmetička ① kos·me·tich·kuh
beautiful krásný kras·nee
beauty salon kosmetický salón ⑩
kos·me·tits·kee suh·lawn
because protože pro·to·zhe
bed postel ① pos·tel
bedding lůžkoviny ① loozh·ko·vi·ni
bed linen ložní prádlo ⑩ lozh·nyee prad·lo
bedroom ložnice ① lozh·nyi·tse
bee včela ① fche·luh
beef hovězí ⑩ ho·vye·zee
beer pivo ⑩ pi·vo
beetroot červená řepa ①
cher·ve·na rzhe·puh
before před przhed
beggar žebrák ⑩ zheb·rak
behind za zuh
Belgium Belgie ① bel·gi·ye
below pod pod
Berlin Berlín ⑩ ber·leen
berth kotviště ⑩ kot·vish·tye
beside vedle ved·le
best nejlepší ney·lep·shee
bet sázka ① saz·kuh
bet v sázet sa·zet
better lepší lep·shee
between mezi me·zi
Bible Bible ① bib·le
bicycle kolo ⑩ ko·lo
big velký vel·kee
bigger větší vyet·shee
biggest největší ney·vyet·shee
bike kolo ⑩ ko·lo
bike chain řetěz na kolo ⑩
rzhe·tyez nuh ko·lo
bike lock zámek na kolo ⑩
za·mek nuh ko·lo
bike path cyklostezka ① tsi·klo·stez·kuh

bike shop obchod s kolama ⑩
op·khod s ko·luh·muh
bill (restaurant) účet ⑩ oo·chet
binoculars dalekohled ⑩ duh·le·ko·hled
bird pták ⑩ ptak
birth certificate rodný list ⑩ rod·nee list
birthday narozeniny ① pl nuh·ro·ze·nyi·ni
biscuit sušenka ① su·shen·kuh
bite (dog) kousnutí ⑩ kohs·nu·tyee
bite (insect) štípnutí ⑩ shtyeep·nu·tyee
bitter hořký horzh·kee
black černý cher·nee
black market černý trh ⑩ cher·nee trh
bladder močový měchýř ⑩
mo·cho·vee mye·kheerzh
blanket deka ① de·kuh
blind a slepý sle·pee
blister puchýř ⑩ pu·kheerzh
blocked ucpaný uts·puh·nee
blood krev ① kref
blood group krevní skupina ①
krev·nyee sku·pi·nuh
blood pressure krevní tlak ①
krev·nyee tluhk
blood test krevní zkouška ①
krev·nyee skohsh·kuh
blue modrý mod·ree
board (plane, ship) v nastoupit
nuhs·toh·pit
boarding house penzion ⑩ pen·zi·on
boarding pass palubní vstupenka ①
puh·lub·nyee fstu·pen·kuh
boat člun ⑩ chlun
body tělo ⑩ tye·lo
boiled vařený vuh·rzhe·nee
bone kost ① kost
book kniha ① knyi·huh
book (make a booking) v objednat
ob·yed·nuht
booked out obsazeno op·suh·ze·no
book shop knihkupectví ⑩
knih·ku·pets·tvee
boot (footwear) bota ① bo·tuh
boots (footwear) boty ① pl bo·ti
border hranice ① hruh·nyi·tse
bored unuděný u·nu·dye·nee
boring nudný nud·nee
borrow půjčit pooy·chit
botanic garden botanická zahrada ①
bo·tuh·nits·ka zuh·hruh·duh
both oba o·buh
bottle láhev ① la·hef

bottle opener *otvírák na láhve* ⓜ
ot·vee·rak nuh *lah*·ve
bottom (body) *zadek* ⓜ *zuh*·dek
bottom (position) *dno* ⓝ dno
bowl (plate) *miska* ⓕ *mis*·kuh
box *krabice* ⓕ *kruh*·bi·tse
boxer shorts *trenýrky* ⓕ pl *tre*·neer·ki
boxing *box* ⓜ boks
boy *chlapec* ⓜ *khluh*·pets
boyfriend *přítel* ⓜ *przhee*·tel
bra *podprsenka* ⓕ *pod*·pr·sen·kuh
brakes *brzdy* ⓕ pl brz·di
brandy *brandy* ⓕ *bruhn*·di
Bratislava *Bratislava* ⓕ *bruh*·tyi·sluh·vuh
brave *odvážný* od·*vazh*·nee
bread *chléb* ⓜ khlairb
bread rolls *pečivo* ⓝ *pe*·chi·vo
break v *zlomit* zlo·mit
break down v *porouchat* po·*roh*·khuht
breakfast *snídaně* ⓕ *snee*·duh·nye
breast (body) *prso* ⓝ *pr*·so
breathe *dýchat* *dee*·khuht
bribe *úplatek* ⓜ *oo*·pluh·tek
bribe v *podplatit* pod·*pluh*·tyit
bridge (structure) *most* ⓜ most
briefcase *aktovka* ⓕ *uhk*·tof·kuh
bring *přinést* *przhi*·nairst
broccoli *brokolice* ⓕ *bro*·ko·li·tse
brochure *brožura* ⓕ *bro*·zhu·ruh
broken *zlomený* zlo·me·nee
broken down *rozbitý* roz·*bi*·tee
bronchitis *zánět průdušek* ⓜ
za·nyet *proo*·du·shek
brother *bratr* ⓜ *bruh*·tr
brown *hnědý* hnye·dee
bruise *modřina* ⓕ *mod*·rzhi·nuh
brush *kartáč* ⓜ *kuhr*·tach
bucket *kbelík* ⓜ *kbe*·leek
Buddhist *buddhista/buddhistka* ⓜ/ⓕ
bud·his·tuh/*bud*·hist·kuh
budget *rozpočet* ⓜ *roz*·po·chet
buffet *bufet* ⓜ *bu*·fet
bug *brouk* ⓜ brohk
build *stavět* *stuh*·vyet
builder *stavbař* ⓜ *stuhf*·buhrzh
building *budova* ⓕ *bu*·do·vuh
bumbag *ledvinka* ⓕ *led*·vin·kuh
burn *spálenina* ⓕ *spa*·le·nyi·nuh
burnt *spálený* spa·le·nee
bus *autobus* ⓜ *ow*·to·bus
business *obchod* ⓜ *op*·khod
business class *business třída* ⓕ
biz·nis *trzhee*·duh

businessperson *obchodník* ⓜ&ⓕ
ob·khod·nyeek
business trip *služební cesta* ⓕ
slu·zheb·nyee *tses*·tuh
busker *pouliční muzikant* ⓜ
po·u·lich·nye *mu*·zi·kuhnt
bus station *autobusové nádraží* ⓝ
ow·to·bu·so·vair *nad*·ruh·zhee
bus stop *autobusová zastávka* ⓕ
ow·to·bu·so·va *zuhs*·taf·kuh
busy *zaneprázdněný* zuh·ne·prazd·nye·nee
but *ale* uh·le
butcher *řezník* ⓜ *rzhez*·nyeek
butcher's shop *řeznictví* ⓝ *rzhez*·nyits·tvee
butter *máslo* ⓝ *mas*·lo
butterfly *motýl* ⓜ *mo*·teel
button *knoflík* ⓜ *knof*·leek
buy v *koupit* koh·pit

C

cabbage *kapusta* ⓕ *kuh*·pus·tuh
cable car *kabinová lanovka* ⓕ
kuh·bi·no·va *luh*·nof·kuh
café *kavárna* ⓕ *kuh*·var·nuh
cafeteria *jídelna* ⓕ *yee*·del·nuh
cake *dort* ⓜ dort
cake shop *cukrárna* ⓕ *tsu*·krar·nuh
calculator *kalkulačka* ⓕ *kuhl*·ku·luhch·kuh
calendar *kalendář* ⓜ *kuh*·len·darzh
call (phone) v *telefonovat* te·le·fo·no·vuht
camera *fotoaparát* ⓜ *fo*·to·uh·puh·rat
camera shop *foto potřeby* ⓕ pl
fo·to *pot*·rzhe·bi
camp v *tábořit* ta·bo·rzhit
camping ground *stanový tábor* ⓜ
stuh·no·vee ta·bor
camping store *obchod s kempingovými*
potřebami ⓜ *op*·khod s
kem·pin·go·vee·mi *pot*·rzhe·buh·mi
camp site *autokempink* ⓜ *ow*·to·kem·pink
can (be able) *umět* u·myet
can (have permission) *moci* mo·tsi
Canada *Kanada* ⓜ *kuh*·nuh·duh
cancel *zrušit* zru·shit
cancer *rakovina* ⓕ *ruh*·ko·vi·nuh
candle *svíčka* ⓕ *sveech*·kuh
candy *kandovaný cukr* ⓜ
kuhn·do·vuh·nee tsu·kr
canoeing *kanoistika* ⓕ *kuh*·no·is·ti·kuh
can opener *otvírák na konzervy* ⓜ
ot·vee·rak nuh kon·zer·vi

cantaloupe *kantalup* Ⓜ kuhn·tuh·lup
capsicum *paprika* Ⓕ puh·pri·kuh
car *auto* Ⓝ ow·to
caravan *karavan* Ⓜ kuh·ruh·vuhn
cardiac arrest *zástava srdce* Ⓕ
  zas·tuh·vuh srd·tse
cards (playing) *karty* Ⓕ pl kuhr·ti
care (for someone) v *starat se (o)*
  stuh·ruht se (o)
car hire *půjčovna aut* Ⓕ
  pooy·chov·nuh owt
car owner's title *doklad o vlastnictví auta*
  Ⓜ dok·luhd o vluhst·nyits·tvee ow·tuh
car park *parkoviště* Ⓝ puhr·ko·vish·tye
carpenter *tesař* Ⓜ te·suhrzh
car registration *osvědčení o registraci* Ⓕ
  os·vyed·che·nyee o re·gis·truh·tsi
carrot *mrkev* Ⓕ mr·kef
carry *nosit* no·sit
carton *kartón* Ⓜ kuhr·tawn
cash *hotovost* Ⓕ ho·to·vost
cash (a cheque) v *inkasovat šek*
  in·kuh·so·vuht shek
cashew *kešů* Ⓝ ke·shoo
cashier *pokladník/pokladní* Ⓜ/Ⓕ
  po·kluhd·nyeek/po·kluhd·nyee
cash register *pokladna* Ⓕ po·kluhd·nuh
casino *kasino* Ⓝ kuh·si·no
cassette *kazeta* Ⓕ kuh·ze·tuh
castle (classical) *zámek* Ⓜ za·mek
castle (medieval) *hrad* Ⓜ hruhd
casual work *příležitostní práce* Ⓕ
  przhe·le·zhi·tost·nyee pra·tse
cat *kočka* Ⓕ koch·kuh
cathedral *katedrála* Ⓕ ka·te·dra·luh
Catholic *katolík* Ⓜ kuh·to·leek
cauliflower *květák* Ⓜ kvye·tak
cave *jeskyně* Ⓕ yes·ki·nye
CD *CD* Ⓝ tsair·dairch·ko
celebration *oslava* Ⓕ o·sluh·vuh
cell phone *mobil* Ⓜ mo·bil
cemetery *hřbitov* Ⓜ hrzh·bi·tov
cent *cent* Ⓜ tsent
centimetre *centimetr* Ⓜ tsen·ti·me·tr
centre *střed* Ⓜ strzhed
ceramics *keramika* Ⓕ ke·ruh·mi·kuh
cereal (breakfast) *cereálie* Ⓕ tse·re·a·li·ye
certificate *osvědčení* Ⓝ os·vyed·che·nyee
chain *řetěz* Ⓜ rzhe·tyez
chair *židle* Ⓕ zhid·le
chairlift (skiing) *sedačka* Ⓕ se·duhch·kuh
champagne *šampaňské* Ⓝ
  shuhm·puhn'·skair

championships *mistrovství* Ⓝ
  mis·trofs·tvee
chance *náhoda* Ⓕ na·ho·duh
change *změna* Ⓕ zmye·nuh
change (coins) *drobné* Ⓝ drob·nair
change (money) v *vyměnit* vi·mye·nyit
changing room *šatna* Ⓕ shuht·nuh
charming *okouzlující* o·koh·zlu·yee·tsee
chat up v *balit* buh·lit
cheap *levný* lev·nee
cheat *podvod* Ⓜ pod·vod
check (banking) *šek* Ⓜ shek
check (bill) *účet* Ⓜ oo·chet
check v *kontrolovat* kon·tro·lo·vuht
check-in (desk) *recepce* Ⓕ re·tsep·tse
checkpoint *kontrolní stanoviště* Ⓝ
  kon·trol·nyee stuh·no·vish·tye
cheese *sýr* Ⓜ seer
cheese shop *obchod se sýrem* Ⓜ
  op·khod se see·rem
chef *šéfkuchař(ka)* Ⓜ/Ⓕ
  shairf·ku·khuhrzh(·kuh)
chemist (pharmacist) *lékárník* Ⓜ
  lair·kar·nyeek
chemist (pharmacy) *lékárna* Ⓕ
  lair·kar·nuh
cheque (banking) *šek* Ⓜ shek
cherry *třešeň* Ⓕ trzhe·shen'
chess *šachy* Ⓜ shuh·khi
chessboard *šachovnice* Ⓕ
  shuh·khov·nyi·tse
chest (body) *hruď* Ⓕ hrud'
chestnut *kaštan* Ⓜ kuhsh·tuhn
chewing gum *žvýkačka* Ⓕ
  zhvee·kuhch·kuh
chicken *kuře* Ⓝ ku·rzhe
chicken pox *plané neštovice* Ⓕ
  pluh·nair nesh·to·vi·tse
chickpea *cizrna* Ⓕ tsi·zr·nuh
child *dítě* Ⓝ dyee·tye
child-minding service
  služba pro hlídání dětí Ⓕ
  sluzh·buh pro hlee·da·nye dyeˇ·tyee
children *děti* Ⓝ pl dye·tyi
child seat *autosedačka* Ⓝ
  ow·to·se·duhch·kuh
chilli *feferon* Ⓜ pfe·fe·ron
chilli sauce *feferonová omáčka* Ⓕ
  pfe·fe·ro·no·va o·mach·kuh
China *Čína* Ⓕ chee·nuh
chiropractor *chiropraktik* Ⓜ
  khi·ro·pruhk·tik
chocolate *čokoláda* Ⓕ cho·ko·la·duh

choose *vybrat si* vi·bruht si

chopping board *prkénko na krájení* ⓝ
pr·kairn·ko nuh kra·ye·nyee

chopsticks *hůlky* ⓣ pl hool·ki

Christian *křesťan* ⓜ krzhes·tyuhn

Christian name *křestní jméno* ⓝ
krzhest·nyee ymair·no

Christmas *Vánoce* ⓜ pl va·no·tse

Christmas Day *Boží hod vánoční* ⓜ
bo·zhee hod va·noch·nyee

Christmas Eve *Štědrý večer* ⓜ
shtyed·ree ve·cher

church *kostel* ⓜ kos·tel

cider *mošt* ⓜ mosht

cigar *doutník* ⓜ doht·nyeek

cigarette *cigareta* ⓣ tsi·guh·re·tuh

cigarette lighter *zapalovač* ⓜ
zuh·puh·lo·vuhch

cinema *kino* ⓝ ki·no

circus *cirkus* ⓜ tsir·kus

citizenship *občanství* ⓝ ob·chuhn·stvee

city *město* ⓝ myes·to

city centre *střed města* ⓜ
strzhed myes·tuh

civil rights *občanská práva* ⓝ pl
ob·chuhns·ka pra·vuh

clarinet *klarinet* ⓜ kluh·ri·net

class (category) *třída* ⓣ trzhee·duh

class system *třídní systém* ⓜ
trzheed·nyee sis·tairm

classical *antický* uhn·tits·kee

clean a *čistý* chis·tee

clean v *čistit* chis·tyit

cleaning *úklid* ⓜ oo·klid

client *zákazník/zákaznice* ⓜ/ⓣ
za·kuhz·nyeek/za·kuhz·nyi·tse

cliff *skála* ⓣ ska·luh

climb v *šplhat* shpl·hut

cloakroom *šatna* ⓣ shuht·nuh

clock *hodiny* ⓣ pl ho·dyi·ni

close a *blízký* bleez·kee

close v *zavírat* zuh·vee·ruht

closed *zavřený* zuh·vrzhe·nee

clothesline *prádelní šňůra* ⓣ
pra·del·nyee shnyoo·ruh

clothing *šaty* ⓜ pl shuh·ti

clothing store *obchod s oblečením* ⓜ
op·khod s o·ble·che·nyeem

cloud *mrak* ⓜ mruhk

cloudy *zataženo* zuh·tuh·zhe·no

clutch (car) *spojka* ⓣ spoy·kuh

coach (bus) *autokar* ⓜ ow·to·kuhr

coach (trainer) *trenér* ⓜ tre·ner

coach v *trénovat* trair·no·vuht

coast *pobřeží* ⓝ pob·rzhe·zhee

coat *kabát* ⓜ kuh·bat

cocaine *kokain* ⓜ ko·kain

cockroach *šváb* ⓜ shvab

cocktail *koktejl* ⓜ kok·teyl

cocoa *kakao* ⓝ kuh·kow

coconut *kokos* ⓜ ko·kos

coffee *káva* ⓣ ka·vuh

coins *mince* ⓣ min·tse

cold (illness) *nachlazení* ⓝ
nuh·khluh·ze·nyee

cold (weather) *zima* ⓣ zi·muh

cold a *chladný* khluhd·nee

colleague *kolega/kolegině* ⓜ/ⓣ
ko·le·guh/ko·le·gi·nye

collect call *hovor na účet volaného* ⓜ
ho·vor nuh oo·chet vo·luh·nair·ho

college *vysoká škola* ⓣ vi·so·ka shko·luh

colour *barva* ⓣ buhr·vuh

comb *hřeben* ⓜ hrzhe·ben

come *přijít* przhi·yeet

comedy *komedie* ⓣ ko·me·di·ye

comfortable *pohodlný* po·ho·dl·nee

commission *zakázka* ⓣ zuh·kaz·kuh

communion *přijímání svátosti oltářní* ⓝ
przhi·yee·ma·nyee sva·tos·tyi
ol·tarzh·nyee

communist *komunista/komunistka* ⓜ/ⓣ
ko·mu·nis·tuh/ko·mu·nist·kuh

companion *společník/společnice* ⓜ/ⓣ
spo·lech·nyeek/spo·lech·nyi·tse

company (firm) *společnost* ⓣ
spo·lech·nost

compass *kompas* ⓜ kom·puhs

complain *stěžovat si* stye·zho·vuht si

complaint *stížnost* ⓣ styeezh·nost

complimentary (free) *bezplatný*
bez·pluht·nee

computer *počítač* ⓜ po·chee·tuhch

computer game *počítačová hra* ⓣ
po·chee·tuh·cho·va hruh

concert *koncert* ⓜ kon·tsert

concussion *otřes mozku* ⓜ
ot·rzhes moz·ku

conditioner (hair) *kondicionér* ⓜ
kon·di·tsi·o·ner

condom *prezervativ* ⓜ pre·zer·vuh·tif

conference (big) *konference* ⓣ
kon·fe·ren·tse

conference (small) *porada* ⓣ po·ruh·duh

confession (religious) *zpověď* ① spo·vyed'

confirm (a booking) *potvrdit* pot·vr·dyit

congratulations *blahopřání* bluh·ho·przha·nyee

conjunctivitis *zánět spojivek* ⓜ za·nyet spo·yi·vek

connection (transport) *spojení* ⓝ spo·ye·nyee

conservative *konzervativec* ⓜ&① kon·zer·vuh·ti·vets

constipation *zácpa* ① zats·puh

consulate *konzulát* ⓜ kon·zu·lat

contact lenses *kontaktní čočky* ① pl kon·tuhkt·nyee choch·ki

contact lens solution *fjozologický roztok* ⓜ fyo·zo·lo·gits·kee roz·tok

contraceptives *antikoncepční prostředky* ⓜ pl uhn·ti·kon·tsep·chnyee prost·rzhed·ki

contract *smlouva* ① smloh·vuh

convenience store (milk bar) *večerka* ① ve·cher·kuh

convent *klášter* ⓜ klash·ter

cook *kuchař(ka)* ⓜ/① ku·kharzh(·kuh)

cook v *vařit* vuh·rzhit

cookie *sušenka* ① su·shen·kuh

cooking *vaření* ⓝ v uh·rzhe·nyee

cool (groovy) *žůžo* zhoo·zho

cool (temperature) *chladný* khluhd·nee

corkscrew *vývrtka* ① vee·vrt·kuh

corn *kukuřice* ① ku·ku·rzhi·tse

corner *roh* ⓜ rawh

cornflakes *kukuřičné lupínky* ⓜ pl ku·ku·rzhich·nair lu·peen·ki

corrupt a *zkorumpovaný* zko·rum·po·vuh·nee

corruption *korupce* ① ko·rup·tse

cost *cena* ① tse·nuh

cost v *stát* stat

cotton *bavlna* ① buh·vl·nuh

cotton balls *kosmetické polštářky* ⓜ pl kos·me·tits·kair polsh·tarzh·kl

cotton buds *vatové tyčinky* ① pl vuh·to·vair ti·chin·ki

couchette *lehátko* ⓝ le·hat·ko

cough *kašel* ⓜ kuh·shel

cough v *kašlat* kuhsh·luht

cough medicine *lék proti kašli* ⓜ lairk pro·tyi kuhsh·li

count v *počítat* po·chee·tat

counter (at bar) *pult* ⓜ pult

country *země* ① ze·mye

countryside *venkov* ⓜ ven·kof

coupon *kupón* ⓜ ku·pawn

courgette *cuketa* ① tsu·ke·tuh

court (legal) *soud* ⓜ sohd

court (tennis) *kurt* ⓜ kurt

couscous *kuskus* ⓜ kus·kus

cover charge *vstupné* ⓝ vstup·nair

cow *kráva* ① kra·vuh

cracker *kreker* ⓜ kre·ker

crafts *umělecké řemesla* ⓝ pl u·mye·lets·kair rzhe·mes·luh

crash *srážka* ① srazh·kuh

crazy *bláznivý* blaz·nyi·vee

cream (food) *smetana* ① sme·tuh·nuh

cream (lotion) *krém* ⓜ krairm

crèche *jesle* ① pl yes·le

credit *úvěr* ⓜ oo·vyer

credit card *kreditní karta* ① kre·dit·nyee kuhr·tuh

cricket (sport) *kriket* ⓜ kri·ket

crop (riding) *bičík* ⓜ bi·cheek

cross (religious) *kříž* ⓜ krzheezh

crowded *nacpaný* nuhts·puh·nee

crystal *krystal* ⓜ kris·tuhl

cucumber *okurka* ① o·kur·kuh

cup *šálek* ⓜ sha·lek

cupboard *kredenc* ① kre·dents

currency exchange *směnárna* ① smye·nar·nuh

current (electricity) *elektrický proud* ⓜ e·lek·trits·kee prohd

current affairs *aktuální události* ① pl uhk·tu·al·nyee u·da·los·tyi

curry *kari* ⓜ kuh·ri

custom *zvyk* ⓜ zvik

customs *celnice* ① tsel·ni·tse

cut *říznutí* ⓝ rzheez·nu·tyee

cut (with knife) v *říznout* rzheez·noht

cut (with scissors) v *stříhat* strzhee·huht

cutlery *příbory* ⓜ pl przhee·bo·ri

CV *životopis* ⓜ zhi·vo·to·pis

cycle (ride) v *jezdit na kole* yez·dit nuh ko·le

cycling *jízda na kole* ① yeez·duh nuh ko·le

cyclist *cyklista* ⓜ tsi·klis·tuh

cystitis *zánět močového měchýře* ⓜ za·nyet mo·cho·vair·ho mye·khee·rzhe

Czech a *český* ches·kee

Czech (language) *čeština* ① chesh·tyi·nuh

Czech (nationality) *Čech/Češka* ⓜ/① chekh/chesh·kuh

Czech Republic *Česká republika* ① ches·ka re·pu·bli·kuh

D

dad *táta* ⓜ ta·tuh
daily adv *denně* de·nye
dance *tanec* ⓜ tuh·nets
dance v *tancovat* tuhn·tso·vuht
dancing *tanec* ⓜ tuh·nets
dangerous *nebezpečný* ne·bez·pech·nee
dark (colour) *tmavý* tmuh·vee
dark (night) *černý* cher·nee
date (appointment) *schůzka* ⓕ
  skhooz·kuh
date (day) *datum* ⓜ duh·tum
date (fruit) *datle* ⓜ duht·le
date (night out) *rande* ⓝ ruhn·de
date of birth *datum narození* ⓝ
  duh·tum nuh·ro·ze·nye
daughter *dcera* ⓕ dtse·ruh
dawn *svítání* ⓝ svee·ta·nye
day *den* ⓜ den
day after tomorrow *pozítří* ⓝ
  po·zeet·rzhee
day before yesterday *předevčírem* ⓝ
  przhe·def·chee·rem
dead *mrtvý* mrt·vee
deaf *hluchý* hlu·khee
deal (cards) v *rozdávat* roz·da·vat
December *prosinec* ⓜ pro·si·nets
decide *rozhodnout* roz·hod·noht
deep (water) *hluboký* hlu·bo·kee
deforestation *odlesňování* ⓝ
  od·les·nyo·va·nye
degrees (temperature) *stupeň* ⓜ stu·pen'
delay *zpoždění* ⓝ zpozh·dye·nye
delicatessen *lahůdky* ⓕ pl luh·hood·ki
deliver *dovézt* do·vairzt
democracy *demokracie* ⓕ
  de·mo·kruh·tsi·ye
demonstration (display) *předvedení* ⓝ
  przhed·ve·de·nye
demonstration (rally) *demonstrace* ⓕ
  de·mons·truh·tse
Denmark *Dánsko* ⓝ dans·ko
dental floss *dentální nit* ⓕ
  den·tal·nyee nyit
dentist *zubař(ka)* ⓜ/ⓕ zu·buhrzh(·kuh)
deodorant *deodorant* ⓜ de·o·do·ruhnt
depart *odjet* od·yet
department store *obchodní dům* ⓜ
  op·khod·nyee doom
departure *odjezd* ⓜ od·yezd
departure gate *východ k letadlům* ⓕ
  vee·khod k le·tuhd·loom

deposit *vklad* ⓜ fkluhd
derailleur *přesmykač* ⓜ przhes·mi·kuhch
descendent *potomek* ⓜ po·to·mek
desert *poušť* ⓜ pohsht'
design *vzor* ⓜ vzor
dessert *moučník* ⓜ mohch·nyeek
destination *cíl cesty* ⓜ tseel tses·ti
details *podrobnosti* ⓕ po·drob·nos·tyi
diabetes *cukrovka* ⓕ tsu·krof·kuh
dial tone *oznamovací tón* ⓜ
  oz·nuh·mo·vuh·tsee tawn
diaper *plénka* ⓕ plairn·kuh
diaphragm (contraceptive) *pesar* ⓜ
  pe·suhr
diarrhoea *průjem* ⓜ proo·yem
diary *denník* ⓜ de·nyeek
dice *kostka* ⓕ kost·kuh
dictionary *slovník* ⓜ slov·nyeek
die v *zemřít* zem·rzheet
diet *strava* ⓕ struh·vuh
different *odlišný* od·lish·nee
difficult *těžký* tyezh·kee
digital *digitální* di·gi·tal·nyee
dining car *jídelní vůz* ⓜ yee·del·nyee vooz
dinner *večeře* ⓕ ve·che·rzhe
direct *přímý* przhee·mee
direct-dial *přímé volání* ⓝ
  przhee·mair vo·la·nyee
direction *směr* ⓜ smyer
director *ředitel(ka)* ⓜ/ⓕ rzhe·dyi·tel(·kuh)
dirty *špinavý* shpi·nuh·vee
disabled *invalidní* in·vuh·lid·nyee
disco *disko* ⓝ dis·ko
discount *sleva* ⓕ sle·vuh
discrimination *diskriminace* ⓕ
  dis·kri·mi·nuh·tse
disease *nemoc* ⓕ ne·mots
dish *pokrm* ⓜ po·krm
disk (CD-ROM) *disk* ⓜ disk
disk (floppy) *disketa* ⓕ dis·ke·tuh
diving *potápění* ⓝ po·ta·pye·nyee
diving equipment *výzbroj na potápění* ⓕ
  veez·broy nuh po·ta·pye·nyee
divorced *rozvedený* roz·ve·de·nee
dizzy *závratný* za·vruht·nee
do *dělat* dye·luht
doctor *doktor(ka)* ⓜ/ⓕ dok·tor(·kuh)
documentary *dokumentární* ⓜ
  do·ku·men·tar·nyee
dog *pes* ⓜ pes
dole *podpora v nezaměstnanosti* ⓕ
  pod·po·ruh v ne·zuh·myest·nuh·nos·tyi
doll *panenka* ⓕ puh·nen·kuh

dollar *dolar* ⓜ do·luhr
door *dveře* ⓕ pl dve·rzhe
dope (drugs) *hňup* ⓜ hnyup
double a *dvojitý* dvo·yi·tee
double bed *manželská postel* ⓕ
   muhn·zhels·ka pos·tel
double room *dvoulůžkový pokoj* ⓜ
   dvoh·loozh·ko·vee po·koy
down *dolů* do·loo
downhill *z kopce* s kop·tse
dozen *tucet* ⓜ tu·tset
drama *činohra* ⓕ chi·no·hruh
dream *sen* ⓜ sen
dress *šaty* pl shuh·ti
dried *sušený* su·she·nee
dried fruit *sušené ovoce* ⓝ
   su·she·nair o·vo·tse
drink *nápoj* ⓜ na·poy
drink v *pít* peet
drink (alcoholic) *alkoholický nápoj* ⓜ
   uhl·ko·ho·lits·kee na·poy
drive v *řídit* rzhee·dyit
drivers licence *řidičský průkaz* ⓜ
   rzhi·dyich·skee proo·kuhz
drug *lék* ⓜ lairk
drug addiction *narkomanie* ⓕ
   nuhr·ko·muh·ni·ye
drug dealer *překupník drog* ⓜ
   przhe·kup·nyeek drog
drugs (illicit) *drogy* ⓕ pl dro·gi
drug trafficking *pašování drog* ⓝ
   puh·sho·va·nyee drog
drug user *narkoman(ka)* ⓜ/ⓕ
   nuhr·ko·muhn(·kuh)
drum *buben* ⓜ bu·ben
drums (kit) *bicí souprava* ⓕ pl
   bi·tsee soh·pruh·vuh
drunk *opilý* o·pi·lee
dry a *suchý* su·khee
dry (clothes) v *sušit* su·shit
dry (oneself) v *utřít se* ut·rzheet se
duck *kachna* ⓕ kuhkh·nuh
dummy (pacifier) *dudlík* ⓜ dud·leek
duty-free *bez cla* bez tsluh
DVD *DVD* ⓝ dee·vee·deech·ko

E

each *každý* kuhzh·dee
ear *ucho* ⓝ u·kho
early adv *časně* chuhs·nye
earn *vydělat* vi·dye·luht

earplugs *ucpávky do ucha* ⓕ pl
   uts·paf·ki do u·khuh
earrings *náušnice* ⓕ pl na·ush·nyi·tse
Earth *Země* ⓕ ze·mye
earthquake *zemětřesení* ⓝ
   ze·myet·rzhe·se·nyee
east *východ* ⓜ vee·khod
Easter *Velikonoce* ve·li·ko·no·tse
easy *lehký* leh·kee
eat v *jíst* yeest
economy class *turistická třída* ⓕ
   tu·ris·tits·ka trzhee·duh
ecstasy (drug) *extáze* ⓕ eks·ta·ze
eczema *ekzém* ⓜ ek·zairm
education *vzdělání* ⓝ vzde·la·nyee
egg *vajíčko* ⓝ vuh·yeech·ko
eggplant *lilek* ⓜ li·lek
election *volby* ⓕ pl vol·bi
electrical store *elektro obchod* ⓜ
   e·lek·tro op·khod
electrician *elektrikář* ⓜ e·lek·tri·karzh
electricity *elektřina* ⓕ e·lek·trzhi·nuh
elevator *výtah* ⓜ vee·tuh
email *email* ⓜ ee·meyl
embarrassed *rozpačitý* roz·puh·chi·tee
embassy *velvyslanectví* ⓝ
   vel·vi·sluh·nets·tvee
emergency *pohotovost* ⓕ po·ho·to·vost
emotional *citový* tsi·to·vee
employee *zaměstnanec/zaměstnankyně*
   ⓜ/ⓕ zuh·myest·nuh·nets/
   zuh·myest·nuhn·ki·nye
employer *zaměstnavatel(kyně)* ⓜ/ⓕ
   zuh·myest·nuh·vuh·tel(·ki·nye)
empty a *prázdný* prazd·nee
encephalitis (tick-borne)
   meningokoková encefalitida ⓕ
   me·nin·go·ko·ko·va en·tse·fuh·li·ti·duh
end *konec* ⓜ ko·nets
endangered species *ohrožené druhy*
   ⓜ pl o hro·zhe·nair dru·hi
engaged (phone) *obsazeno* ob·suh·ze·no
engaged (to be married) *zasnoubený*
   zuh·snoh·be·nee
engagement (to marry) *zasnoubení* ⓝ
   zuh·snoh·be·nyee
engine *motor* ⓜ mo·tor
engineer *inženýr(ka)* ⓜ/ⓕ
   in·zhe·neer(·kuh)
engineering *strojírenství* ⓝ
   stro·yee·rens·tvee
England *Anglie* ⓕ uhn·gli·ye

English (language) *angličtina* ①
   uhn-glich-tyi-nuh
English (nationality) *Angličan(ka)* ⑩/①
   uhn-gli-chuhn(-kuh)
enjoy (oneself) *užívat u*-zhee-vuht
enough *dost* dost
enter *vstoupit* vstoh-pit
entertainment guide
   přehled kulturních pořadů ⑩
   przhe-hled *kul*-tur-nyeekh po-rzha-doo
entry *vstup* ⑩ vstup
envelope *obálka* ① o-bal-kuh
environment *prostředí* ⑪ *prost*-rzhe-dyee
epilepsy *epilepsie* ① e-pi-lep-si-ye
equality *rovnost* ① rov-nost
equal opportunity *rovné příležitosti* ① pl
   rov-nair przhe-le-zhi-tos-tyi
equipment *výstroj* ① vees-troy
escalator *eskalátor* ⑩ es-kuh-la-tor
estate agency *realitní kancelář* ①
   re-uh-lit-nyee kuhn-tse-larzh
euro *euro* ⑪ e-u-ro
Europe *Evropa* ① e-vro-puh
European Union *Evropská unie* ①
   e-vrops-ka u-ni-ye
euthanasia *euthanasie* ①
   e-u-tuh-nuh-si-ye
evening *večer* ⑩ ve-cher
every a *každý* kuzh-dee
everyone *všichni* vshikh-nyi
everything *všechno* ⑪ vshekh-no
exactly *přesně* przhes-nye
example *příklad* ⑩ przhee-kluhd
excellent *výborný* vee-bor-nee
excess baggage *nadměrné zavazadlo* ⑪
   nuhd-myer-nair zuh-vuh-zuhd-lo
exchange *výměna* ① vee-mye-nuh
exchange v *vyměnit* vi-mye-nyit
exchange rate *směnný kurs* ⑩
   smye-nee kurz
excluded *vynechaný* vi-ne-khuh-nee
exhaust (car) *výfuk* ⑩ vee-fuk
exhibition *výstava* ① vees-tuh-vuh
exit *východ* ⑩ vee-khod
expensive *drahý* druh-hee
experience *zkušenost* ① sku-she-nost
exploitation *vykořisťování* ⑪
   vi-ko-rzhis-tyo-va-nyee
export permit *vývozní povolení* ⑪
   vee-voz-nyee po-vo-le-nyee
express a *expresní* eks-pres-nyee
express mail *expresní zásilka* ①
   eks-pres-nyee za-sil-kuh

extension (visa) *prodloužení* ⑪
   prod-loh-zhe-nyee
eye *oko* ⑪ o-ko
eye drops *oční kapky* ① pl
   och-nyee kuhp-ki

F

fabric *látka* ① lat-kuh
face *obličej* ⑩ ob-li-chey
face cloth *žínka* ① zheen-kuh
factory *továrna* ① to-var-nuh
factory worker *dělník* ⑩ dyel-nyeek
fall (autumn) *podzim* ⑩ pod-zim
fall (down) *pád* ⑩ pad
family *rodina* ① ro-dyi-nuh
family name *příjmení* ① przheey-me-nyee
famous *slavný* sluhv-nee
fan (machine) *větrák* ⑩ vye-trak
fan (sport) *fanoušek* ⑩ fuh-noh-shek
fan belt *klínový řemen* ⑩
   klee-no-vee rzhe-men
far *daleko* duh-le-ko
fare *jízdné* ⑪ yeezd-nair
farm *statek* ⑩ stuh-tek
farmer *zemědělec/zemědělkyně* ⑩/①
   ze-mye-dye-lets/ze-mye-dyel-ki-nye
fashion *móda* ① maw-duh
fast a *rychlý* rikh-lee
fat a *tlustý* tlus-tee
father *otec* ⑩ o-tets
father-in-law *tchán* ⑩ tkhan
faucet *kohoutek* ⑩ ko-hoh-tek
fault (someone's) *chyba* ① khi-buh
faulty *vadný* vuhd-nee
fax machine *fax* ⑩ fuhks
February *únor* ⑩ oo-nor
feed *krmit* kr-mit
feel (touch) v *sáhnout* sah-noht
feeling (physical) *cit* ⑩ tsit
feelings *city* ⑩ pl tsi-ti
female a *ženský* zhens-kee
fence *plot* ⑩ plot
fencing (sport) *šerm* ⑩ sherm
ferry *trajekt* ⑩ truh-yekt
festival *festival* ⑩ fes-ti-vuhl
fever *horečka* ① ho-rech-kuh
few *málo* ma-lo
fiancé *snoubenec* ⑩ snoh-be-nets
fiancée *snoubenka* ① snoh-ben-kuh
fiction *beletrie* ① be-le-tri-ye
fig *fík* ⑩ feek
fight *rvačka* ① rvuhch-kuh

fill v *plnit* pl·nyit
fillet *filé* ⓝ fi·lair
film (cinema) *film* ⓜ film
film (for camera) *film* ⓜ film
film speed *citlivost* ⓕ tsit·li·vost
filtered *filtrovaný* fil·tro·vuh·nee
find v *najít* nuh·yeet
fine *vynikající* vi·nyi·kuh·yee·tsee
fine *pokuta* ⓕ po·ku·tuh
finger *prst* ⓜ prst
finish *konec* ⓜ ko·nets
finish v *dokončit* do·kon·chit
Finland *Finsko* ⓝ fin·sko
fire *oheň* o·hen'
firewood *palivové dřevo* ⓝ
    puh·li·vo·vair drzhe·vo
first a *první* prv·nyee
first-aid kit *lékárnička* ⓕ lair·kar·nyich·kuh
first class *první třída* ⓕ
    prv·nyee trzhee·duh
first name *křestní jméno* ⓝ
    krzhest·nyee ymair·no
fish *ryba* ⓕ ri·buh
fishing *rybolov* ⓜ ri·bo·lov
fishmonger *prodavač ryb* ⓜ
    pro·duh·vuhch rib
fish shop *obchod s rybami* ⓕ
    op·khod s ri·buh·mi
flag *vlajka* ⓕ vlai·kuh
flannel (face cloth) *žínka* ⓕ zheen·kuh
flash (camera) *blesk* ⓜ blesk
flashlight *baterka* ⓕ buh·ter·kuh
flat (apartment) *byt* ⓜ bit
flat a *rovný* rov·nee
flea *blecha* ⓕ ble·khuh
fleamarket *bleší trh* ⓜ ble·shee trh
flight *let* ⓜ let
flood *povodeň* ⓕ po·vo·den'
floor *podlaha* ⓕ pod·luh·huh
floor (storey) *poschodí* ⓝ pos·kho·dyee
florist *květinář* ⓜ kvye·tyi·narzh
flour *mouka* ⓕ moh·kuh
flower *květina* ⓕ kvye·tyi·nuh
flu *chřipka* ⓕ khrzhip·kuh
flute *flétna* ⓕ flairt·nuh
fly *moucha* ⓕ moh·khuh
fly v *létat* lair·tuht
foggy *mlhavý* ml·huh·vee
follow *následovat* nas·le·do·vuht
food *jídlo* ⓝ yeed·lo
food supplies *zásoby potravin* ⓕ pl
    za·so·bi po·truh·vin
foot (body) *chodidlo* ⓝ kho·dyid·lo

football (soccer) *fotbal* ⓜ fot·buhl
footpath *chodník* ⓜ khod·nyeek
foreign *cizí* tsi·zee
forest *les* ⓜ les
forever *navždy* nuhv·zhdi
forget *zapomenout* zuh·po·me·noht
forgive *prominout* pro·mi·noht
fork *vidlička* ⓕ vid·lich·kuh
fortnight *čtrnáct dní* chtr·natst dnyee
fortune teller *věštkyně* ⓕ vyesht·ki·nye
foul (soccer) *faul* ⓜ fowl
foyer *předsíň* ⓕ przhed·seen'
fragile *křehký* krzheh·kee
France *Francie* ⓕ fruhn·tsi·ye
free (available) a *volný* vol·nee
free (gratis) a *bezplatný* bez·pluht·nee
free (not bound) a *svobodný* svo·bod·nee
freeze v *zmrznout* zmrz·noht
fresh *čerstvý* cherst·vee
Friday *pátek* ⓜ pa·tek
fridge *lednička* ⓕ led·nyich·kuh
fried *smažený* smuh·zhe·nee
friend *přítel* ⓜ przhee·tel
from *z* z
frost *mráz* ⓜ mraz
frozen *zmrzlý* zmrz·lee
fruit *ovoce* ⓝ o·vo·tse
fruit picking *trhání ovoce* ⓝ
    tr·ha·nyee o·vo·tse
fry v *smažit* smuh·zhit
frying pan *pánev* ⓕ pa·nef
full *plný* pl·nee
full-time *na plný úvazek*
    nuh pl·nee oo·vuh·zek
fun *zábavný* za·buhv·nee
funeral *pohřeb* ⓜ po·hrzheb
funny *legrační* le·gruhch·nyee
furniture *nábytek* ⓜ na·bi·tek
future *budoucnost* ⓕ bu·dohts·nost

G

game (general) *hra* ⓕ hruh
game (sport) *zápas* ⓜ za·puhs
garage *garáž* ⓕ guh·razh
garbage *odpadky* ⓜ pl od·puhd·ki
garbage can *popelnice* ⓕ po·pel·nyi·tse
garden *zahrada* ⓕ zuh·hruh·duh
gardener *zahradník* ⓜ zuh·hrud·nyeek
gardening *zahradničení* ⓝ
    zuh·hruhd·nyi·che·nyee
garlic *česnek* ⓜ ches·nek
garnet *granát* ⓜ gruh·nat

gas **(for cooking)** *plyn* ⓜ plin
gas **(petrol)** *benzín* ⓜ ben·zeen
gas cartridge *plynová bomba* ⓕ
  pli·no·va bom·buh
gastroenteritis *gastroenteritida* ⓕ
  guhs·tro·en·te·ri·ti·duh
gate **(airport)** *výstup k letadlům* ⓜ
  vees·tup k le·tuhd·loom
gauze *gáza* ⓕ ga·zuh
gay **(homosexual)** *homosexuální*
  ho·mo·sek·su·al·nyee
gearbox *rychlostní skříň* ⓕ
  ri·khlost·nyee skrzheen'
Germany *Německo* ⓝ nye·mets·ko
get *dostat* dos·tuht
get off **(bus, train)** *vystoupit* vis·toh·pit
gift *dar* ⓜ duhr
gig *koncert* ⓜ kon·tsert
gin *džin* ⓜ dzhin
girl *dívka* ⓕ dyeef·kuh
girlfriend *přítelkyně* ⓕ przhe·tel·ki·nye
give *dát* dat
given name *křestní jméno* ⓝ
  krzhest·nyee ymair·no
glandular fever *mononukleóza* ⓕ
  mo·no·nu·kle·aw·zuh
glass **(drinking)** *sklenička* ⓕ skle·nyich·kuh
glasses **(spectacles)** *brýle* ⓕ pl bree·le
glassware *skleněné zboží* ⓝ
  skle·nye·nair zbo·zhee
gloves **(clothing)** *rukavice* ⓕ pl
  ru·kuh·vi·tse
gloves **(latex)** *gumové rukavice* ⓕ pl
  gu·mo·vair ru·kuh·vi·tse
glue *lepidlo* ⓝ le·pid·lo
go *jít* yeet
goal **(sport)** *gól* ⓜ gawl
goalkeeper *brankář* ⓜ bruhn·karzh
goat *koza* ⓕ ko·zuh
god **(general)** *bůh* ⓜ booh
goggles **(skiing)** *lyžařské brýle* ⓕ pl
  li·zharzh·skair bree·le
goggles **(swimming)** *plavecké brýle* ⓕ pl
  pluh·vets·kair bree·le
gold *zlato* ⓝ zluh·to
golf ball *golfový míček* ⓜ
  gol·fo·vee mee·chek
golf course *golfové hřiště* ⓝ
  gol·fo·vair hrzhish·tye
good *dobrý* do·bree
goodbye *na shledanou* nuh·skhle·duh·noh
go out *vyjít* vi·yeet
go out with **(date)** *chodit s* kho·dyit s

go shopping *jít na nákupy*
  yeet nuh na·ku·pi
government *vláda* ⓕ vla·duh
gram *gram* ⓜ gruhm
grandchild *vnuk/vnučka* ⓜ/ⓕ
  vnuk/vnuch·kuh
grandfather *dědeček* ⓜ dye·de·chek
grandmother *babička* ⓕ buh·bich·kuh
grapes *hrozny* ⓜ pl hroz·ni
grass **(lawn)** *tráva* ⓕ tra·vuh
grateful *vděčný* vdyech·nee
grave *hrob* ⓜ hrob
great **(fantastic)** *báječný* ba·yech·nee
green *zelený* ze·le·nee
greengrocer *zelinář* ⓜ ze·li·narzh
grey *šedivý* she·dyi·vee
grocery *potravina* ⓕ pot·ruh·vi·nuh
grocery store *konzum* ⓜ kon·zum
groundnut *podzemnice olejná* ⓕ
  pod·zem·nyi·tse o·ley·na
grow *růst* roost
guarantee *záruka* ⓕ za·ru·kuh
guess v *odhadovat* od·huh·do·vuht
guesthouse *penzion* ⓜ pen·zi·on
guide **(audio)** *audio guide* ⓜ ow·di·o gaid
guide **(person)** *průvodce* ⓜ proo·vod·tse
guidebook *průvodce* ⓜ proo·vod·tse
guide dog *slepecký pes* ⓜ sle·pets·kee pes
guided tour *okružní jízda* ⓕ
  o·kruzh·nyee yeez·duh
guilty *vinný* vi·nee
guitar *kytara* ⓕ ki·tuh·ruh
gum *dáseň* ⓕ da·sen'
gun **(pistol)** *pistole* ⓕ pis·to·le
gun **(rifle)** *puška* ⓕ push·kuh
gym **(place)** *tělocvična* ⓕ tye·lots·vich·nuh
gymnastics *gymnastika* ⓕ gim·nuhs·ti·kuh
gynaecologist *gynekolog* ⓜ gi·ne·ko·log

H

hair *vlasy* ⓜ pl vluh·si
hairbrush *kartáč na vlasy* ⓜ
  kuhr·tach nuh vluh·si
haircut *ostříhání vlasů* ⓝ
  ost·rzhee·ha·nyee vluh·soo
hairdresser **(for men)** *holič* ⓜ ho·lich
hairdresser **(for women)**
  kadeřník/kadeřnice ⓜ/ⓕ
  kuh·derzh·nyeek/kuh·derzh·nyi·tse
halal *halal* huh·luhl
half *polovina* ⓕ po·lo·vi·nuh

hallucination *halucinace* ⓕ
huh·lu·tsi·nuh·tse
ham *šunka* ⓕ shun·kuh
hammer *kladivo* ⓝ kluh·dyi·vo
hammock *hamak* ⓜ huh·muhk
hand *ruka* ⓕ ru·kuh
handbag *kabelka* ⓕ kuh·bel·kuh
handball *házená* ⓕ ha·ze·na
handicraft *umělecké řemeslo* ⓝ
u·mye·lets·kair rzhe·mes·lo
handkerchief *kapesník* ⓜ kuh·pes·nyeek
handlebars *řidítka* ⓝ rzhi·dyeet·kuh
handmade *ručně vyrobeno* ⓝ
ruch·nye vi·ro·be·no
handsome *hezký* hez·kee
happy *šťastný* shtyast·nee
harassment *obtěžování* ⓝ
ob·tye·zho·va·nyee
harbour *přístav* ⓜ przhe·stuhf
hard (not soft) *tvrdý* tvr·dee
hard-boiled *natvrdo uvařený*
nuh·tvr·do u·vuh·rzhe·nee
hardware store *železářství* ⓝ
zhe·le·zarzh·stvee
hashish *hašiš* ⓜ huh·shish
hat (hard) *klobouk* ⓜ klo·bohk
hat (soft) *čepice* ⓕ che·pi·tse
have *mít* meet
have a cold *být nastydlý* beet nuh·stid·lee
have fun *bavit se* buh·vit se
hay fever *senná rýma* ⓕ se·na ree·muh
hazelnut *lískový oříšek* ⓜ
lees·ko·vee o·rzhee·shek
he *on* on
head *hlava* ⓕ hluh·vuh
headache *bolení hlavy* ⓝ
bo·le·nyee hluh·vi
headlights *reflektor* ⓜ re·flek·tor
health *zdraví* ⓝ zdra·vee
hear *slyšet* sli·shet
hearing aid *naslouchátko* ⓝ
nuh·sloh·khat·ko
heart *srdce* ⓝ srd·tse
heart attack *srdeční infarkt* ⓜ
sr·dech·nyee in·fuhrkt
heart condition *srdeční porucha* ⓕ
sr·dech·nyee po·ru·khuh
heat *horko* ⓝ hor·ko
heated *vytápěný* vi·ta·pye·nee
heater *ohřívač* ⓜ o·hrzhee·vuhch
heating *topení* ⓝ to·pe·nyee
heavy (weight) *těžký* tyezh·kee
helmet *helma* ⓕ hel·muh

help *pomoc* ⓕ po·mots
help v *pomoci* po·mo·tsi
hepatitis *žloutenka* ⓕ zhloh·ten·kuh
her (possessive) *její* ye·yee
herb *bylina* ⓕ bi·li·nuh
herbalist *kořenář* ⓜ ko·rzhe·narzh
here *tady* tuh·di
heroin *heroin* ⓝ he·ro·in
herring *sleď* ⓕ sled'
high (height) *vysoký* vi·so·kee
highchair *dětská stolička* ⓕ
dyet·ska sto·lich·kuh
high school *střední škola* ⓕ
strzhed·nyee shko·luh
highway *dálnice* ⓕ dal·nyi·tse
hike v *trampovat* truhm·po·vuht
hiking *turistika* ⓕ tu·ris·ti·kuh
hiking boots *trekingová obuv* ⓕ
tre·kin·go·va o·buf
hiking route *turistická stezka* ⓕ
tu·ris·tits·ka stez·kuh
hill *kopec* ⓜ ko·pets
Hindu *hind/hindka* ⓜ/ⓕ hind/hind·kuh
hire v *vypůjčit* vi·pooy·chit
his *jeho* ye·ho
historical *historický* his·to·rits·kee
history *dějiny* ⓕ pl dye·yi·ni
hitchhike *stopovat* sto·po·vuht
HIV *HIV* ⓝ ha·ee·vair
hockey *hokej* ⓝ ho·key
holiday *svátek* ⓜ sva·tek
holidays *dovolená* ⓕ do·vo·le·na
home *domov* ⓜ do·mof
homeless (person) *bezdomovec* ⓜ&ⓕ
bez·do·mo·vets
homemaker *manželka* ⓕ muhn·zhel·kuh
homeopathy *homeopatie* ⓕ
ho·me·o·puh·ti·ye
homesick *tesknící po domově*
tesk·nyee·tsee po do·mo·vye
homosexual *homosexuál* ⓜ
ho·mo·sek·su·al
honey *med* ⓜ med
honeymoon *svatební cesta* ⓕ
svuh·teb·nyee tses·tuh
horoscope *horoskop* ⓜ ho·ros·kop
horse *kůň* koon'
horse racing *dostihy* ⓜ pl dos·tyi·hi
horse riding *jízda na koni* ⓕ
yeez·duh nuh ko·nyi
hospital *nemocnice* ⓕ ne·mots·nyi·tse
hospitality *pohostinství* ⓝ
po·hos·tyins·tvee

hot *horký* hor·kee
hotel *hotel* ho·tel
hot water *teplá voda* ① tep·la vo·duh
hot water bottle *ohřívací láhev* ①
o·hrzhee·vuh·tsee la·hef
hour *hodina* ① ho·dyi·nuh
house *dům* ⑩ doom
housework *práce v domácnosti* ①
pra·tse v do·mats·nos·tyi
how *jak* yuhk
how much *kolik* ko·lik
hug v *objemout* o·bey·moht
huge *ohromný* o·hrom·nee
humanities *humanitní vědy* ① pl
hu·muh·nit·nyee vye·di
human resources *lidské zdroje* ⑩ pl
lid·skair zdro·ye
human rights *lidská práva* ① pl
lid·ska pra·vuh
hundred *sto* ⑩ sto
hungry *hladový* hluh·do·vee
hunting *lov* ⑩ lov
hurt v *uhodit se* u·ho·dyit se
husband *manžel* ⑩ muhn·zhel

I

I *já* ya
ice *led* ⑩ led
ice axe *cepín* ⑩ tse·peen
ice cream *zmrzlina* ① zmrz·li·nuh
ice-cream parlour
cukrárna ①/*ovocný bar* ⑩
tsu·krar·nuh/o·vots·nee buhr
ice hockey *lední hokej* ⑩ led·nyee ho·key
identification *osobní doklad* ①
o·sob·nyee dok·luhd
identification card (ID) *doklad totožnosti*
⑩ dok·luhd to·tozh·nos·tyi
if *jestliže* yest·li·zhe
ill *nemocný* ne·mots·nee
immigration *imigrace* ① i·mi·gruh·tse
important *důležitý* doo·le·zhi·tee
impossible *nemožný* ne·mozh·nee
in *v* v
in a hurry *spěšně* spyesh·nye
included *včetně* fchet·nye
income tax *daň z příjmu* ①
duhn' z przheey·mu
indicator *blinkr* ⑩ blin·kr

indigestion *zažívací poruchy* ① pl
zuh·zhee·vuh·tsee po·ru·khi
indoor *halový* huh·lo·vee
industry *průmysl* ⑩ proo·mi·sl
infection *infekce* ① in·fek·tse
inflammation *zánět* ⑩ za·nyet
influenza *chřipka* ① khrzhip·kuh
information *informace* ① in·for·muh·tse
in front of *před* przhed
ingredient *příměs* ① przhee·myes
inject *aplikovat injekci*
uh·pli·ko·vuht in·yek·tsi
injection *injekce* ① in·yek·tse
injured *zraněný* zruh·nye·nee
injury *zranění* ① zruh·nye·nyee
inner tube *duše* ① du·she
innocent *nevinný* ne·vi·nee
insect *hmyz* ⑩ hmiz
insect repellent *repelent (prostředek
na hubení hmyzu)* ⑩ re·pe·lent
(prost·rzhe·dek nuh hu·be·nyee hmi·zu)
inside adv *vnitřní* vnyi·trzh·nyee
instructor *instruktor(ka)* ⑩/①
ins·truk·tor(·kuh)
insurance *pojištění* ①
po·yish·tye·nyee
interesting *zajímavý* zuh·yee·muh·vee
intermission *přestávka* ① przhe·staf·kuh
international *mezinárodní*
me·zi·na·rod·nyee
Internet *internet* ⑩ in·ter·net
Internet café *internetová kavárna* ①
in·ter·ne·to·va kuh·var·nuh
interpreter *tlumočník/tlumočnice* ⑩/①
tlu·moch·nyeek/tlu·moch·nyi·tse
interview *pohovor* ⑩ po·ho·vor
invite *pozvat* poz·vuht
Ireland *Irsko* ⑩ ir·sko
iron (for clothes) *žehlička* ①
zheh·lich·kuh
island *ostrov* ⑩ os·trov
it *to* to
IT (information technology) *IT
(informuční technologie)* ① ee·tair
(in·for·muhch·nyec tekh·no·lo·gi·ye)
Italy *Itálie* ① i·ta·li·ye
itch *svědění* ⑩ svye·dye·nyee
itemised *rozepsaný* ro·zep·suh·nee
itinerary *itinerář* ① i·ti·ne·rarzh
IUD *nitroděložní tělísko* ⑩
nyi·tro·dye·lozh·nyee tye·lees·ko

J

jacket *sako* ⓝ suh·ko
jail *věznice* ⓕ vyez·ni·tse
jam *džem* ⓜ dzhem
January *leden* ⓜ le·den
Japan *Japonsko* ⓝ yuh·pon·sko
jar *sklenice* ⓕ skle·nyi·tse
jaw *čelist* ⓕ che·list
jealous *žárlivý* ⓜ zhar·li·vee
jeans *džíny* ⓟ pl dzhee·ni
jeep *džíp* ⓜ dzheep
jet lag *pásmová nemoc* ⓕ
  pas·mo·va ne·mots
jewellery *šperky* ⓜ pl shper·ki
Jewish *židovský* zhi·dof·skee
job *zaměstnání* ⓝ zuh·myest·na·nyee
jogging *kondiční běh* ⓜ
  kon·dich·nyee byeh
joke *vtip* ⓜ ftyip
journalist *novinář(ka)* ⓜ/ⓕ
  no·vi·narzh(·kuh)
journey *cesta* ⓕ tses·tuh
judge *soudce* ⓜ sohd·tse
juice *šťáva* ⓕ shtya·vuh
July *červenec* ⓜ cher·ve·nets
jump v *skočit* sko·chit
jumper (sweater) *svetr* ⓜ sve·tr
jumper leads *startovací kabely* ⓜ
  stuhr·to·vuh·tsee kuh·be·li
June *červen* ⓜ cher·ven

K

kayaking *kajakování* ⓝ
  kuh·yuh·ko·va·nyee
ketchup *kečup* ⓜ ke·chup
key (door etc) *klíč* ⓜ kleech
keyboard *klávesnice* ⓕ kla·ves·nyi·tse
kick v *kopat* ko·puht
kidney *ledvina* ⓕ led·vi·nuh
kill v *zabít* zuh·beet
kilogram *kilogram* ⓜ ki·lo·gruhm
kilometre *kilometr* ⓜ ki·lo·me·tr
kind (nice) *laskavý* luhs·kuh·vee
kindergarten *školka* ⓕ shkol·kuh
king *král* ⓜ kral
kiosk *stánek* ⓜ sta·nek
kiss *polibek* ⓜ po·li·bek
kiss v *líbat* lee·buht
kitchen *kuchyň* ⓕ ku·khin'

L

labourer *pomocný dělník* ⓜ
  po·mots·nee dyel·nyeek
lace (fabric) *krajka* ⓕ krai·kuh
lake *jezero* ⓝ ye·ze·ro
lamb (meat) *jehněčí* ⓝ yeh·nye·chee
land *země* ⓕ ze·mye
landlady *paní domácí* ⓕ
  puh·nyee do·ma·tsee
landlord *pan domácí* ⓜ puhn do·ma·tsee
language *jazyk* ⓜ yuh·zik
laptop *notebook* ⓜ noht·buk
large *velký* vel·kee
last (final) *poslední* pos·led·nyee
last (previous) *předešlý* przhe·desh·lee
late adv *pozdě* poz·dye
later *později* poz·dye·yi
laugh v *smát se* smat se
launderette (samoobslužná) pradlenka ⓕ
  (suh·mo·ob·sluzh·na) pruhd·len·kuh
laundry (clothes) *prádlo* ⓝ prad·lo
laundry (place/room) *prádelna* ⓕ
  pra·del·nuh
law (legislation) *zákon* ⓜ za·kon
law (study/profession) *právo* ⓝ pra·vo
lawyer *advokát(ka)* ⓜ/ⓕ uhd·vo·kat(·kuh)
laxative *projímadlo* ⓝ pro·yee·muhd·lo
lazy *líný* lee·nee
leader *vůdce/vůdkyně* ⓜ/ⓕ
  vood·tse/vood·ki·nye
leaf *list* ⓜ list
learn *učit se* u·chit se
leather *kůže* ⓕ koo·zhe
lecturer *lektor(ka)* ⓜ/ⓕ lek·tor(·kuh)
ledge *lišta* ⓕ lish·tuh
left (direction) *levý* le·vee
left luggage *zavazadlo v úschovně* ⓕ
  zuh·vuh·zuhd·lo v oos·khov·nye
left-luggage office *úschovna zavazadel*
  ⓕ oos·khov·nuh zuh·vuh·zuh·del
left-wing *levicový* le·vi·tso·vee
leg (body) *noha* ⓕ no·huh
legal *legální* le·gal·nyee
legislation *legislativa* ⓕ le·gis·luh·ti·vuh
legume *luštěnina* ⓕ lush·tye·nyi·nuh
lemon *citron* ⓜ tsi·tron
lemonade *limonáda* ⓕ li·mo·na·duh

lens (camera) objektiv @ ob·yek·tif
lentil čočka ① choch·ka
lesbian lesbička ① les·bich·kuh
less menší men·shee
letter (mail) dopis @ do·pis
lettuce hlávkový salát @ hlaf·ko·vec suh·lal
liar lhář @ lharzh
librarian knihovník/knihovnice @/① knyi·hov·nyeek/knyi·hov·nyi·tse
library knihovna ① knyi·hov·nuh
lice veš ① vesh
licence povolení @ po·vo·le·nyee
license plate number tabulka se státní poznávací značkou ① tuh·bul·kuh se stat·nyee poz·na·vuh·tsee znuch·koh
lie (not stand) v ležet le·zhet
lie (not tell the truth) v lhát lhat
life život @ zhi·vot
life jacket plovací vesta ① plo·vuh·tsee ves·tuh
lift (elevator) výtah @ vee·tah
light světlo @ svyet·lo
light (colour) světlý svyet·lee
light (weight) lehký leh·kee
light bulb žárovka ① zha·rof·kuh
lighter (cigarette) zapalovač @ zuh·puh·lo·vuhch
light meter expozimetr @ eks·po·zi·me·tr
like v mít rád meet rad
lime limeta ① li·me·tuh
linen (material) lněná tkanina ① lnye·na tkuh·nyi·nuh
linen (sheets) ložní prádlo @ pl lozh·nyee prad·lo
linguist lingvista @ ling·vis·tuh
lip balm pomáda na rty ① po·ma·duh nuh rti
lips rty ① pl rti
lipstick rtěnka ① rtyen·kuh
listen poslouchat po·sloh·khuht
little (quantity) málo @ ma·lo
little (size) a malý muh·lee
live (life) žít zheet
live (somewhere) bydlet bid·let
liver játra ① ya·truh
lizard ještěrka ① yesh·tyer·kuh
local a místní meest·nyee
lock zámek @ za·mek
lock v zamknout zuhm·knoht
locked zamknutý zuhm·knu·tee
lollies lízátka @ pl lee·zat·kuh
long dlouhý dloh·hee

look v dívat se dyee·vuht se
look after starat se stuh·ruht se
look for hledat hle·duht
lookout vyhlídka ① vih·leed·kuh
loose volný vol·nee
loose change drobné @ pl drob·nair
lose ztratit ztruh·tyit
lost ztracený ztruh·tse·nee
lost-property office ztráty a nálezy ① ztra·ti uh na·le·zi
(a) lot hodně hod·nye
loud hlasitý hluh·si·tee
love láska ① las·kuh
love v milovat mi·lo·vuht
lover milenec/milenka @/① mi·le·nets/mi·len·kuh
low nízký nyeez·kee
lubricant mazivo @ muh·zi·vo
luck štěstí @ shtyes·tyee
lucky šťastný shtyast·nee
luggage zavazadlo @ zuh·vuh·zuhd·lo
luggage locker zavazadlová schránka ① zuh·vuh·zuhd·lo·va skhran·kuh
luggage tag zavazadlový lístek @ zuh·vuh·zuhd·lo·vee lees·tek
lump boule ① boh·le
lunch oběd @ o·byed
lung plíce ① plee·tse
luxurious přepychový przhe·pi·kho·vee

M

machine stroj @ stroy
magazine časopis @ chuh·so·pis
mail (letters/postal system) pošta ① posh·tuh
mail v odeslat o·des·luht
mailbox poštovní schránka ① posh·tov·nyee skhran·kuh
main a hlavní hluhv·nyee
main road hlavní silnice ① hluhv·nyee sil·nyi·tse
make v dělat dye·luht
make-up líčidlo @ lee·chid·lo
mammogram mamogram @ muh·mo·gruhm
man muž @ muzh
manager (business) ředitel(ka) @/① rzhe·dyi·tel(·kuh)
manager (sport) manažer(ka) @/① muh·nuh·zher(·kuh)
mandarin mandarinka ① muhn·duh·rin·kuh

mango *mango* ⓝ muhn-go
manual worker *dělník* dyel-nyeek
many *mnohý* mno-hee
map (of country) *mapa* ⓕ muh-puh
map (of town) *plán* ⓜ plan
March *březen* ⓜ brzhe-zen
margarine *margarín* ⓜ muhr-guh-reen
marijuana *marihuana* ⓕ muh-ri-hu-uh-nuh
marital status *rodinný stav* ⓜ
    ro-dyi-nee stuhf
market *trh* ⓜ trh
marriage *manželství* ⓝ muhn-zhels-tvee
married (man) *ženatý* zhe-nuh-tee
married (woman) *vdaná* f-duh-na
marry (man) *oženit se* o-zhe-nyit se
marry (woman) *vdát se* f-dat se
martial arts *bojová umění* ⓝ pl
    bo-yo-va u-mye-nyee
mass (Catholic) *mše* ⓕ mshe
massage *masáž* ⓕ muh-sazh
masseur *masér* ⓜ muh-ser
masseuse *masérka* ⓕ muh-ser-kuh
mat *rohožka* ⓕ ro-hozh-kuh
match (sports) *zápas* ⓜ za-puhs
matches (for lighting) *zápalky* ⓕ pl
    za-puhl-ki
mattress *matrace* ⓕ muh-truh-tse
May *květen* ⓜ kvye-ten
maybe *možná* mozh-na
mayonnaise *majonéza* ⓕ muh-yo-nair-zuh
mayor *starosta/starostka* ⓜ/ⓕ
    stuh-ros-tuh/stuh-rost-kuh
me *mě* mye
meal *jídlo* ⓝ yeed-lo
measles *spalničky* ⓕ pl spuhl-nyich-ki
meat *maso* ⓝ muh-so
mechanic *mechanik* ⓜ me-khuh-nik
media *média* ⓝ pl mair-di-yuh
medicine (medication) *lék* ⓜ lairk
medicine (profession) *lékařství* ⓝ
    lair-kuhrzh-stvee
medicine (study) *medicína* ⓕ
    me-di-tsee-nuh
meditation *meditace* ⓕ me-di-tuh-tse
meet (first time) v *potkat* pot-kuht
meet (get together) v *sejít se* se-yeet se
melon *meloun* ⓜ me-lohn
member *člen/členka* ⓜ/ⓕ
    chlen/chlen-kuh
memory card *paměťová karta* ⓕ
    puh-mye-to-va kuhr-tuh
menstruation *menstruace* ⓕ
    men-stru-uh-tse

menu *jídelní lístek* ⓜ yee-del-nyee lees-tek
message *zpráva* ⓕ zpra-vuh
metal *kov* ⓜ kov
metre *metr* ⓜ me-tr
metro (train) *metro* ⓝ met-ro
metro station *stanice metra* ⓕ
    stuh-nyi-tse met-ruh
microwave oven *mikrovlná trouba* ⓕ
    mi-kro-vl-na troh-buh
midday *poledne* ⓝ po-led-ne
midnight *půlnoc* ⓕ pool-nots
migraine *migréna* ⓕ mi-grair-nuh
military *branná moc* ⓕ bruh-na mots
military service *vojenská služba* ⓕ
    vo-yens-ka sluzh-buh
milk *mléko* ⓝ mlair-ko
millimetre *milimetr* ⓜ mi-li-me-tr
million *milion* ⓜ mi-li-yon
mince meat *mleté maso* ⓝ mle-tair muh-so
mineral water *minerálka* ⓕ mi-ne-ral-kuh
minute *minuta* ⓕ mi-nu-tuh
mirror *zrcadlo* ⓝ zr-tsuhd-lo
miscarriage *samovolný potrat* ⓜ
    suh-mo-vol-nee po-truht
Miss *slečna* ⓕ slech-nuh
miss (feel absence of) *postrádat*
    pos-tra-duht
miss (not catch train etc) *zmeškat*
    zmesh-kuht
mistake *chyba* ⓕ khi-buh
mix v *míchat* mee-khuht
mobile phone *mobil* ⓜ mo-bil
modem *modem* ⓜ mo-dem
modern *moderní* mo-der-nyee
moisturiser *hydratační krém* ⓜ
    hi-druh-tuhch-nyee krairm
monastery *klášter* ⓜ klash-ter
Monday *pondělí* ⓝ pon-dye-lee
money *peníze* ⓝ pl pe-nyee-ze
monk *mnich* ⓜ mnyikh
month *měsíc* ⓜ mye-seets
monument *pomník* ⓜ pom-nyeek
moon *měsíc* ⓜ mye-seets
more *více* vee-tse
morning *ráno* ⓝ ra-no
morning sickness *ranní nevolnost* ⓕ
    ruh-nyee ne-vol-nost
mosque *mešita* ⓕ me-shi-tuh
mosquito *komár* ⓜ ko-mar
mosquito net *moskitiéra* ⓕ
    mos-ki-ti-yair-ruh
motel *motel* ⓜ mo-tel
mother *matka* ⓕ muht-kuh

mother-in-law *tchýně* ① *tkhee·nye*
motorbike *motorka* ① *mo·tor·kuh*
motorboat *motorový člun* ②
  mo·to·ro·vee chlun
motorway (tollway) *dálnice* ① *dal·nyi·tse*
mountain *hora* ① *ho·ruh*
mountain bike *horské kolo* ②
  hors·kair ko·lo
mountaineering *horolezectví* ②
  ho·ro·le·zets·tvee
mountain path *horská stezka* ①
  hors·ka stez·kuh
mountain range *pohoří* ② *po·ho·rzhee*
mouse *myš* ① *mish*
mouth *ústa* ② *oos·tuh*
movie *film* ② *film*
Mr *pan* ⑨ *puhn*
Mrs *paní* ① *puh·nyee*
Ms *slečna* ① *slech·nuh*
mud *bahno* ② *buh·no*
muesli *muesli* ② *mis·li*
mum *máma* ① *ma·muh*
mumps *příušnice* ① pl *przhi·ush·nyi·tse*
murder *vražda* ① *vruhzh·duh*
murder v *vraždit* *vruhzh·dyit*
muscle *sval* ② *svuhl*
museum *muzeum* ② *mu·ze·um*
mushroom *houba* ① *hoh·buh*
music *hudba* ① *hud·buh*
musician *hudebník/hudebnice* ⑨/①
  hu·deb·nyeek/hu·deb·nyi·tse
music shop *obchod s hudebninami* ②
  op·khod s hu·deb·nyi·nuh·mi
Muslim *muslim(ka)* ⑨/① *mus·lim(·kuh)*
mussel *slávka jedlá* ① *slaf·kuh yed·la*
mustard *hořčice* ① *horzh·chi·tse*
mute a *němý* *nye·mee*
my *můj* *mooy*

N

nail clippers *kleštičky na nehty* ① pl
  klesh·tyich·ki nuh nekh·ti
name *jméno* ② *ymair·no*
napkin *ubrousek* ⑨ *u·broh·sek*
nappy *plenka* ① *plen·kuh*
nappy rash *vyrážka* ① *vi·razh·kuh*
nationality *národnost* ① *na·rod·nost*
national park *národní park* ⑨
  na·rod·nyee puhrk
nature *příroda* ① *przhee·ro·duh*
naturopathy *přírodní medicína* ①
  przhee·rod·nyee me·di·tsee·nuh

nausea *nevolnost* ① *ne·vol·nost*
near prep *blízko* *bleez·ko*
nearby *nedaleko* *ne·duh·le·ko*
nearest *nejbližší* *ney·blizh·shee*
necessary *nutný* *nut·nee*
neck *krk* ⑨ *krk*
necklace *náhrdelník* ⑨ *na·hr·del·nyeek*
nectarine *nektarínka* ① *nek·tuh·reen·kuh*
need v *potřebovat* *pot·rzhe·bo·vuht*
needle (sewing/syringe) *jehla* ① *yeh·luh*
negative a *záporný* *za·por·nee*
negatives (photos) *negativy* ⑨ pl
  ne·guh·ti·vi
neither adv *také ne* *tuh·kair ne*
net *síť* ① *seet'*
Netherlands *Nizozemí* ② *nyi·zo·ze·mee*
network (phone) *síť* ① *seet'*
never *nikdy* *nyik·di*
new *nový* *no·vee*
news *zprávy* ① pl *zpra·vi*
newsagency *tisková agentura* ①
  tyis·ko·va uh·gen·tu·ruh
newspaper *noviny* ① pl *no·vi·ni*
newsstand *novinový stánek* ⑨
  no·vi·no·vee sta·nek
New Year's Day *Nový rok* ⑨ *no·vee rok*
New Year's Eve *Silvestr* ⑨ *sil·ves·tr*
New Zealand *Nový Zéland* ⑨
  no·vee zair·luhnd
next (following) *následující*
  nas·le·du·yee·tsee
next to *vedle* *ved·le*
nice *příjemný* *przhee·yem·nee*
nickname *přezdívka* ① *przhez·dyeef·kuh*
night *noc* ① *nots*
nightclub *noční klub* ⑨ *noch·nyee klub*
night out (party) *večírek/mejdan* ⑨
  ve·chee·rek/mey·duhn
no *ne* *ne*
noisy *hlučný* *hluch·nee*
none *žádný* *zhad·nee*
nonsmoking *nekuřácký* *ne·ku·rzhats·kee*
noodles *nudle* ① *nud·le*
noon *poledne* ② *po·led·ne*
north *sever* ⑨ *se·ver*
Norway *Norsko* ② *nors·ko*
nose *nos* ⑨ *nos*
not *ne* *ne*
notebook *zápisník* ⑨ *za·pis·nyeek*
nothing *nic* ② *nyits*
no vacancy *obsazeno* *op·suh·ze·no*
November *listopad* ⑨ *lis·to·puhd*
now *teď* *ted'*

nuclear energy *jaderná energie* ①
  yuh·der·na *e*·ner·gi·ye
nuclear testing *atomové pokusy* ⓜ pl
  uh·to·mo·vair po·ku·si
nuclear waste *atomový odpad* ⓜ
  uh·to·mo·vee od·puhd
number *číslo* ① chees·lo
numberplate *poznávací značka* ①
  poz·na·vuh·tsee znuhch·kuh
nun *jeptiška* ① yep·tyish·kuh
nurse *zdravotní sestra* ①
  zdruh·vot·nyee ses·truh
nut (food) *ořech* ⓜ o·rzhekh

O

oats *oves* ① o·ves
ocean *oceán* ⓜ o·tse·an
October *říjen* ⓜ rzhee·yen
off (power) *zhasnuto* zhuhs·nu·to
off (spoilt) *zkažený* zkuh·zhe·nee
office *kancelář* ① kuhn·tse·larzh
office worker *administrativní
  pracovník/pracovnice* ⓜ/①
  uhd·mi·ni·struh·tiv·nyee
  pruh·tsov·nyeek/pruh·tsov·nyi·tse
often *často* chuhs·to
oil (cooking) *stolní olej* ⓜ stol·nyee o·ley
oil (petrol) *benzín* ⓜ ben·zeen
old *starý* stuh·ree
olive *oliva* ① o·li·vuh
olive oil *olivový olej* ⓜ o·li·vo·vee o·ley
Olympic Games *olympijské hry* ① pl
  o·lim·piy·skair hri
omelette *omeleta* ① o·me·le·tuh
on *na* nuh
on (power) *zapnuto* zuhp·nu·to
once *jednou* yed·noh
one *jeden* ye·den
one-way ticket *jednoduchá jízdenka* ①
  yed·no·du·kha yeez·den·kuh
onion *cibule* ① tsi·bu·le
only *jen* yen
on time *včas* fchuhs
open (business) a *otevřený* o·tev·rzhe·nee
open v *otevřít* o·tev·rzheet
opening hours *otevírací hodiny* ① pl
  o·te·vee·ruh·tsee ho·dyi·ni
opera *opera* ① o·pe·ruh
opera house *opera* ① o·pe·ruh
operation (medical) *operace* ①
  o·pe·ruh·tse

operator (telephone) *operátor* ⓜ
  o·pe·ra·tor
opinion *názor* ⓜ na·zor
opposite prep *proti* pro·tyi
optometrist *oční lékař* ①
  och·nyee lair·kuhrzh
or *nebo* ne·bo
orange (fruit) *pomeranč* ⓜ po·me·ruhnch
orange (colour) *oranžový* o·ruhn·zho·vee
orange juice *pomerančový džus* ⓜ
  po·me·ruhn·cho·vee dzhus
orchestra *orchestr* ⓜ or·khes·tr
order *pořadí* ① po·rzha·dyee
order v *objednat* ob·yed·nuht
ordinary *obyčejný* o·bi·chey·nee
orgasm *orgasmus* ⓜ or·guhs·mus
original a *původní* poo·vod·nyee
other *další* duhl·shee
our *náš* nash
out of order *nefunguje* ne·fun·gu·ye
outside adv *venku* ven·ku
ovarian cyst *vaječníková cysta* ①
  vuh·yech·nyee·ko·va tsis·tuh
ovary *vaječník* ⓜ vuh·yech·nyeek
oven *trouba* ① troh·buh
overcoat *svrchník* ⓜ svrkh·nyeek
overdose *nadměrná dávka* ①
  nuhd·myer·na daf·kuh
overnight adv *přes noc* przhes nots
overseas *v zámoří* v za·mo·rzhee
owe *dlužit* dlu·zhit
owner *majitel(ka)* ⓜ/① muh·yi·tel(·kuh)
oxygen *kyslík* ⓜ kis·leek
oyster *ústřice* ① oost·rzhi·tse
ozone layer *ozónová vrstva* ①
  o·zaw·no·va vrst·vuh

P

pacemaker *kardiostimulátor* ⓜ
  kuhr·di·o·sti·mu·la·tor
pacifier (dummy) *dudlík* ⓜ dud·leek
package *balík* ⓜ buh·leek
packet (general) *balíček* ⓜ buh·lee·chek
padlock *visací zámek* ⓜ vi·suh·tsee za·mek
page *strana* ① struh·nuh
pain *bolest* ① bo·lest
painful *bolestivý* bo·les·tyi·vee
painkiller *lék proti bolestem* ⓜ
  lairk pro·tyi bo·les·tem
painter (artist) *malíř(ka)* ⓜ/①
  muh·leerzh(·kuh)

painter (tradesperson) *malíř pokojů* ⓜ
  muh·leerzh po·ko·yoo
painting (a work) *natírání* ⓝ
  nuh·tyee·ra·nyee
painting (the art) *malování* ⓝ
  muh·lo·va·nyee
pair (couple) *pár* ⓜ par
palace *palác* ⓜ puh·lats
pan *pánev* ⓕ pa·nef
pants (trousers) *kalhoty* ⓕ pl kuhl·ho·ti
pantyhose *punčochové kalhoty* ⓕ pl
  pun·cho·kho·vair kuhl·ho·ti
panty liner *podšívkovina* ⓕ
  pod·sheef·ko·vi·nuh
paper *papír* ⓜ puh·peer
paperwork *doklady* ⓜ pl do·kluh·di
pap smear *stěr hrdla* ⓜ styer hrd·luh
paraplegic *paraplegik* ⓜ puh·ruh·ple·gik
parcel *balíček* ⓜ buh·lee·chek
parents *rodiče* ⓜ pl ro·dyi·che
park *park* ⓜ puhrk
park (a car) v *parkovat* puhr·ko·vuht
parliament *parlament* ⓜ puhr·luh·ment
part (component) *část* ⓕ chast
part-time *na zkrácený úvazek*
  nuh zkra·tse·nee oo·vuh·zek
party (night out) *večírek/mejdan* ⓜ
  ve·chee·rek/mey·duhn
party (politics) *strana* ⓕ struh·nuh
pass (go by) v *projet* pro·yet
pass (kick/throw) v *přihrát* przhi·hrat
passenger *cestující* ⓜ&ⓕ tses·tu·yee·tsee
passionfruit *pasiflora* ⓕ puh·si·flo·ruh
passport *pas* ⓜ puhs
passport number *číslo pasu* ⓝ
  chees·lo puh·su
past *minulost* ⓕ mi·nu·lost
pasta *těstovina* ⓕ tyes·to·vi·nuh
path *stezka* ⓕ stez·kuh
pay v *platit* pluh·tyit
payment *placení* ⓝ pluh·tse·nyee
pea *hrách* ⓜ hrakh
peace *mír* ⓜ meer
peach *broskev* ⓕ bros·kef
peak (mountain) *vrchol* ⓜ vr·khol
peanut *arašíd* ⓜ uh·ruh·sheed
pear *hruška* ⓕ hrush·kuh
pedal *pedál* ⓜ pe·dal
pedestrian *chodec/chodkyně* ⓜ/ⓕ
  kho·dets/khod·ki·nye
pen (ballpoint) *propiska* ⓕ pro·pis·kuh
pencil *tužka* ⓕ tuzh·kuh
penis *penis* ⓜ pe·nis

penknife *kapesní nůž* ⓜ
  kuh·pes·nyee noozh
pensioner *důchodce/důchodkyně* ⓜ/ⓕ
  doo·khod·tse/doo·khod·ki·nye
people *lid* ⓜ pl lid
pepper *pepř* ⓜ pe·przh
pepper (bell) *paprika* ⓕ puh·pri·kuh
per (day) *na* nuh
per cent *procento* ⓝ pro·tsen·to
perfect a *dokonalý* do·ko·nuh·lee
performance *představení* ⓝ
  przhed·stuh·ve·nyee
perfume *parfém* ⓜ puhr·fairm
period pain *menstruační bolest* ⓕ
  men·stru·uhch·nyee bo·lest
permission *dovolení* ⓝ do·vo·le·nyee
permit *povolení* ⓝ po·vo·le·nyee
person *osoba* ⓕ o·so·buh
petition *petice* ⓕ pe·ti·tse
petrol *benzín* ⓜ ben·zeen
petrol station *benzínová pumpa* ⓕ
  ben·zee·no·va pum·puh
pharmacist *lékárník* ⓜ lair·kar·nyeek
pharmacy *lékárna* ⓕ lair·kar·nuh
phone book *telefonní seznam* ⓜ
  te·le·fo·nyee sez·nuhm
phone box *telefonní budka* ⓕ
  te·le·fo·nyee bud·kuh
phonecard *telefonní karta* ⓕ
  te·le·fo·nyee kuhr·tuh
photo *fotka* ⓕ fot·kuh
photograph v *fotografovat*
  fo·to·gruh·fo·vuht
photographer *fotograf* ⓜ fo·to·gruhf
photography *fotografie* ⓕ fo·to·gruh·fi·ye
phrasebook *konverzační příručka* ⓕ
  kon·ver·zuhch·nyee przhee·ruch·kuh
piano *klavír* ⓜ kluh·veer
pickaxe *krumpáč* ⓜ krum·pach
pickles *nakládaná zelenina* ⓕ
  nuh·kla·duh·na ze·le·nyi·nuh
picnic *piknik* ⓜ pik·nik
piece *kus* ⓜ kus
pig *prase* ⓝ pruh·se
pill *pilulka* ⓕ pi·lul·kuh
(the) pill *antikoncepční pilulka* ⓕ
  uhn·ti·kon·tsep·chnyee pi·lul·kuh
pillow *polštář* ⓜ polsh·tarzh
pillowcase *povlak na polštář* ⓜ
  po·vluhk nuh polsh·tarzh
pineapple *ananas* ⓜ uh·nuh·nuhs
pink *růžový* roo·zho·vee
pistachio *pistácie* ⓕ pis·ta·tsi·ye

place *místo* ⓝ *mees·*to
place of birth *místo narození* ⓝ
  *mees·*to nuh·ro·ze·nyee
plane *letadlo* ⓝ *le·*tuhd·lo
planet *planeta* ⓕ *pluh·*ne·tuh
plant *rostlina* ⓕ *rost·*li·nuh
plastic a *plastický* *pluhs·*tits·kee
plate *talíř* ⓜ tuh·*leerzh*
plateau *náhorní plošina* ⓕ
  *na·*hor·nyee plo·shi·nuh
platform *nástupiště* ⓝ *nas·*tu·pish·tye
play (cards) v *hrát* hrat
play (guitar) v *hrát na* hrat nuh
play (theatre) *hra* ⓕ hruh
plug (bath) *zátka* ⓕ *zat·*kuh
plug (electricity) *zdstrčka* ⓕ *zas·*trch·kuh
plum *švestka* ⓕ *shvest·*kuh
plumber *instalatér* ⓜ *ins·*tuh·luh·ter
poached (egg) *vařit ve skle*
  *vuh·*rzhit ve skle
pocket *kapsa* ⓕ *kuhp·*suh
pocket knife *kapesní nůž* ⓜ
  *kuh·*pes·nyee noozh
poetry *poezie* ⓕ *po·*e·zi·ye
point v *ukazovat* u·*kuh·*zo·vuht
poisonous *jedovatý* ye·do·vuh·tee
Poland *Polsko* *pols·*ko
police *policie* ⓕ *po·*li·tsi·ye
police officer (in city) *městský policista* ⓜ
  *myest·*skee po·li·tsis·tuh
police officer (in country) *policista* ⓜ
  *po·*li·tsis·tuh
police station *policejní stanice* ⓕ
  *po·*li·tsey·nyee stuh·nyi·tse
policy *politická linie* ⓕ *po·*li·tits·ka li·ni·ye
politician *politik/politička* ⓜ/ⓕ
  *po·*li·tik/po·li·tich·kuh
politics *politika* ⓕ *po·*li·ti·kuh
pollen *pyl* ⓜ pil
pollution *znečistění* ⓝ *zne·*chis·tye·nyee
pool (game) *kulečník* ⓜ *ku·*lech·nyeek
pool (swimming) *bazén* ⓜ *buh·*zairn
poor (wealth) *chudý* khu·dee
popular *populární* po·pu·lar·nye
porcelain *porcelán* ⓜ *por·*tse·lan
pork *vepřové maso* ⓝ
  *vep·*rzho·vair muh·so
pork sausage *vuřt* ⓜ vurzht
port (river/sea) *přístav* ⓜ *przhees·*tuhf
positive a *kladný* kluhd·nee
possible *možný* mozh·nee
post (mail) *pošta* ⓜ *posh·*tuh
post v *odeslat* o·des·luht

postage *poštovné* ⓝ *posh·*tov·nair
postcard *pohled* ⓜ *po·*hled
postcode *poštovní směrovací číslo* ⓝ
  *posh·*tov·nyee smye·ro·vuh·tsee chee·slo
poster *plakát* ⓜ *pluh·*kat
post office *pošta* ⓕ *posh·*tuh
pot (ceramics) *nádoba* ⓕ *na·*do·buh
pot (cooking) *hrnec* ⓜ *hr·*nets
potato *brambor* ⓜ *bruhm·*bor
pottery *keramika* ⓕ *ke·*ruh·mi·kuh
pound (money) *libra šterlinků* ⓕ
  *lib·*ruh shter·lin·koo
pound (weight) *libra* ⓕ *lib·*ruh
poverty *chudoba* ⓕ *khu·*do·buh
powder *prášek* ⓜ *pra·*shek
power *síla* ⓕ *see·*luh
Prague *Praha* ⓕ *pruh·*huh
prawn *kreveta* ⓕ *kre·*ve·tuh
prayer *modlitba* ⓕ *mod·*lit·buh
prayer book *modlitební knížka* ⓕ
  *mod·*li·teb·nyee knyeezh·kuh
prefer *dávat přednost* da·vuht przhed·nost
pregnancy test kit *těhotenský test* ⓜ
  *tye·*ho·ten·skee test
pregnant *těhotná* tye·hot·na
premenstrual tension *premenstruální*
  tenze ⓕ *pre·*mens·tru·al·nyee ten·ze
prepare *připravit* przhi·pruh·vit
prescription *lékařský předpis* ⓜ
  *lair·*kuhrzh·skee przhed·pis
present (gift) *dárek* ⓜ *da·*rek
present (time) *přítomnost* ⓕ
  *przhee·*tom·nost
president *president(ka)* ⓜ/ⓕ
  *pre·*zi·dent(·kuh)
pressure (tyre) *tlak* ⓜ tluhk
pretty *hezký* hez·kee
price *cena* ⓕ *tse·*nuh
priest *kněz* ⓜ knyez
prime minister *premiér(ka)* ⓜ/ⓕ
  *pre·*mi·yer(·kuh)
printer (computer) *tiskárna* ⓕ *tyis·*kar·nuh
prison *vězení* ⓝ *vye·*ze·nyee
prisoner *vězeň(kyně)* ⓜ/ⓕ *vye·*zen'(·ki·nye)
private *soukromý* soh·kro·mee
produce v *vyrobit* vi·ro·bit
profit *zisk* ⓜ zisk
program *program* ⓜ *pro·*gruhm
projector *projektor* ⓜ *pro·*yek·tor
promise v *slíbit* slee·bit
prostitute *prostitut(ka)* ⓜ/ⓕ
  *pros·*ti·tut(·kuh)
protect v *chránit* khra·nyit

protected *chráněný* khra·nye·nee
protest *protest* ⓜ pro·test
protest v *protestovat* pro·tes·to·vuht
provisions *potraviny* ⓕ pl po·truh·vi·ni
pub (bar) *hospoda* ⓕ hos·po·duh
public gardens *veřejné zahrady* ⓕ pl
   ve·rzhey·nair zuh·hruh·di
public phone *veřejná telefonní budka* ⓕ
   ve·rzhey·na te·le·fo·nyee bud·kuh
public relations *styk s veřejností* ⓜ pl
   stik s ve·rzhey·nos·tyee
public toilet *veřejné toalety* ⓕ pl
   ve·rzhey·nair to·uh·le·ti
pull v *táhnout* tah·noht
pump *hustilka* ⓕ hus·tyil·kuh
pumpkin *dýně* ⓕ dee·nye
puncture *defekt* ⓜ de·fekt
puppet *loutka* ⓕ loht·kuh
puppet show *loutkové představení* ⓝ
   loht·ko·vair przhed·stuh·ve·nyee
puppet theatre *loutkové divadlo* ⓝ
   loht·ko·vair dyi·vuhd·lo
pure *čistý* chis·tee
purple *fialový* fi·yuh·lo·vee
purse *peněženka* ⓕ pe·nye·zhen·kuh
push v *tlačit* tluh·chit
put *dát* dat

Q

quadriplegic *kvadruplegik* ⓜ
   kvuh·drup·le·gik
qualifications *vzdělání* ⓝ pl vzdye·la·nyee
quality *kvalita* ⓕ kvuh·li·tuh
quarantine *karanténa* ⓕ
   kuh·ruhn·tair·nuh
quarter *čtvrtina* ⓕ chtvr·tyi·nuh
queen *královna* ⓕ kra·lov·nuh
question *otázka* ⓕ o·taz·kuh
queue *fronta* ⓕ fron·tuh
quick *rychlý* rikh·lee
quiet *tichý* tyi·khee
quit *nechat* ne·khuht

R

rabbit *králík* ⓜ kra·leek
rabies *vzteklina* ⓕ vztek·li·nuh
race (sport) *závod* ⓜ za·vod
racetrack *dostihová dráha* ⓕ
   dos·tyi·ho·va dra·huh

racing bike *závodní kolo* ⓝ
   za·vod·nyee ko·lo
racism *rasismus* ⓜ ruh·sis·mus
racquet *raketa* ⓕ ruh·ke·tuh
radiator *chladič* ⓜ khlu·dyich
radio *rádio* ⓝ ra·di·yo
radish *ředkvička* ⓕ rzhed·kvich·kuh
railway station *železniční nádraží* ⓝ
   zhe·lez·nyich·nyee na·druh·zhee
rain *déšť* ⓜ dairsht'
raincoat *pláštěnka* ⓕ plash·tyen·kuh
raisin *hrozinka* ⓕ hro·zin·kuh
rally (protest) *manifestace* ⓕ
   muh·ni·fes·tuh·tse
rape *znásilnění* ⓝ zna·sil·nye·nyee
rape v *znásilnit* zna·sil·nyit
rare (steak) *krvavý* kr·vuh·vee
rare (uncommon) *vzácný* vzats·nee
rash *vyrážka* ⓕ vi·razh·kuh
raspberry *malina* ⓕ muh·li·nuh
rat *krysa* ⓕ kri·suh
rave (party) *techno party* ⓕ tekh·no par·ti
raw *syrový* si·ro·vee
razor *břitva* ⓕ brzhit·vuh
razor blade *žiletka* ⓕ zhi·let·kuh
read v *číst* cheest
reading *čtení* ⓝ chte·nyee
ready a *připravený* przhi·pruh·ve·nee
real estate agent *realitní kancelář* ⓕ
   re·uh·lit·nyee kuhn·tse·larzh
realistic *realistický* re·uh·lis·tits·kee
rear (location) a *zadní* zuhd·nyee
reason *důvod* ⓜ doo·vod
receipt *stvrzenka* ⓕ stvr·zen·kuh
recently *nedávno* ne·dav·no
recommend *doporučit* do·po·ru·chit
record v *zaznamenat* zuhz·nuh·me·nuht
recording *nahrávka* ⓕ nuh·hraf·kuh
recyclable *recyklovatelný*
   re·tsi·klo·vuh·tel·nee
recycle *recyklovat* re·tsi·klo·vuht
red *červený* cher·ve·nee
red wine *červené víno* ⓝ cher·ve·nair
   vee·no
referee *rozhodčí* ⓜ roz·hod·chee
reference *zmínka* ⓕ zmeen·kuh
reflexology *reflexní terapie* ⓕ
   re·fleks·nee te·ruh·pi·ye
refrigerator *lednička* ⓕ led·nyich·kuh
refugee *uprchlík/uprchlice* ⓜ/ⓕ
   u·pr·khleek/u·pr·khli·tse
refund *vrácení peněz* ⓝ
   vruh·tse·nyee pe·nyez

refuse v odmítnout od·meet·noht
regional oblastní o·blust·nyee
registered mail doporučená zásilka ①
do·po·ru·che·na za·sil·kuh
rehydration salts iontový nápoj ⑩
yon·to·vee na·poy
reiki reiki ⑩ rey·ki
relationship vztah ⑩ vztah
relax uvolnit se u·vol·nyit se
relic relikvie ① re·lik·vi·ye
religion náboženství ⑪ na·bo·zhens·tvee
religious náboženský na·bo·zhens·kee
remote a vzdálený vzda·le·nee
remote control dálkový ovládač ⑩
dal·ko·vee ov·la·duch
rent činže ① chin·zhe
rent v pronajmout pro·nai·moht
repair v opravit o·pruh·vit
republic republika ① re·pu·bli·kuh
reservation (booking) rezervace ①
re·zer·vuh·tse
rest v odpočinout si od·po·chi·noht si
restaurant restaurace ① res·tow·ruh·tse
résumé (CV) životopis ⑩ zhi·vo·to·pis
retired důchodový doo·kho·do·vee
return v vrátit se vra·tyit se
return ticket zpáteční jízdenka ①
zpa·tech·nyee yeez·den·kuh
review kritika ① kri·ti·kuh
rhythm rytmus ① rit·mus
rib (body) žebro ⑪ zheb·ro
rice rýže ① ree·zhe
rich (wealthy) bohatý bo·huh·tee
ride jízda ① yeez·duh
ride (bike, horse) v jezdit na yez·dyit nuh
right (correct) správný sprav·nee
right (direction) pravý pruh·vee
right-wing pravicový pruh·vi·tso·vee
ring (jewellery) prsten ⑩ prs·ten
ring (phone) v zvonit zvo·nyit
rip-off zloděina ① zlo·dyey·nuh
risk riziko ⑪ ri·zi·ko
river řeka ① rzhe·kuh
road silnice ① sil·nyi·tse
road map automapa ① ow·to·muh·puh
rob okrást o·krast
rock skála ① ska·luh
rock (music) bigbít ⑩ big·beet
rock climbing horolezectví ⑪
ho·ro·le·zets·tvee
rock group rocková skupina ①
ro·ko·va sku·pi·nuh
rockmelon kantalup ⑩ kuhn·tuh·lup

rollerblading jízda na kolečkových
bruslích ① yeez·duh nuh
ko·lech·ko·veekh brus·leekh
romantic a romantický ro·muhn·tits·kee
room pokoj ⑩ po·koy
room number číslo pokoje ⑩
chees·lo po·ko·ye
rope provaz ⑩ pro·vuhz
round (drinks) runda ① run·duh
round a kulatý ku·luh·tee
roundabout kruhový objezd ⑩
kru·ho·vee ob·yezd
route trasa ① truh·suh
rowing veslování ⑪ ves·lo·va·nyee
rubbish odpad ⑩ od·puhd
rubella zarděnky ① pl zuhr·dyen·ki
rug kobereček ⑩ ko·be·re·chek
rugby ragby ① ruhg·bi
ruins zřícenina ① zrzhee·tse·nyi·nuh
rule pravidlo ⑪ pruh·vid·lo
rum rum ⑩ rum
run v běžet bye·zhet
running běh ⑩ byeh
runny nose rýma ① ree·muh

S

sad smutný smut·nee
saddle sedlo ⑪ sed·lo
safe trezor ⑩ tre·zor
safe a bezpečný bez·pech·nee
safe sex bezpečný sex ⑩ bez·pech·nee seks
sailboarding surfing ⑩ sur·fing
saint svatý ⑩ svuh·tee
salad salát ⑩ suh·lat
salami salám ⑩ suh·lam
salary plat ⑩ pluht
sale prodej ⑩ pro·dey
sales assistant prodavač(ka) ⑩/①
pro·duh·vuhch(·kuh)
sales tax daň z obratu ① duhn' z o·bruh·tu
salmon losos ⑩ lo·sos
salt sůl ① sool
same stejný stey·nee
sand písek ⑩ pee·sek
sandals sandále ⑩ pl suhn·da·le
sandwich sendvič ⑩ send·vich
sandwich shop lahůdky ① pl luh·hood·ki
sanitary napkins dámské vložky ① pl
dams·kair vlozh·ki
sardine sardinka ① suhr·din·kuh
Saturday sobota ① so·bo·tuh
sauce omáčka ① o·mach·kuh

saucepan *kastrol* ⓜ *kuhs·*trol
sauna *sauna* ① *sow·*nuh
saxophone *saxofon* ⓜ *suhk·so·*fon
say v *říci* rzhee·tsi
scalp *kůže na hlavě* ①
　*koo·*zhe nuh *hluh·*vye
scarf *šála* ① *sha·*luh
school *škola* ① *shko·*luh
science *věda* ① *vye·*duh
scientist *vědec/vědkyně* ⓜ/①
　*vye·*dets/*vyed·*ki·nye
scissors *nůžky* ① pl *noozh·*ki
score v *bodovat* bo·do·vuht
scoreboard *ukazatel skóre* ①
　u·kuh·zuh·tel *skaw·*re
Scotland *Skotsko* ① *skots·*ko
scrambled *míchaný* mee·khuh·nee
sculpture *socha* ① *so·*khuh
sea *moře* ⓝ *mo·*rzhe
seaside *pobřeží* ⓝ pob·rzhe·zhee
season *roční období* ⓝ
　*roch·*nyee ob·do·bee
seat (place) *místo* ⓝ *mees·*to
seatbelt *bezpečnostní pás* ⓜ
　bez·pech·nost·nyee pas
second *vteřina* ① fte·rzhi·nuh
second a *druhý* dru·hee
second class *druhá třída* ①
　*dru·*ha trzhee·duh
secondhand *použitý* po·u·zhi·tee
secondhand shop *bazar* ⓜ buh·zuhr
secretary *sekretář(ka)* ⓜ/①
　se·kre·tarzh(·kuh)
see v *vidět* vi·dyet
self-employed *samostatně výdělečně*
　činný suh·mos·tuht·nye
　vee·dye·lech·nye chi·nee
selfish *sobecký* so·bets·kee
self-service a *samoobslužný*
　suh·mo·ob·sluzh·nee
sell v *prodávat* pro·da·vuht
send *poslat* pos·luht
sensible *rozumný* ro·zum·nee
sensual *senzuální* sen·zu·al·nyee
separate a *oddělený* od·dye·le·nee
September *září* ⓝ za·rzhee
serious *vážný* vazh·nee
service *služba* ① sluzh·buh
service charge *přirážka za obsluhu* ①
　przhi·razh·kuh zuh op·slu·hu
service station *benzínová pumpa* ①
　ben·zee·no·va pum·puh
serviette *ubrousek* ⓜ u·broh·sek

several *několik* nye·ko·lik
sew *šít* sheet
sex *pohlaví* ⓝ po·hluh·vee
sexism *sexismus* ⓜ sek·sis·mus
sexy *erotický* e·ro·tits·kee
shade *odstín* ⓜ od·styeen
shadow *stín* ⓜ styeen
shampoo *šampon* ⓜ shuhm·pon
shape *tvar* ⓜ tvuhr
share (accommodation) v *spoluobývat*
　spo·lu·o·bee·vuht
share (with) v *bydlet spolu* bid·let spo·lu
shave v *holit* ho·lit
shaving cream *pěna na holení* ①
　pye·nuh nuh ho·le·nyee
she *ona* o·nuh
sheep *ovce* ① of·tse
sheet (bed) *prostěradlo* ⓝ pros·tye·ruhd·lo
shelf *police* ① po·li·tse
shiatsu *shiatsu* ① shi·uh·tsu
shingles (illness) *pásový opar* ⓜ
　pa·so·vee o·puhr
ship *loď* ① lod'
shirt *košile* ① ko·shi·le
shoe *bota* ① bo·tuh
shoelace *tkanička* ① tkuh·nyich·kuh
shoes *boty* ① pl bo·ti
shoe shop *obchod s obuví* ⓜ
　op·khod s o·bu·vee
shoot v *střelit* strzhe·lit
shop *obchod* ⓜ op·khod
shop v *nakupovat* nuh·ku·po·vuht
shopping *nakupování* ⓝ
　nuh·ku·po·va·nye
shopping centre *nákupní centrum* ⓝ
　na·kup·nyee tsen·trum
short (height) *malý* muh·lee
short (length) *krátký* krat·kee
shortage *nedostatek* ⓜ ne·dos·tuh·tek
shorts *šortky* ① pl short·ki
shoulder *rameno* ⓝ ruh·me·no
shout v *křičet* krzhi·chet
show *představení* ⓝ przhed·stuh·ve·nyee
show v *ukázat* u·ka·zuht
shower *sprcha* ① spr·khuh
shrine *svatyně* ① svuh·ti·nye
shut a *zavřený* zuhv·rzhe·nee
shy *stydlivý* stid·li·vee
sick *nemocný* ne·mots·nee
side *strana* ① struh·nuh
sign *nápis* ⓜ na·pis
sign v *podepsat* po·dep·suht
signature *podpis* ⓜ pod·pis

silk *hedvábí* ⓝ hed·va·bee
silver *stříbro* ⓝ strzee·bro
SIM card *SIM karta* ⓕ sim kuhr·tuh
similar *podobný* po·dob·nee
simple *jednoduchý* yed·no·du·khee
since (time) *od* od
sing v *zpívat* zpee·vuht
singer *zpěvák/zpěvačka* ⓜ/ⓕ
  spye·vak/spye·vuhch·kuh
single (person) *svobodný* svo·bod·nee
single room *jednolůžkový pokoj* ⓜ
  yed·no·loozh·ko·vee po·koy
singlet *nátělník* ⓜ na·tyel·nyeek
sister *sestra* ⓕ ses·truh
sit *posadit* po·suh·dyit
size (general) *velikost* ⓕ ve·li·kost
skate v *bruslit* brus·lit
skateboarding *skateboarding* ⓜ
  skeyt·bor·ding
ski *lyže* ⓕ li·zhe
ski v *lyžovat* li·zho·vuht
skiing *lyžování* ⓝ li·zho·va·nyee
skim milk *odstředěné mléko* ⓝ
  od·strzhe·dye·nair mlair·ko
skin *kůže* ⓕ koo·zhe
skirt *sukně* ⓕ suk·nye
skull *lebka* ⓕ leb·kuh
sky *nebe* ⓝ ne·be
sleep *spánek* ⓜ spa·nek
sleep v *spát* spat
sleeping bag *spací pytel* ⓜ spuh·tsee pi·tel
sleeping berth *lehátko* ⓝ le·hat·ko
sleeping car *spací vůz* ⓜ spuh·tsee vooz
sleeping pills *prášek na spaní* ⓝ
  pra·shek nuh spuh·nyee
sleepy *ospalý* os·puh·lee
slice *krajíc* ⓜ kruh·yeets
slide film *diapozitivní film* ⓜ
  di·uh·po·zi·tiv·nyee film
Slovakia *Slovensko* ⓝ slo·ven·sko
slow a *pomalý* po·muh·lee
slowly *pomalu* po·muh·lu
small *malý* muh·lee
smaller *menší* men·shee
smallest *nejmenší* ney·men·shee
smell *pach* ⓜ puhkh
smile v *usmát se* us·mat se
smoke v *kouřit* koh·rzhit
snack *svačina* ⓕ svuh·chi·nuh
snail *šnek* ⓜ shnek
snake *had* ⓜ huhd
snorkelling *šnorchlování* ⓝ
  shnor·khlo·va·nyee

snow *sníh* ⓜ snyeeh
snowboarding *snowboarding* ⓝ
  snoh·bor·ding
snow pea *císařský lusk* ⓜ
  tsee·suhrzh·skee lusk
soap *mýdlo* ⓝ meed·lo
soap opera *telenovela* ⓕ te·le·no·ve·luh
soccer *fotbal* ⓜ fot·buhl
socialist *socialista/socialistka* ⓜ/ⓕ
  so·tsi·uh·lis·tuh/so·tsi·uh·list·kuh
social welfare *sociální péče* ⓕ
  so·tsi·al·nyee pair·che
socks *ponožky* ⓕ pl po·nozh·ki
soft-boiled *na měkko* nuh mye·ko
soft drink *nealkoholický nápoj* ⓜ
  ne·uhl·ko·ho·lits·kee na·poy
soldier *voják* ⓜ vo·yak
some *několik* nye·ko·lik
someone *někdo* nyek·do
something *něco* nye·tso
sometimes *někdy* nyek·di
son *syn* ⓜ sin
song *píseň* ⓕ pee·sen'
soon *brzy* br·zi
sore a *bolestivý* bo·les·tyi·vee
soup *polévka* ⓕ po·lairf·kuh
sour cream *kyselá smetana* ⓕ
  ki·se·la sme·tuh·nuh
south *jih* ⓜ yih
souvenir *suvenýr* ⓜ su·ve·neer
souvenir shop *obchod se suvenýry* ⓜ
  op·khod se su·ve·nee·ri
soy milk *sójové mléko* ⓝ
  saw·yo·vair mlair·ko
soy sauce *sójová omáčka* ⓕ
  saw·yo·va o·mach·kuh
space (room) *prostor* ⓜ pros·tor
Spain *Španělsko* ⓝ shpuh·nyels·ko
sparkling wine *šumivé víno* ⓝ
  shu·mi·vair vee·no
speak *říci* rzhee·tsi
special a *mimořádný* mi·mo·rzhad·nee
specialist *odborník* ⓜ od·bor·nyeek
speed (drug) *amfetamin* ⓜ
  uhm·fe·tuh·min
speed (travel) *rychlost* ⓕ rikh·lost
speed limit *omezená rychlost* ⓕ
  o·me·ze·na rikh·lost
speedometer *tachometr* ⓜ tuh·kho·me·tr
spider *pavouk* ⓜ puh·vohk
spinach *špenát* ⓜ shpe·nat
spoilt (food) *zkažený* skuh·zhe·nee
spoke *říkal* ⓜ rzhee·kuhl

english–czech

S

spoon *lžíce* ① *lzhee*·tse

sport *sport* ⑩ sport

sportsperson *sportovec/sportovkyně*
⑩/① *spor*·to·vets/*spor*·tof·ki·nye

sports store *obchod se sportovními
potřebami* ⑩ *op*·khod se
spor·tov·nyee·mi pot·rzhe·buh·mi

sprain *výron* ⑦ *vee*·ron

spring (coil) *spirálová pružina* ①
spi·ra·lo·va *pru*·zhi·nuh

spring (season) *jaro* ⑩ *yuh*·ro

square (town) *náměstí* ⑩ *na*·myes·tyee

stadium *stadion* ⑩ *stuh*·di·yon

stairway *schodiště* ⑩ *skho*·dyish·tye

stale *okoralý* o·ko·ruh·lee

stamp (postage) *známka* ① *znam*·kuh

star *hvězda* ① *hvyez*·duh

(four-)star *(čtyř) hvězdičkový*
(chtirzh) *hvyez*·dyich·ko·vee

start *začátek* ⑩ *zuh*·cha·tek

start v *začít* zuh·cheet

station *nádraží* ⑩ *na*·druh·zhee

stationer *papírnictví* ⑦ *puh*·peer·nits·tvee

statue *socha* ① *so*·khuh

stay (at a hotel) v *bydlet* bid·let

stay (in one place) v *zůstat* zoos·tuht

steak (beef) *biftek* ⑩ *bif*·tek

steal v *ukrást* u·krast

steep *strmý* str·mee

step *krok* ⑩ krok

stereo *stereo* ⑩ *ste*·re·o

still water *neperlivá voda* ①
ne·per·li·va *vo*·duh

stock (food) *zásoba* ① *za*·so·buh

stockings *punčochy* ⑩ pl *pun*·cho·khi

stolen *kradený* kruh·de·nee

stomach *žaludek* ⑩ *zhuh*·lu·dek

stomachache *bolesti žaludku* ⑩ pl
bo·les·tyi zhuh·lud·ku

stone *kámen* ⑩ *ka*·men

stoned (drugged) *zhulený* zhu·le·nee

stop (bus, tram) *zastávka* ① *zuhs*·taf·kuh

stop (cease) v *zastavit* zuhs·tuh·vit

stop (prevent) v *zabránit* zuh·bruh·nyit

storm *bouře* ① *boh*·rzhe

story *příběh* ⑩ *przhee*·byeh

stove *kamna* ① *kuhm*·nuh

straight *rovný* rov·nee

strange *cizí* tsi·zee

stranger *neznámý/á* ⑩/① *nez*·na·mee/a

strawberry *jahoda* ① *yuh*·ho·duh

stream *potok* ⑩ *po*·tok

street *ulice* ① *u*·li·tse

street market *pouliční trh* ⑩
po·u·*lich*·nyee trh

strike *stávka* ① *staf*·kuh

string *provázek* ① *pro*·va·zek

stroke (health) *mrtvice* ① *mrt*·vi·tse

stroller *sportovní skládací kočárek* ⑩
spor·tov·nyee *skla*·da·tsee ko·cha·rek

strong *silný* sil·nee

stubborn *tvrdohlavý* tvr·do·hluh·vee

student *student(ka)* ⑩/① *stu*·dent(·kuh)

studio *ateliér* ⑩ *uh*·te·li·yer

stupid *hloupý* hloh·pee

style *styl* ⑩ stil

subtitles *titulky* ⑩ pl *ti*·tul·ki

suburb *čtvrť* ① chtvrt'

subway (train) *metro* ⑩ *me*·tro

sugar *cukr* ⑩ *tsu*·kr

suitcase *kufr* ⑩ ku·fr

sultana *rozinka* ① *ro*·zin·kuh

summer *léto* ⑩ *lair*·to

sun *slunce* ① slun·tse

sunblock *opalovací krém* ⑩
o·*puh*·lo·vuh·tsee krairm

sunburn *spálený sluncem* ⑩
spa·le·nee slun·tsem

Sunday *neděle* ① *ne*·dye·le

sunglasses *sluneční brýle* ① pl
slu·nech·nyee *bree*·le

sunny *slunečný* slu·nech·nee

sunrise *východ slunce* ⑩ *vee*·khod slun·tse

sunset *západ slunce* ⑩ *za*·puhd slun·tse

sunstroke *úžeh* ⑩ *oo*·zheh

supermarket *samoobsluha* ①
suh·mo·ob·slu·huh

superstition *pověra* ① *po*·vye·ruh

supporter (politics) *stoupenec* ⑩
stoh·pe·nets

supporter (sport) *fanoušek* ⑩
fuh·noh·shek

surf (sport) *surfing* ⑩ *sur*·fing

surf (wave) *vlny* ⑩ *vl*·ni

surf v *surfovat* sur·fo·vuht

surface mail (land) *obyčejná pošta* ①
o·bi·*chey*·na *posh*·tuh

surface mail (sea) *obyčejná pošta lodí* ①
o·bi·*chey*·na posh·tuh lo·dyee

surfboard *surfovací prkno* ⑩
sur·fo·vuh·tsee prk·no

surfing *surfing* ⑩ *sur*·fing

surname *příjmení* ① *przheey*·me·nyee

surprise *překvapení* ① *przhek*·vuh·pe·nyee

sweater *svetr* ⑩ *sve*·tr

Sweden *Švédsko* ⑩ *shvaird*·sko

sweet a *sladký* sluhd·kee
sweets *cukroví* ⓝ pl tsu·kro·vee
swelling *otok* ⓜ o·tok
swim v *plavat* pluh·vuht
swimming *plavání* ⓝ pluh·va·nyee
swimming pool *bazén* ⓜ buh·zairn
swimsuit *plavky* ① pl pluhf·ki
Switzerland *Švýcarsko* ⓝ shvee·tsuhr·sko
synagogue *synagoga* ① si·nuh·go·guh
synthetic a *syntetický* sin·te·tits·kee
syringe *stříkačka* ① strzhee·kuhch·kuh

T

table *stůl* ⓜ stool
tablecloth *ubrus* ⓜ ub·rus
table tennis *stolní tenis* ⓜ stol·nyee te·nis
tail *ocas* ⓜ o·tsuhs
tailor *krejčí/krejčová* ⓜ/① krey·chee/krey·cho·va
take v *vzít* vzeet
take a photo *vyfotit* vi·fo·tyit
talk v *mluvit* mlu·vit
tall *vysoký* vi·so·kee
tampon *tampon* ⓜ tuhm·pon
tanning lotion *opalovací mléko* ⓝ o·puh·lo·vuh·tsee mlair·ko
tap *kohoutek* ⓜ ko·hoh·tek
tap water *voda z kohoutku* ① vo·duh s ko·hoht·ku
tasty *chutný* khut·nee
tax *daň* ① duhn'
taxi *taxík* ⓜ tuhk·seek
taxi stand *taxi stanoviště* ⓝ tuhk·si stuh·no·vish·tye
tea *čaj* ⓜ chai
teacher *učitel(ka)* ⓜ/① u·chi·tel(·kuh)
team *mužstvo* ⓝ muzh·stvo
teaspoon *lžička* ① lzhich·kuh
technique *metoda* ① me·to·duh
teeth *zuby* ⓜ pl zu·bi
telegram *telegram* ⓜ te·le·gruhm
telephone *telefon* ⓜ te·le·fon
telephone v *telefonovat* te·le·fo·no·vuht
telephone centre *telefonní centrum* ⓝ te·le·fo·nyee tsen·trum
telescope *dalekohled* ⓜ duh·le·ko·hled
television *televize* ① te·le·vi·ze
tell *povědět* po·vye·dyet
temperature (fever) *horečka* ① ho·rech·kuh
temperature (weather) *teplota* ① te·plo·tuh

temple (body) *spánek* ⓜ spa·nek
temple (building) *chrám* ⓜ khram
tennis *tenis* ⓜ te·nis
tennis court *tenisový kurt* ⓜ te·ni·so·vee kurt
tent *stan* ⓜ stuhn
tent peg *stanový kolík* ⓜ stuh·no·vee ko·leek
terrible *hrozný* hroz·nee
terrorism *terorismus* ⓜ te·ro·ris·mus
test *zkouška* ① skohsh·kuh
thank *poděkovat* po·dye·ko·vuht
that a *ten* ten
that (one) pron *tamten* tuhm·ten
theatre *divadlo* ⓝ dyi·vuhd·lo
their *jejich* ye·yikh
there *tam* tuhm
they *oni* o·nyi
thick *silný* sil·nee
thief *zloděj* ⓜ zlo·dyey
thin *tenký* ten·kee
think *myslet* mis·let
third a *třetí* trzhe·tyee
thirsty *žíznivý* zheez·nyi·vee
this a *tento* ten·to
this (one) pron *tenhle* ten·hle
thread *nit* ① nyit
throat *hrdlo* ⓝ hrd·lo
thrush (health) *mykóza* ① mi·kaw·zuh
thunderstorm *bouře* ① boh·rzhe
Thursday *čtvrtek* ⓜ chtvr·tek
ticket *vstupenka* ① fstu·pen·kuh
ticket collector *výběrčí lístků* ⓜ vee·byer·chee leest·koo
ticket machine *automat na lístky* ⓜ ow·to·muht nuh leest·ki
ticket office *pokladna* ① po·kluhd·nuh
tide (high) *příliv* ⓜ przhee·lif
tide (low) *odliv* ⓜ od·lif
tight *těsný* tyes·nee
time *čas* ⓜ chuhs
time difference *časový rozdíl* ⓜ chuh·so·vee roz·dyeel
timetable *jízdní řád* ⓜ yeezd·nyee rzhad
tin (can) *plechovka* ① ple·khof·kuh
tin opener *otvírač konzerv* ⓜ ot·vee·ruhch kon·zerf
tiny *maličký* muh·lich·kee
tip (gratuity) *spropitné* ⓝ spro·pit·nair
tire *pneumatika* ① pne·u·muh·ti·kuh
tired *unavený* u·nuh·ve·nee
tissues *kosmetické kapesníčky* ⓜ pl kos·me·tits·kair kuh·pes·neech·ki

to *do/na* do/nuh
toast (food) *toast* ⑩ tohst
toaster *toastovač* ⑩ tohs-to-vuhch
tobacco *tabák* ⑩ tuh-bak
tobacconist *trafikant* ⑩ truh-fi-kuhnt
tobogganing *sáňkování* ⑪ san'-ko-va-nyee
today *dnes* dnes
toe *prst u nohy* ⑩ prst u no-hi
tofu *sójový tvaroh* ⑩ saw-yo-vee tvuh-rawh
together *spolu* spo-lu
toilet *toaleta* ⑪ to-uh-le-tuh
toilet paper *toaletní papír* ⑩
  to-uh-let-nyee puh-peer
tomato *rajské jablko* ⑪ rais-kair yuh-bl-ko
tomato sauce *rajská omáčka* ⑪
  rais-ka o-mach-kuh
tomorrow *zítra* zeet-ruh
tomorrow afternoon *zítra odpoledne*
  zeet-ruh od-po-led-ne
tomorrow evening *zítra večer*
  zeet-ruh ve-cher
tomorrow morning *zítra ráno*
  zeet-ruh ra-no
tonight *dnes večer* dnes ve-cher
too (also) *také* tuh-kair
too (much) *příliš mnoho*
  przhee-lish mno-ho
tooth *zub* ⑩ zub
toothache *bolení zubu* ⑪ bo-le-nyee zu-bu
toothbrush *zubní kartáček* ⑩
  zub-nyee kuhr-ta-chek
toothpaste *zubní pasta* ⑪
  zub-nyee puhs-tuh
toothpick *párátko* ⑪ pa-rat-ko
torch (flashlight) *baterka* ⑪ buh-ter-kuh
touch v *dotknout se* dot-knoht se
tour *okružní jízda* ⑪ o-kruzh-nyee yeez-duh
tourist *turista* ⑩ tu-ris-tuh
tourist office *turistická informační*
  kancelář ⑪ tu-ris-tits-ka
  in-for-muhch-nyee kuhn-tse-larzh
towards *směrem k* smye-rem k
towel *ručník* ⑩ ruch-nyeek
tower *věž* ⑪ vyezh
toxic waste *toxický odpad* ⑩
  tok-sits-kee od-puhd
toy shop *hračkářství* ⑪ hruch-karzh-stveé
track (path) *stezka* ⑪ stez-kuh
track (sport) *dráha* ⑪ dra-huh
trade *obchod* ⑩ op-khod
tradesperson *řemeslník/řemeslnice* ⑩/⑪
  rzhe-me-sl-nyeek/rzhe-me-sl-nyi-tse
traffic *doprava* ⑪ do-pruh-vuh

traffic lights *semafor* ⑩ se-muh-for
trail *stezka* ⑪ stez-kuh
train *vlak* ⑩ vluhk
train station *nádraží* ⑪ na-druh-zhee
tram *tramvaj* ⑪ truhm-vai
transit lounge *tranzitní salónek* ⑩
  truhn-zit-nyee suh-law-nek
translate *přeložit* przhe-lo-zhit
translator *překladatel(ka)* ⑩/⑪
  przhe-kluh-duh-tel(-kuh)
transport *přeprava* ⑪ przhe-pruh-vuh
travel v *cestovat* tses-to-vuht
travel agency *cestovní kancelář* ⑪
  tses-tov-nyee kuhn-tse-larzh
travellers cheque *cestovní šek* ⑩
  tses-tov-nyee shek
travel sickness *nevolnost při cestování* ⑪
  ne-vol-nost przhi tses-to-va-nyee
tree *strom* ⑩ strom
trip (journey) *výlet* ⑩ vee-let
trolley *vozík* ⑩ vo-zeek
trolleybus *trolejbus* ⑩ tro-ley-bus
trousers *kalhoty* ⑪ pl kuhl-ho-ti
truck *nákladní auto* ⑪
  na-kluhd-nyee ow-to
trumpet *trumpeta* ⑪ trum-pe-tuh
trust v *důvěřovat* doo-vye-rzho-vuht
try (attempt) v *zkusit* sku-sit
T-shirt *tričko* ⑪ trich-ko
tube (tyre) *duše* ⑪ du-she
Tuesday *úterý* ⑩ oo-te-ree
tumour *nádor* ⑩ na-dor
tuna *tuňák* ⑩ tu-nyak
tune *melodie* ⑪ me-lo-di-ye
turkey *krůta* ⑪ kroo-tuh
turn v *zahnout* zuh-hnoht
TV *televize* ⑪ te-le-vi-ze
tweezers *pinzeta* ⑪ pin-ze-tuh
twice *dvakrát* dvuh-krat
twin beds *dvoupostel* ⑪ dvoh-pos-tel
twins *dvojčata* ⑪ pl dvoy-chuh-tuh
two *dva* dvuh
type *druh* ⑩ drooh
typical *typický* ti-pits-kee
tyre *pneumatika* ⑪ pne-u-muh-ti-kuh

U

ultrasound *ultrazvuk* ⑩ ul-truh-zvuk
umbrella *deštník* ⑩ desht-nyeek
uncomfortable *nepohodlný*
  ne-po-ho-dl-nee
understand *rozumět* ro-zu-myet

underwear *spodní prádlo* ⓝ
spod·nyee prad·lo
unemployed *nezaměstnaný*
ne·zuh·myest·nuh·nee
unfair *nespravedlivý* ne·spruh·ve·dli·vee
uniform *uniforma* ⓕ u·ni·for·muh
universe *vesmír* ⓜ ves·meer
university *univerzita* ⓕ u·ni·ver·zi·tuh
unleaded petrol *natural* ⓜ nuh·tu·ruhl
unsafe *nebezpečný* ne·bez·pech·nee
until *až do* uhzh do
unusual *neobvyklý* ne·ob·vik·lee
up *nahoru* nuh·ho·ru
uphill *do kopce* do kop·tse
urgent *naléhavý* nuh·lair·huh·vee
urinary infection *infekce močových cest*
ⓕ in·fek·tse mo·cho·veech tsest
USA *Spojené státy americké*
spo·ye·nair sta·ti uh·me·rits·kair
useful *užitečný* u·zhi·tech·nee

V

vacancy *volno* ⓝ vol·no
vacant *volný* vol·nee
vacation (from school) *prázdniny* ⓕ
prazd·nyi·ni
vacation (from work) *dovolená* ⓕ
do·vo·le·na
vaccination *očkování* ⓝ och·ko·va·nyee
vagina *vagína* ⓕ vuh·gi·nuh
validate *označit* oz·nuh·chit
valley *údolí* ⓝ oo·do·lee
valuable *cenný* tse·nee
value (price) *cena* ⓕ tse·nuh
van *dodávka* ⓕ do·daf·kuh
veal *telecí* te·le·tsee
vegetable *zelenina* ⓕ ze·le·nyi·nuh
vegetarian *vegetarián(ka)* ⓜ/ⓕ
ve·ge·tuh·ri·yan(·kuh)
vegetarian a *vegetariánský*
ve·ge·tuh·ri·yans·kee
vein *žíla* ⓕ zhee·luh
venereal disease *pohlavní nemoc* ⓕ
po·hlav·nyee ne·mots
venue *zábavný podnik* ⓜ
za·buhv·nee pod·nik
very *velmi* vel·mi
video camera *videokamera* ⓕ
vi·de·o·kuh·me·ruh
video recorder *videonahrávač* ⓜ
vi·de·o·nuh·hra·vuhch
video tape *videopásek* ⓜ vi·de·o·pa·sek

Vienna *Vídeň* ⓕ vee·den'
view *pohled* ⓜ po·hled
village *vesnice* ⓕ ves·nyi·tse
vine *vinná réva* ⓕ vi·na rair·vuh
vinegar *ocet* ⓜ o·tset
vineyard *vinice* ⓕ vi·nyi·tse
violin *housle* ⓕ pl hoh·sle
virus *vir* ⓜ vir
visa *vízum* ⓝ vee·zum
visit v *navštívit* nuhf·shtyee·vit
visually impaired *slabozraký*
sluh·bo·zruh·kee
vitamins *vitamíny* ⓜ pl vi·tuh·mi·ni
vodka *vodka* ⓕ vod·kuh
voice *hlas* ⓜ hluhs
volleyball *odbíjená* ⓕ od·bee·ye·na
volume (sound) *hlasitost* ⓕ hluh·si·tost
vote v *hlasování* hluh·so·va·nyee

W

wage *mzda* ⓕ mzduh
wait *čekat* che·kuht
waiter *číšník/číšnice* ⓜ/ⓕ
cheesh·nyeek/cheesh·nyi·tse
waiting room *čekárna* ⓕ che·kar·nuh
wake (someone) up *probudit* pro·bu·dyit
walk v *jít* yeet
wall *zeď* ⓕ zed'
want v *chtít* khtyeet
war *válka* ⓕ val·kuh
wardrobe *skříň* ⓕ skrzheen'
warm a *teplý* tep·lee
warn *varovat* vuh·ro·vuht
Warsaw *Varšava* ⓕ vuhr·shuh·vuh
wash (oneself) v *mýt se* meet se
wash (something) v *umýt* u·meet
wash cloth (flannel) *utěrka* ⓕ u·tyer·kuh
washing machine *pračka* ⓕ pruhch·kuh
wasp *vosa* ⓕ vo·suh
watch *hodinky* ⓕ pl ho·dyin·ki
watch v *dívat se* dyee·vuht se
water *voda* ⓕ vo·duh
water bottle *láhev na vodu* ⓕ
la·hef nuh vo·du
waterfall *vodopád* ⓜ vo·do·pad
watermelon *meloun* ⓜ me·lohn
waterproof *nepromokavý*
ne·pro·mo·kuh·vee
water-skiing *vodní lyžování* ⓝ
vod·nyee li·zho·va·nyee
wave (beach) *vlna* ⓕ vl·nuh
way *cesta* ⓕ tses·tuh

we *my* mi
weak *slabý* sluh·bee
wealthy *bohatý* bo·huh·tee
wear *nosit* no·sit
weather *počasí* ⊙ po·chuh·see
wedding *svatba* ① svuht·buh
wedding cake *svatební dort* ⊚
   svuh·teb·nyee dort
wedding present *svatební dar* ⊚
   svuh·teb·nyee duhr
Wednesday *středa* ① strzhe·duh
week *týden* ⊚ tee·den
weekend *víkend* ⊚ vee·kend
weigh *vážit* va·zhit
weight *váha* ① va·huh
weights *činky* ① pl chin·ki
welcome v *uvítat* u·vee·tuht
welfare *sociální péče* ①
   so·tsi·al·nyee pair·che
well adv *dobře* dob·rzhe
west *západ* ⊚ za·puhd
wet a *mokrý* mok·ree
what *co* tso
wheel *kolo* ⊚ ko·lo
wheelchair *invalidní vozík* ⊚
   in·vuh·lid·nyee vo·zeek
when *kdy* gdi
where *kde* gde
which *který* kte·ree
whisky *whisky* ① vis·ki
white *bílý* bee·lee
white wine *bílé víno* ⊚ bee·lair vee·no
who *kdo* gdo
wholemeal bread *celozrný chléb* ⊚
   tse·lo·zr·nee khlairb
why *proč* proch
wide *široký* shi·ro·kee
wife *manželka* ① muhn·zhel·kuh
win v *vyhrát* vih·rat
wind *vítr* vee·tr
window *okno* ⊚ ok·no
windscreen *přední sklo* ⊚
   przhed·nyee sklo
wine *víno* ⊚ vee·no
wings *křídla* ⊚ pl krzheed·luh
winner *vítěz* ⊚ vee·tyez
winter *zima* ① zi·muh
wire *drát* ⊚ drat
wish v *přát* przhat
with *s* s
within (time) *do* do
without *bez* bez
wok *wok* ⊚ wok

woman *žena* ① zhe·nuh
wonderful *báječný* ba·yech·nee
wood *dřevo* ⊚ drzhe·vo
wool *vlna* ① vl·nuh
word *slovo* ⊚ slo·vo
work *práce* ① pra·tse
work v *pracovat* pruh·tso·vuht
work experience *praxe* ① pruhk·se
workout *cvičení* ⊚ tsvi·che·nyee
work permit *pracovní povolení* ⊚
   pruh·tsov·nyee po·vo·le·nyee
workshop *dílna* ① dyeel·nuh
world *svět* ⊚ svyet
World Cup *světový pohár* ⊚
   svye·to·vee po·har
worms (intestinal) *cizopasník* ⊚
   tsi·zo·puhs·nyeek
worried *ustaraný* us·tuh·ruh·nee
worship v *uctívat* uts·tyee·vuht
wrist *zápěstí* ① za·pyes·tee
write *psát* p·sat
writer *spisovatel(ka)* ⊚/①
   spi·so·vuh·tel(·kuh)
wrong a *nesprávný* nes·prav·nee

Y

year *rok* ⊚ rok
yellow *žlutý* zhlu·tee
yes *ano* uh·no
yesterday *včera* fche·ruh
yet *ještě* yesh·tye
yoga *jóga* ① yaw·guh
yogurt *jogurt* ⊚ yo·gurt
you sg inf *ty* ti
you sg pol&pl *vy* vi
young a *mladý* mluh·dee
your sg inf *tvůj* tvooy
your sg pol&pl *váš* vash
youth hostel *mládežnická ubytovna* ①
   mla·dezh·nyits·ka u·bi·tov·nuh

Z

zip/zipper *zdrhovadlo* ⊚ zdr·ho·vuhd·lo
zodiac *zvěrokruh* ⊚ zvye·ro·krooh
zoo *zoo* ① zo·o
zoom lens *zůmový objektiv* ⊚
   zoo·mo·vee ob·yek·tif
zucchini *cuketa* ① tsu·ke·tuh

This dictionary is arranged acording to the Czech alphabetical order (shown below). Czech nouns in the **dictionary** have their gender indicated by ⓜ (masculine), ⓕ (feminine) or ⓝ (neuter). If it's a plural noun, you'll also see pl. When a word that could be either a noun or a verb has no gender indicated, it's a verb. For added clarity, certain words are marked as adjectives a or verbs v. Adjectives, however, are given in the masculine form only. Both nouns and adjectives are provided in the nominative case only. For information on case and gender, refer to the **phrasebuilder**. For any food terms, refer to the **culinary reader**.

alphabet

Aa	Áá	Bb	Cc	Čč	Dd	Ďď	Ee	Éé	Ěě	Ff	Gg	Hh	Chch
Ii	Íí	Jj	Kk	Ll	Mm	Nn	Ňň	Oo	Óó	Pp	Qq	Rr	Řř
Ss	Šš	Tt	Ťť	Uu	Úú	Ůů	Vv	Ww	Xx	Yy	Ýý	Zz	Žž

A

a uh *and*
adresa ⓕ uh·dre·suh *address*
advokát(ka) ⓜ/ⓕ uhd·vo·kat(·kuh) *lawyer*
aerolinie ⓕ uh·e·ro·li·ni·ye *airline*
aktovka ⓕ uhk·tof·kuh *briefcase*
ale uh·le *but*
alergie ⓕ uh·ler·gi·ye *allergy*
alkoholický nápoj ⓜ uhl·ko·ho·lits·kee na·poy *alcoholic drink*
angličan(ka) ⓜ/ⓕ uhn·gli·chuhn(·kuh) *English (nationality)*
angličtina ⓕ uhn·glich·tyi·nuh *English (language)*
Anglie ⓕ uhn·gli·ye *England*
ano uh·no *yes*
antický uhn·tits·kee *classical*
auto ⓝ ow·to *car*
autobus ⓜ ow·to·bus *bus*
autobusová zastávka ⓕ ow·to·bu·so·va zuhs·taf·kuh *bus stop*
autobusové nádraží ⓝ ow·to·bu·so·vair nad·ruh·zhee *bus station*
autokar ⓜ ow·to·kuhr *bus • coach*

automat na lístky ⓜ ow·to·muht nuh *leest·*ki *ticket machine*
autosedačka ⓝ ow·to·se·duhch·kuh *child seat*
až do uhzh do *until*

B

babička ⓕ buh·bich·kuh *grandmother*
báječný ba·yech·nee *great (wonderful)*
balíček ⓜ buh·lee·chek *packet • parcel*
banka ⓕ buhn·kuh *bank*
bankomat ⓜ buhn·ko·muht *ATM*
bankovka ⓕ buhn·kof·kuh *banknote*
bankovní účet ⓜ buhn·kov·nyee oo·chet *bank account*
barva ⓕ buhr·vuh *colour*
baterie ⓕ buh·te·ri·ye *battery*
baterka ⓕ buh·ter·kuh *flashlight (torch)*
batoh ⓜ buh·tawh *backpack*
bavlna ⓕ buh·vl·nuh *cotton*
bazén ⓜ buh·zairn *swimming pool*
benzín ⓜ ben·zeen *gas (petrol)*
benzínová pumpa ⓕ ben·zee·no·va pum·puh *petrol station*
bez bez *without*
bez cla bez tsluh *duty-free*

bezpečnostní pás ⓜ
bez·pech·nost·nyee pas seatbelt
bezpečný *bez·pech·nee safe* a
bezplatný *bez·pluht·nee
complimentary (free)*
bigbit ⓜ *big·beet rock music*
bílý *bee·lee white*
blahopřání *bluh·ho·przha·nyee
congratulations*
bleší trh *ble·shee trh fleamarket*
blízko *bleez·ko near* prep
blízký *bleez·kee close* a
bolení hlavy *bo·le·nyee hluh·vi headache*
bolení zubu *bo·le·nyee zu·bu toothache*
bolest ① *bo·lest pain*
bolesti žaludku ⓜ pl
bo·les·tyi zhuh·lud·ku stomachache
bolestivý *bo·les·tyi·vee painful*
bota ① *bo·tuh boot · shoe*
boty ① pl *bo·ti shoes*
bratr ⓜ *bruh·tr brother*
brožura ① *bro·zhu·ruh brochure*
brýle ① pl *bree·le glasses (spectacles)*
brzdy ① pl *brz·di brakes*
brzy *br·zi soon*
břitva ① *brzhit·vuh razor*
budík ⓜ *bu·dyeek alarm clock*
budova ① *bu·do·vuh building*
business třída ① *biz·nis trzhee·duh
business class*
bydlet spolu *bid·let spo·lu share (with)* v
byt ⓜ *bit apartment*
být *beet be*

C

celnice ① *tsel·ni·tse customs*
cena ① *tse·nuh cost (price)*
cenný *tse·nee valuable*
centrum ⓝ *tsen·trum city centre*
cesta ① *tses·tuh journey*
cestovní kancelář ① *tses·tov·nyee
kuhn·tse·larzh travel agency*
cestovní šek ⓜ *tses·tov·nyee shek
travellers cheque*
cestující ⓜ&① *tses·tu·yee·tsee
passenger*
chráněný *khra·nye·nee protected*
cigareta ① *tsi·guh·re·tuh cigarette*
cíl cesty ⓜ *tseel tses·ti destination*
cit ⓜ *tsit feeling (physical)*
citlivost ① *tsi·tli·vost film speed*
cizí *tsi·zee foreign*

co *tso what*
cukrárna ① *tsu·krar·nuh cake shop*
cukrovka ① *tsu·krof·kuh diabetes*

Č

čas ⓜ *chuhs time*
časně *chuhs·nye early* adv
časový rozdíl ⓜ *chuh·so·vee roz·dyeel
time difference*
často *chuhs·to often*
Čech/Češka ⓜ/① *chekh/chesh·kuh
Czech (nationality)*
čekárna ① *che·kar·nuh waiting room*
čekat *che·kuht wait*
čepice ① *che·pi·tse soft hat*
černobílý *cher·no·bee·lee B&W (film)*
černý *cher·nee black · dark (night)*
čerstvý *cherst·vee fresh*
červený *cher·ve·nee red*
Česká republika ① *ches·ka re·pu·bli·kuh
Czech Republic*
český *ches·kee Czech* a
čeština ① *chesh·tyi·nuh Czech (language)*
činže ① *chin·zhe rent*
číslo ⓝ *chees·lo number*
číslo pasu ⓝ *chees·lo puh·su
passport number*
číslo pokoje ⓝ *chees·lo po·ko·ye
room number*
čistit *chis·tyit clean* v
čistý *chis·tee clean* a
číšník/číšnice ⓜ/①
cheesh·nyeek/cheesh·nyi·tse waiter
člun ⓜ *chlun boat*

D

daleko *duh·le·ko far*
dálkový ovládač ⓜ
dal·ko·vee o·vla·duhch remote control
dálnice ① *dal·nyi·tse
highway · motorway (tollway)*
další *duhl·shee another · other*
dámské vložky ① pl *dams·kair vlozh·ki
sanitary napkin*
daň ① *duhn' tax*
dar ⓜ *duhr gift*
dárek ⓜ *da·rek present (gift)*
datum ⓜ *duh·tum date (day)*
datum narození ⓝ
duh·tum nuh·ro·ze·nyee date of birth

E

dcera ① *dtse*·ruh *daughter*
dědeček ① *dye*·de·chek *grandfather*
deka ① *De*·kuh *blanket*
den ⓜ den *day*
denně *de*·nye *daily* adv
denník ⓜ *de*·nyek *diary*
dentální nit ① *den*·tal·nyee nyit *dental floss*
déšť ① dairsht' *rain*
deštník ⓜ desht·nyeek *umbrella*
děti ① pl *dye*·tyi *children*
dětská výživa ① *dyets*·ka *vee*·zhi·vuh *baby food*
diapozitivní film ⓜ *di*·uh·po·zi·tiv·nyee film *slide film*
disketa ① *dis*·ke·tuh *floppy disk*
dítě ① *dyee*·tye *child*
divadlo ① *dyi*·vuhd·lo *theatre*
dívka ① *dyeef*·kuh *girl*
dlouhý *dloh*·hee *long*
dnes dnes *today*
dnes večer dnes ve·cher *tonight*
dno ① dno *bottom (position)*
dobře dob·rzhe *well* adv
dobrý *do*·bree *good*
doklad o vlastnictví auta ⓜ *dok*·luhd o *vluhst*·nyits·tvee ow·tuh *car owner's title*
doklad totožnosti ⓜ *dok*·luhd to·tozh·nos·tyi *identification card (ID)*
doklady ⓜ pl *do*·kluh·di *paperwork*
doktor(ka) ⓜ/① *dok*·tor(·kuh) *doctor*
dolů *do*·loo *down*
domov ⓜ *do*·mof *home*
dopis ⓜ *do*·pis *letter (mail)*
doporučená zásilka ① *do*·po·ru·che·na za·sil·kuh *registered mail*
doporučit *do*·po·ru·chit *recommend*
dort ⓜ dort *cake*
dost dost *enough*
dotknout se *dot*·knoht se *touch* v
doutník ⓜ *doht*·nyeek *cigar*
dovézt *do*·vairzt *deliver*
dovolená ① *do*·vo·le·na *holidays • vacation (from work)*
drahý *druh*·hee *expensive*
drobné ① *drob*·nair *change (coins)*
drogy ① pl *dro*·gi *drugs (illicit)*
druhá třída ① *dru*·ha *trzhee*·duh *second class*
dudlík ⓜ *dud*·leek *dummy (pacifier)*

důchodce/důchodkyně ⓜ/① *doo*·khod·tse/*doo*·khod·ki·nye *pensioner*
důležitý *doo*·le·zhi·tee *important*
dům ⓜ doom *house*
dva dvuh *two*
dveře ① pl dve·rzhe *door*
dvojitý *dvo*·yi·tee *double* a
dvoulůžkový pokoj ⓜ *dvoh*·loozh·ko·vee po·koy *double room*
dvoupostel ① *dvoh*·pos·tel *twin beds*
džíny ⓜ pl *dzhee*·ni *jeans*

E

elektrický proud ⓜ *e*·lek·trits·kee prohd *current (electricity)*
elektro obchod ⓜ *e*·lek·tro op·khod *electrical store*
elektřina ① *e*·lek·trzhi·nuh *electricity*
Evropa ① *e*·vro·puh *Europe*
Evropská unie ① *e*·vrops·ka *u*·ni·ye *European Union*
expozimetr ⓜ *eks*·po·zi·me·tr *light meter*
expresní zásilka ① *eks*·pres·nyee za·sil·kuh *express mail*

F

fialový *fi*·yuh·lo·vee *purple*
fotka ① *fot*·kuh *photo*
fotoaparát ⓜ *fo*·to·uh·puh·rat *camera*
fotograf ⓜ *fo*·to·gruhf *photographer*
fotografie ① *fo*·to·gruh·fi·ye *photography*
fronta ① *fron*·tuh *queue*

G

galerie ① *guh*·le·ri·ye *art gallery*
golfové hřiště ⓜ *gol*·fo·vair hrzhish·tye *golf course*
granát ⓜ *gruh*·nat *garnet*

H

hedvábí ⓜ *hed*·va·bee *silk*
herec/herečka ⓜ/① *he*·rets/*he*·rech·kuh *actor*
hezký *hez*·kee *handsome • pretty*
historický *his*·to·rits·kee *historical*

235

hladový *hluh·do·vee* hungry
hlasitý *hluh·si·tee* loud
hlava ① *hluh·vuh* head
hlavní silnice ① *hluhv·nyee sil·nyi·tse* main road
hlučný *hluch·nee* noisy
hnědý *hnye·dee* brown
hňup ⓜ *hnyup* dope (drugs)
hodina ① *ho·dyi·nuh* hour
hodinky ① pl *ho·dyin·ki* watch
hodně *hod·nye* (a) lot
holič ⓜ *ho·lich* hairdresser for men
holit *ho·lit* shave v
hora ① *ho·ruh* mountain
horko ⓝ *hor·ko* heat
horký *hor·kee* hot
hořký *horzh·kee* bitter
hospoda ① *hos·po·duh* pub (bar)
hotovost ① *ho·to·vost* cash
hovor na účet volaného ⓜ *ho·vor nuh oo·chet vo·luh·nair·ho* collect call
hra ① *hruh* game (general) • play (theatre)
hrad ⓜ *hruhd* castle
hranice ① *hruh·nyi·tse* border
hrdlo ⓝ *hrd·lo* throat
hrnec ⓜ *hr·nets* pot (cooking)
hrozný *hroz·nee* awful
hruď ① *hrud'* chest (body)
hřbitov ⓜ *hrzh·bi·tov* cemetery
hřeben ⓜ *hrzhe·ben* comb
hudebník/hudebnice ⓜ/① *hu·deb·nyeek/hu·deb·nyi·tse* musician
hudba ① *hud·buh* music

Ch

chladný *khluhd·nee* cold a
chlapec ⓜ *khluh·pets* boy
chléb ⓜ *khlairb* bread
chodidlo ⓝ *kho·dyid·lo* foot (body)
chodník ⓜ *khod·nyeek* footpath
chřipka ① *khrzhip·kuh* flu • influenza
chutný *khut·nee* tasty
chůva ① *khoo·vuh* babysitter
chyba ① *khi·buh* mistake

I

infekce ① *in·fek·tse* infection
informace ① *in·for·muh·tse* information
injekce ① *in·yek·tse* injection

inkasovat šek *in·kuh·so·vuht shek* cash a cheque v
internetová kavárna ① *in·ter·ne·to·va kuh·var·nuh* Internet café
invalidní *in·vuh·lid·nyee* disabled
invalidní vozík ⓜ *in·vuh·lid·nyee vo·zeek* wheelchair
inženýr(ka) ⓜ/① *in·zhe·neer(·kuh)* engineer
itinerář ① *i·ti·ne·rarzh* itinerary

J

já *ya* I
jak *yuhk* how
jaro ⓝ *yuh·ro* spring (season)
jazyk ⓜ *yuh·zik* language
jeden *ye·den* one
jednoduchá jízdenka ① *yed·no·du·kha yeez·den·kuh* one-way ticket
jednolůžkový pokoj ⓜ *yed·no·loozh·ko·vee po·koy* single room
jedovatý *ye·do·vuh·tee* poisonous
jehla ① *yeh·luh* needle (sewing/syringe)
jeho *ye·ho* his
její *ye·yee* her (possessive)
jejich *ye·yikh* their
jen *yen* only
jezero ⓝ *ye·ze·ro* lake
jídelna ① *yee·del·nuh* cafeteria
jídelní lístek ⓜ *yee·del·nyee lees·tek* menu
jídelní vůz ⓜ *yee·del·nyee vooz* dining car
jídlo ⓝ *yeed·lo* food • meal
jih ⓜ *yih* south
jíst *yeest* eat v
jít *yeet* go • walk v
jít na nákupy *yeet nuh na·ku·pi* go shopping
jízda na koni ① *yeez·duh nuh ko·nyi* horse riding
jízdné ⓝ *yeezd·nair* fare
jízdní řád ⓜ *yeezd·nyee rzhad* timetable
jméno ⓝ *ymair·no* name

K

kabát ⓜ *kuh·bat* coat
kabelka ① *kuh·bel·kuh* handbag
kadeřník ⓜ *kuh·derzh·nyeek* hairdresser for women
kajakování ⓝ *kuh·yuh·ko·va·nyee* kayaking

kalhoty ① pl *kuhl*·ho·ti *pants (trousers)*
kalkulačka ① *kuhl*·ku·luhch·kuh *calculator*
kancelář ① *kuhn*·tse·larzh *office*
kanoistika ① *kuh*·no·is·ti·kuh *canoeing*
kapesní nůž ⓜ *kuh*·pes·nyee noozh *penknife*
kapesník ⓜ *kuh*·pes·nyek *handkerchief*
kartáč ⓜ *kuhr*·tach *brush*
kašlat *kuhsh*·luht *cough* v
káva ① *ka*·vuh *coffee*
kavárna ① *kuh*·var·nuh *café*
kazeta ① *kuh*·ze·tuh *cassette*
každý *kuhzh*·dee *each • every* a
kde gde *where*
kdo gdo *who*
kdy gdi *when*
kino ⓝ *ki*·no *cinema*
klíč ⓜ kleech *key (door etc)*
klimatizovaný *kli*·muh·ti·zo·vuh·nee *air-conditioned*
klobouk ⓜ *klo*·bohk *hard hat*
kniha ① *knyi*·huh *book*
knihkupectví ⓝ *knikh*·ku·pets·tvee *book shop*
knihovna ① *knyi*·hov·nuh *library*
knoflík ⓜ *knof*·leek *button*
kohoutek ⓜ *ko*·hoh·tek *faucet (tap)*
kolega/kolegyně ⓜ/①
  ko·le·guh/*ko*·le·gi·nye *colleague*
koleno ⓝ *ko*·le·no *knee*
kulik *ku*·lik *how much*
kolo ⓝ *ko*·lo *bicycle*
konec ⓜ *ko*·nets *finish*
kontaktní čočky ① pl
  kon·tuhkt·nyee choch·ki *contact lenses*
konverzační příručka ①
  kon·ver·zuhch·nyee przhee·ruch·kuh *phrasebook*
konzum ⓜ *kon*·zum *grocery store*
kopec ⓜ *ko*·pets *hill*
kosmetické kapesníčky ⓝ pl
  kos·me·tits·kair kuh·pes·neech·ki *tissues*
kosmetické polštářky ⓝ pl
  kos·me·tits·kair polsh·tarzh·ki *cotton balls*
kosmetický salón ⓜ
  kos·me·tits·kee suh·lawn *beauty salon*
kost ① kost *bone*
kostel ⓜ *kos*·tel *church*
košile ① *ko*·shi·le *shirt*
kotník ⓜ *kot*·nyeek *ankle*
kotviště ⓝ *kot*·vish·tye *berth*
koupel ① *koh*·pel *bath*

koupelna ① *koh*·pel·nuh *bathroom*
koupit *koh*·pit *buy* v
kouřit koh·rzhit *smoke* v
krabice ① *kruh*·bi·tse *box*
kradený *kruh*·de·nee *stolen*
krajíc ⓜ *kruh*·yeets *slice*
krásný kras·nee *beautiful*
krátký *krat*·kee *short (length)*
kreditní karta ① *kre*·dit·nyee *kuhr*·tuh *credit card*
krejčí/krejčová ⓜ/①
  krey·chee/*krey*·cho·va *tailor*
krev ① kref *blood*
krevní skupina ① *krev*·nyee *sku*·pi·nuh *blood group*
krk ⓜ krk *neck*
křehký *krzheh*·kee *fragile*
křestní jméno ⓝ *krzhest*·nyee ymair·no *first name*
který *kte*·ree *which*
kufr ⓜ *ku*·fr *suitcase*
kuchař(ka) ⓜ/① *ku*·kharzh(·kuh) *cook*
kuchyň ① *ku*·khin' *kitchen*
kurt ⓜ kurt *tennis court*
kůže ① *koo*·zhe *leather*
květinář ⓜ *kvye*·tyi·narzh *florist*
kyselý déšť ⓜ *ki*·se·lee desht' *acid rain*
kytara ① *ki*·tuh·ruh *guitar*

L

láhev ① *la*·hef *bottle*
lahůdky ① pl *luh*·hood·ki *delicatessen • sandwich shop*
láska ① *las*·kuh *love*
laskavý *luhs*·kuh·vee *kind (nice)*
látka ① *lat*·kuh *fabric*
led ⓜ led *ice*
lednička ① *led*·nyich·kuh *refrigerator*
lední hokej ⓜ *led*·nyee *ho*·key *ice hockey*
legrační *le*·gruh·nyee *funny*
lehátko ① *le*·hat·ko *couchette • sleeping berth*
lehký *leh*·kee *light (weight)*
lék ⓜ lairk *drug (medication)*
lék proti bolestem lairk *pro*·tyi bo·les·tem *painkiller*
lék proti kašli ⓜ lairk *pro*·tyi *kuhsh*·li *cough medicine*
lékárna ① *lair*·kar·nuh *pharmacy*
lékárnička ① *le*·kar·nyich·kuh *first-aid kit*
lékárník ⓜ *lair*·kar·nyeek *pharmacist*

lékařský předpis ⑩
lair-kuhrzh-skee przhed-pis prescription
lékařství ⑩ *lair-kuhrzh-stvee*
medicine (profession)
lepší *lep-shee better*
les ⑪ *les forest*
lesbička ① *les-bich-kuh lesbian*
let ⑪ *let flight*
letadlo ⑩ *le-tuhd-lo airplane*
létat *lair-tuht fly v*
letecká pošta ① *le-tets-ka posh-tuh*
airmail
letiště ⑩ *le-tyish-tye airport*
letištní poplatek ⑩
le-tyisht-nyee po-pluh-tek airport tax
léto ⑩ *lair-to summer*
leukoplast ⑩ *leu-ko-pluhst Band-Aid*
levný *lev-nee cheap*
levý *le-vee left (direction)*
libra šterlinků ① *lib-ruh shter-lin-koo*
pound (money)
líčidlo ⑩ *lee-chid-lo make-up*
lid ⑩ pl lid *people*
lněná tkanina ① *lnye-na tkuh-nyi-nuh*
linen (material)
loutka ① *loht-kuh puppet*
loutkové divadlo ⑩
loht-ko-vair dyi-vuh-dlo puppet theatre
loutkové představení ⑩ *loht-ko-vair*
przhed-stuh-ve-nyee puppet show
ložní prádlo ⑩ *lozh-nyee prad-lo*
bed linen (sheets)
ložnice ① *lozh-nyi-tse bedroom*
lyže ① *li-zhe ski*
lyžování ⑩ *li-zho-va-nyee skiing*
lžíce ① *lzhee-tse spoon*
lžička ① *lzhich-kuh teaspoon*

M

majitel(ka) ⑩/① *muh-yi-tel(-kuh) owner*
malíř(ka) ⑩/① *muh-leerzh(-kuh)*
painter (artist)
málo *ma-lo few • little (quantity)*
malý *muh-lee short (height) • small*
manžel ⑩ *muhn-zhel husband*
manželka ① *muhn-zhel-kuh wife*
manželská postel ①
muhn-zhels-ka pos-tel double bed
mapa ① *muh-puh map of country*
masér ⑩ *muh-ser masseur*
masérka ① *muh-ser-kuh masseuse*
maso ⑩ *muh-so meat*

matka ① *muht-kuh mother*
matrace ① *muh-truh-tse mattress*
mazivo ⑩ *muh-zi-vo lubricant*
mě *mye me*
medicína ① *me-di-tsee-nuh*
medicine (study)
mejdan ⑩ *mey-duhn party (entertainment)*
menší *men-shee less • smaller*
měsíc ⑩ *mye-seets month*
město ⑩ *myes-to city*
městský policista ⑩
myest-skee po-li-tsis-tuh city police officer
metr ⑩ *me-tr metre*
metro ⑩ *me-tro subway (train)*
mezi *me-zi between*
mikrovlná trouba ①
mi-kro-vl-na troh-buh microwave oven
milovat *mi-lo-vuht love v*
mimořádný *mi-mo-rzhad-nee special a*
mince ① *min-tse coins*
minerálka ① *mi-ne-ral-kuh mineral water*
minuta ① *mi-nu-tuh minute*
miska ① *mis-kuh bowl (plate)*
místní *meest-nyee local a*
místo ⑩ *mees-to seat*
místo narození ①
mees-to nuh-ro-ze-nyee place of birth
mít *meet have*
mít rád *meet rad like v*
mládežnická ubytovna ①
mla-dezh-nyits-ka u-bi-tov-nuh
youth hostel
mladý *mluh-dee young a*
mléko ⑩ *mlair-ko milk*
mnohý *mno-hee many*
mobil ⑩ *mo-bil mobile phone*
móda ① *maw-duh fashion*
moderní *mo-der-nyee modern*
modrý *mod-ree blue*
mokrý *mok-ree wet a*
moře ⑩ *mo-rzhe sea*
most ⑩ *most bridge (structure)*
motor ⑩ *mo-tor engine*
moučník ⑩ *mohch-nyeek dessert*
možná *mozh-na maybe*
možný *mozh-nee possible*
můj *mooy my*
muzeum ⑩ *mu-ze-um museum*
muž ⑩ *muzh man*
my *mi we*
mýdlo ⑩ *meed-lo soap*

DICTIONARY

N

na nuh *at • on • per • to*
náboženství ⓝ *na*-bo-zhens-tvee *religion*
nad nuhd *above*
na palubě nuh *puh*-lu-bye *aboard*
na shledanou nuh-skhle-duh-noh *goodbye*
nábytek ⓜ *na*-bi-tek *furniture*
nacpaný nuhts-puh-nee *crowded*
nadměrné zavazadlo ⓝ nuhd-*myer*-nair zuh-vuh-zuhd-lo *excess baggage*
nádraží ⓝ *na*-druh-zhee *station*
nahoru nuh-*ho*-ru *up*
náhrdelník ⓜ *na*-hr-del-nyeek *necklace*
nachlazení ⓝ nuh-khluh-ze-nyee *cold (illness)*
nákupní centrum ⓝ *na*-kup-nyee *tsen*-trum *shopping centre*
nakupovat nuh-ku-po-vuht *shop* v
naléhavý nuh-*lair*-huh-vee *urgent*
náměstí ⓝ *na*-myes-tyee *town square*
nápoj ⓜ *na*-poy *drink*
národnost ⓕ *na*-rod-nost *nationality*
narozeniny ⓕ pl nuh-*ro*-ze-nyi-ni *birthday*
následující nas-le-du-yee-tsee *next (following)*
nastoupit nuhs-*toh*-pit *board (plane, ship)* v
nástupiště ⓝ *nas*-tu-pish-tye *platform*
náš nash *our*
náušnice ⓕ *na*-ush-nyi-tse *earrings*
ne ne *no*
nebe ⓝ *ne*-be *sky*
nebezpečný ne-*bez*-pech-nee *dangerous*
nedaleko ne-duh-*le*-ko *nearby*
nefunguje ne-fun-gu-ye *out of order*
nehoda ⓕ *ne*-ho-duh *accident*
nejbližší ney-*blizh*-shee *nearest*
nejlepší ney-*lep*-shee *best*
nejmenší ney-*men*-shee *smallest*
největší ney-*vyet*-shee *biggest*
někdy *nyeg*-di *sometimes*
několik nye-*ko*-lik *several • some*
nekuřácký ne-ku-*rzhats*-kee *nonsmoking*
nemluvně ⓝ *nem*-luv-nye *baby*
nemocnice ⓕ *ne*-mots-nyi-tse *hospital*
nemocný ne-mots-nee *ill • sick*
nemožný ne-mozh-nee *impossible*
nepohodlný ne-po-ho-dl-nee *uncomfortable*
nesprávný nes-*prav*-nee *wrong* a

nevolnost ⓕ *ne*-vol-nost *nausea*
nevolnost při cestování ⓕ *ne*-vol-nost przhi tses-to-va-nyee *travel sickness*
nic ⓝ nyits *nothing*
nikdy nyik-di *never*
nízký *nyeez*-kee *low*
noc ⓕ nots *night*
noční klub ⓜ *noch*-nyee klub *nightclub*
noha ⓕ *no*-huh *leg (body)*
nos ⓜ nos *nose*
novinář(ka) ⓜ/ⓕ *no*-vi-narzh(-kuh) *journalist*
noviny ⓕ pl *no*-vi-ni *newspaper*
nový *no*-vee *new*
nudný *nud*-nee *boring*
nůž ⓜ noozh *knife*
nůžky ⓕ pl *noozh*-ki *scissors*

O

o o *about*
oba *o*-buh *both*
obálka ⓕ *o*-bal-kuh *envelope*
oběd ⓜ *o*-byed *lunch*
obchod ⓜ *op*-khod *business • shop* v
obchod s hudebninami ⓜ *op*-khod s hu-deb-nyi-nuh-mi *music shop*
obchod s oblečením ⓜ *op*-khod s o-ble-che-nyeem *clothing store*
obchod s obuví ⓜ *op*-khod s o-bu-vee *shoe shop*
obchod s rybami ⓕ *op*-khod s *ri*-buh-mi *fish shop*
obchod se sportovními potřebami ⓜ *op*-khod se *spor*-tov-nyee-mi po-trzhe-buh-mi *sports store*
obchod se suvenýry ⓜ *op*-khod se su-ve-nee-ri *souvenir shop*
obchodní dům ⓜ *op*-khod-nyee doom *department store*
objednat ob-*yed*-nuht *order* v
objektiv ⓜ *ob*-yek-tif *lens (camera)*
obličej ⓜ *o*-bli-chey *face*
obsazeno op-suh-ze-no *booked out*
obvaz ⓜ *ob*-vuhz *bandage*
obyčejná pošta ⓕ *o*-bi-chey-na *posh*-tuh *surface mail (land)*
obyčejná pošta lodí ⓕ *o*-bi-chey-na *posh*-tuh lo-dyee *surface mail (sea)*
očkování ⓝ *och*-ko-va-nyee *vaccination*
od od *since (time)*
oddělený od-dye-le-nee *separate* a
odjet od-*yet* *depart*

odjezd ⓜ *od*-yezd departure
odlišný *od*-lish-nee different
odpoledne ⓝ *ot*-po-led-ne afternoon
odpověď ⓕ *ot*-po-vyed' answer
oheň ⓜ *o*-hen' fire
ohřívací láhev ⓕ *o*-hrzhee-vuh-tsee *la*-hef
    hot water bottle
ohřívač ⓜ *o*-hrzhee-vuhch heater
okno ⓝ *ok*-no window
oko ⓝ *o*-ko eye
okoralý *o*-ko-ruh-lee stale
okružní jízda ⓕ *o*-kruzh-nyee *yeez*-duh
    tour
omezená rychlost ⓕ *o*-me-ze-na *rikh*-lost
    speed limit
on on he
ona *o*-nuh she
oni *o*-nyi they
opalovací krém ⓜ
    o-puh-lo-vuh-tsee krairm sunblock
opalovací mléko ⓝ
    o-puh-lo-vuh-tsee *mlair*-ko tanning lotion
opěradlo ⓝ *o*-pye-ruhd-lo back (position)
opilý *o*-pi-leee drunk
opravit *o*-pruh-vit repair v
oranžový *o*-ruhn-zho-vee orange (colour)
osoba ⓕ *o*-so-buh person
osobní doklad ⓝ *o*-sob-nyee *dok*-luhd
    identification
ostrov ⓜ *os*-trov island
ostříhání vlasů ⓝ
    os-trzhee-ha-nyee vluh-soo haircut
osvědčení o registraci ⓝ
    o-svyed-che-nee o *re*-gis-truh-tsi
    car registration
otázka ⓕ *o*-taz-kuh question
otec ⓜ *o*-tets father
otřes mozku ⓜ *o*-trzhes *moz*-ku
    concussion
otvírací hodiny ⓕ pl ot-vee-ruh-tsee
    ho-dyi-ni opening hours
otvírák na konzervy ⓜ ot-vee-rak nuh
    kon-zer-vi can (tin) opener
otvírák na láhve ⓜ ot-vee-rak nuh *lah*-ve
    bottle opener
ovoce ⓝ *o*-vo-tse fruit
ovocný bar ⓜ *o*-vots-nee buhr
    ice-cream parlour
označit *oz*-nuh-chit validate
oznamovací tón ⓜ *oz*-nuh-mo-vuh-tsee
    tawn dial tone

pach ⓜ pukh smell
palác ⓜ *puh*-lats palace
palubní vstupenka ⓕ *puh*-lub-nyee
    fstu-pen-kuh boarding pass
pan ⓜ puhn Mr
panenka ⓕ *puh*-nen-kuh doll
pánev ⓕ *pa*-nef frying pan
paní ⓕ *puh*-nyee Mrs
papír ⓜ *puh*-peer paper
papírnictví ⓝ *puh*-peer-nits-tvee
    stationer
parfém ⓜ *puhr*-fairm perfume
parkovat *puhr*-ko-vuht park a car v
pas ⓜ puhs passport
pásmová nemoc ⓕ pas-mo-va ne-mots
    jet lag
paže ⓕ *puh*-zhe arm (body)
pekárna ⓕ *pe*-kar-nuh bakery
pěna na holení ⓕ
    pye-nuh nuh *ho*-le-nyee shaving cream
peněženka ⓕ *pe*-nye-zhen-kuh purse
peníze ⓜ pl pe-nyee-ze money
penzion ⓜ *pen*-zi-on
    boarding house • guesthouse
pes ⓜ pes dog
pilulka ⓕ *pi*-lul-kuh pill
pinzeta ⓕ *pin*-ze-tuh tweezers
pít peet drink v
pivo ⓝ *pi*-vo beer
placení ⓝ *pluh*-tse-nyee payment
plán ⓜ plan map of town
plastický *pluhs*-tits-kee plastic a
pláštěnka ⓕ *plash*-tyen-kuh raincoat
platit *pluh*-tyit pay v
plavat *pluh*-vuht swim v
plechovka ⓕ *ple*-khof-kuh tin (can)
plenka ⓕ *plen*-kuh nappy (diaper)
plný *pl*-nee full
plovací vesta ⓕ *plo*-vuh-tsee ves-tuh
    life jacket
pneumatika ⓕ *pne*-u-muh-ti-kuh tire (tyre)
po po after
počasí ⓝ *po*-chuh-see weather
počítač ⓜ *po*-chee-tuhch computer
pod pud below
podepsat po-dep-suht sign v
podobný po-dob-nee similar
podprsenka ⓕ pod-pr-sen-kuh bra
podrobnosti ⓕ po-drob-nos-tyi details
pohlaví ⓝ *po*-hluh-vee sex
pohled ⓜ *poh*-led postcard • view

pohodlný *po-ho-dl-nee comfortable*
pohotovost ① *po-ho-to-vost emergency*
pojištění ⑩ *po-yish-tye-nyee insurance*
pokladna ① *po-kluhd-nuh*
  cash register • ticket office
pokladník ⑩ *po-kluhd-nyeek cashier*
pokoj ⑩ *po-koy room*
pokrm ⑩ *po-krm dish*
pokuta ① *po-ku-tuh fine*
poledne ⑩ *po-led-ne noon*
policejní stanice ①
  po-li-tsey-nyee stuh-nyi-tse police station
policie ① *po-li-tsi-ye police*
policista ⑩ *po-li-tsis-tuh*
  police officer in country
polovina ① *po-lo-vi-nuh half*
polštář ⑩ *polsh-tarzh pillow*
pomalu *po-muh-lu slowly*
pomník ⑩ *pom-nyeek monument*
pomoc ① *po-mots help*
pomoci *po-mo-tsi help v*
ponožky ① pl *po-nozh-ki socks*
popelnice ① *po-pel-nyi-tse garbage can*
popelník ⑩ *po-pel-nyeek ashtray*
populární *po-pu-lar-nyee popular*
porada ① *po-ruh-duh small conference*
porcelán ⑩ *por-tse-lan porcelain*
poschodí ⑩ *pos-kho-dyee floor (storey)*
poslední *pos-led-nyee last (final)*
poslouchat *po-sloh-khuht listen*
postel ① *pos-tel bed*
pošta ⑩ *posh-tuh post office*
poštovní schránka ①
  posh-tov-nyee skhran-kuh mailbox
poštovní směrovací číslo ⑩
  posh-tov-nyee smye-ro-vuh-tsee
  chee-slo postcode
potravina ① *pot-ruh-vi-nuh grocery*
potvrdit *po-tvr-dyit confirm (a booking)*
pouliční trh ⑩ *po-u-lich-nyee trh*
  street market
použití *po-u-zhi-tee secondhand*
povlak na polštář ⑩
  po-vluhk nuh polsh-tarzh pillowcase
povolená váha zavazadel ①
  po-vo-le-na va-huh zuh-vuh-zuh-del
  baggage allowance
povolení ⑩ *po-vo-le-nyee permit*
pozdě *poz-dye late adv*
později *poz-dye-yi later*
pozítří ⑩ *po-zee-trzhee*
  day after tomorrow
práce ① *pra-tse work*

pračka ① *pruhch-kuh washing machine*
prádelna ① *pra-del-nuh laundry (place)*
(samoobslužná) prádelna ①
  (suh-mo-ob-sluzh-na) pruhd-len-kuh
  launderette
prádlo ⑩ *prad-lo laundry (clothes)*
Praha ① *pruh-huh Prague*
právo ⑩ *pra-vo law (study/profession)*
pravý *pruh-vee right (direction)*
prázdniny ① *prazd-nyi-ni*
  vacation (from school)
prázdný *prazd-nee empty a*
překvapení ⑩ *przhe-kvuh-pe-nyee surprise*
přes *przhez across*
prezervativ ⑩ *pre-zer-vuh-tif condom*
probudit *pro-bu-dyit wake (someone) up*
proč *proch why*
prodej ⑩ *pro-dey sale*
projímadlo ⑩ *pro-yee-muhd-lo laxative*
pronajmout *pro-nai-moht rent v*
propiska ① *pro-pis-kuh ballpoint pen*
prostěradlo ⑩ *pros-tye-ruhd-lo sheet (bed)*
proti *pro-tyi opposite prep*
prso ⑩ *pr-so breast (body)*
prst ⑩ *prst finger*
prst u nohy ⑩ *prst u no-hi toe*
prsten ⑩ *prs-ten ring (jewellery)*
průjem ⑩ *proo-yem diarrhoea*
průvodce ⑩ *proo-vod-tse*
  guide (person) • guidebook
první třída ① *prv-nyee trzhee-duh*
  first class
před *przhed before • in front of*
předešlý *przhe-desh-lee last (previous)*
předevčírem ⑩ *przhe-def-chee-rem*
  day before yesterday
představení ⑩ *przhed-stuh-ve-nyee*
  show
přehled kulturních pořadů ⑩
  przhe-hled kul-tur-nyeekh po-rzha-doo
  entertainment guide
přeložit *przhe-lo-zhit translate*
přepychový *przhe-pi-kho-vee luxurious*
přes noc *przhes nots overnight adv*
přesně *przhes-nye exactly*
přestávka ① *przhe-staf-kuh intermission*
příbory ⑩ pl *przhee-bo-ri cutlery*
příjemný *przhee-yem-nee nice*
příjezd ⑩ *przhee-yezd arrivals*
příjmení ⑩ *przhee-y-me-nyee*
  family name (surname)
příliš mnoho *przhee-lish mno-ho*
  too (much)

přímé volání ⑩ *przhee*·mair *vo*·la·nyee direct-dial

přímý *przhee*·mee *direct* a

připravený *przhi*·pruh·ve·nee *ready* a

přirážka za obsluhu ① *przhi*·razh·kuh zuh *op*·slu·hu *service charge*

příroda ① *przhee*·ro·duh *nature*

přítel ⑩ *przhee*·tel *boyfriend* • *friend*

přítelkyně ① *przhee*·tel·ki·nye *girlfriend*

psát *p*·sat *write*

puchýř ⑩ *pu*·kheerzh *blister*

půjčovna aut ① *pooy*·chov·nuh *owt car hire*

půlnoc ① *pool*·nots *midnight*

punčochy ① pl *pun*·cho·khi *stockings*

původní *poo*·vod·nyee *original* a

R

rada ① *ruh*·duh *advice*

rameno ⑩ *ruh*·me·no *shoulder*

ráno ⑩ *ra*·no *morning*

realitní kancelář ① *re*·uh·lit·nyee *kuhn*·tse·larzh *estate agency*

recepce ① *re*·tsep·tse *check-in (desk)*

reflektor ⑩ *re*·flek·tor *headlights*

restaurace ① *res*·tow·ruh·tse *restaurant*

rezervace ① *re*·zer·vuh·tse *reservation (booking)*

riziko ⑩ *ri*·zi·ko *risk*

rocková skupina ① *ro*·ko·va *sku*·pi·nuh *rock group*

roční období ⑩ *roch*·nyee *ob*·do·bee *season*

rodiče ⑩ pl *ro*·dyi·che *parents*

rodina ① *ro*·dyi·nuh *family*

roh ⑩ *rokh* *corner*

rok ⑩ *rok* *year*

romantický *ro*·muhn·tits·kee *romantic* a

rovný *rov*·nee *straight*

rozbitý *roz*·bi·tee *broken down*

rozhněvaný *roz*·hnye·vuh·nee *angry*

rozpočet ⑩ *roz*·po·chet *budget*

rozumět *ro*·zu·myet *understand*

rozvedený *roz*·ve·de·nee *divorced*

rtěnka ① *rtyen*·kuh *lipstick*

ručně vyrobeno *ruch*·nye *vi*·ro·be·no *handmade*

ručník ⑩ *ruch*·nyeek *towel*

ruka ① *ru*·kuh *hand*

rukavice ① pl *ru*·kuh·vi·tse *gloves (clothing)*

růžový *roo*·zho·vee *pink*

rybolov ⑩ *ri*·bo·lov *fishing*

rychlostní skříň ① *ri*·khlost·nyee *skrzheen'* *gearbox*

rychlý *rikh*·lee *fast* a

Ř

ředitel(ka) ⑩/① *rzhe*·dyi·tel(·kuh) *manager (business)*

řeka ① *rzhe*·kuh *river*

řeznictví ① *rzhez*·nyits·tvee *butcher's shop*

říci *rzhee*·tsi *speak*

řidičský průkaz ⑩ *rzhi*·dyich·skee proo·kuhz *drivers licence*

řídit *rzhee*·dyit *drive* v

říznout *rzheez*·noht *cut (with knife)* v

S

s s *with*

sáhnout *sah*·noht *feel (touch)* v

sako ⑩ *suh*·ko *jacket*

sám sam *alone*

samoobsluha ① *suh*·mo·ob·slu·huh *supermarket*

samoobslužný *suh*·mo·ob·sluzh·nee *self-service* a

sedačka ① *se*·duch·kuh *chairlift (skiing)*

semafor ⑩ *se*·muh·for *traffic lights*

sen ⑩ *sen dream*

senná rýma ① *se*·na *ree*·muh *hay fever*

sestra ① *ses*·truh *sister*

sever ⑩ *se*·ver *north*

schodiště ⑩ *skho*·dyish·tye *stairway*

schůzka ① *skhooz*·kuh *appointment*

silnice ① *sil*·nyi·tse *road*

silný *sil*·nee *strong* • *thick*

skleněné zboží ⑩ *skle*·nye·nair *zbo*·zhee *glassware*

sklenička ① *skle*·nyich·kuh *glass (drinking)*

skupina ① *sku*·pi·nuh *band (music)*

sladký *sluhd*·kee *sweet* a

slečna ① *slech*·nuh *Miss* • *Ms*

sleva ① *sle*·vuh *discount*

Slovensko ⑩ *slo*·ven·sko *Slovakia*

slovník ⑩ *slov* nyeek *dictionary*

slovo ⑩ *slo*·vo *word*

slunce ⑩ *slun*·tse *sun*

sluneční brýle ① pl *slu*·nech·nee *bree*·le *sunglasses*

slunečný *slu*·nech·nee *sunny*

služba ① *sluzh*·buh *service*

služba pro hlídání dětí ①
  sluzh·buh pro *hlee*·da·nye *dye*·tyee
  child-minding service
služební cesta ① *slu*·zheb·nyee *tses*·tuh
  business trip
smažit *smuh*·zhit *fry* v
směnárna ① *smye*·nar·nuh
  currency exchange
směnný kurs ⓜ *smye*·nee kurz
  exchange rate
směr ⓜ smyer *direction*
smutný *smut*·nee *sad*
snídaně ① *snee*·duh·nye *breakfast*
sníh ⓜ snyeeh *snow*
snoubenec ⓜ *snoh*·be·nets *fiancé*
snoubenka ① *snoh*·ben·kuh *fiancée*
socha ① *so*·khuh *sculpture*
soukromý *soh*·kro·mee *private*
spací pytel ⓜ *spuh*·tsee *pi*·tel *sleeping bag*
spací vůz ⓜ *spuh*·tsee vooz *sleeping car*
spálenina ① *spa*·le·nyi·nuh *burn*
spálený sluncem ⓜ *spa*·le·nee *slun*·tsem
  sunburn
spát spat *sleep* v
spěšně *spyesh*·nye *in a hurry*
spisovatel(ka) ⓜ/① *spi*·so·vuh·tel(·kuh)
  writer
spodní prádlo ⓝ *spod*·nyee *prad*·lo
  underwear
spojení ⓝ *spo*·ye·nyee
  connection (transport)
společník/společnice ⓜ/①
  spo·lech·nyeek/*spo*·lech·nyi·tse
  companion
společnost ① *spo*·lech·nost
  company (firm)
spolu *spo*·lu *together*
spoluobývat *spo*·lu·o·bee·vuht
  share (accommodation) v
sportovní skládácí kočárek ⓜ
  spor·tov·nyee *skla*·da·tsee *ko*·cha·rek
  stroller
správný *sprav*·nee *right (correct)*
sprcha ① spr·khuh *shower*
spropitné ⓝ *spro*·pit·nair *tip (gratuity)*
srdce ⓝ *srd*·tse *heart*
srdeční porucha ①
  sr·dech·nyee *po*·ru·khuh *heart condition*
stan ⓜ stuhn *tent*
stánek ⓜ *sta*·nek *kiosk*
stanice metra ① *stuh*·nyi·tse *met*·ruh
  metro station

stanový tábor ⓜ *stuh*·no·vee *ta*·bor
  camping ground
starožitnost ① *stuh*·ro·zhit·nost *antique*
starý *stuh*·ree *old*
stát stat *cost* v
stávka ① *staf*·kuh *strike*
stejný *stey*·nee *same*
stezka ① *stez*·kuh *path*
stín ⓜ styeen *shade*
stížnost ① *styeezh*·nost *complaint*
stolní olej ⓜ *stol*·nyee *o*·ley *oil (cooking)*
stopovat *sto*·po·vuht *hitchhike*
strana ① *struh*·nuh *side*
strojírenství ⓝ *stro*·yee·rens·tvee
  engineering
střed ⓜ strzhed *centre*
střed města ⓜ/ⓝ strzhed *myes*·tuh
  city centre
stříbro ⓝ *strzee*·bro *silver*
stříhat *strzhee*·hut *cut (with scissors)* v
stupeň ⓝ *stu*·pen' *degrees (temperature)*
stůl ⓜ stool *table*
stvrzenka ① *stvr*·zen·kuh *receipt*
stydlivý *stid*·li·vee *shy*
styl ⓜ stil *style*
suchý *su*·khee *dry* a
sukně ① *suk*·nye *skirt*
sušit *su*·shit *dry (clothes)* v
svačina ① *svuh*·chi·nuh *snack*
svatební cesta ① *svuh*·teb·nyee *tses*·tuh
  honeymoon
svědění ⓝ *svye*·dye·nyee *itch*
světlo ⓝ *svyet*·lo *light*
světlý *svyet*·lee *light (colour)*
svetr ⓜ *sve*·tr *jumper (sweater)*
svítání ⓝ *svee*·ta·nyee *dawn*
svobodný *svo*·bod·nee *single (person)*
syn ⓜ sin *son*

Š

šála ① *sha*·luh *scarf*
šálek ⓜ *sha*·lek *cup*
šampaňské ⓝ *shuhm*·puhn'·skair
  champagne
šatna ① *shuht*·nuh
  changing room · cloakroom
šaty ⓜ pl *shuh*·ti *clothing · dress*
šedivý *she*·dyi·vee *grey*
šéfkuchař(ka) ⓜ/①
  shairf·ku·khuhrzh(·kuh) *chef*
šek ⓜ shek *check (banking)*
šortky ① pl *short*·ki *shorts*

špatný *shpuht*·nee *bad*
šperky ⓜ pl *shper*·ki *jewellery*
špinavý *shpi*·nuh·vee *dirty*
šťastný *shtyast*·nee *happy*

T

tady *tuh*·di *here*
také *tuh*·kair *also*
talíř ⓜ *tuh*·leerzh *plate*
tam *tuhm* *there*
tam ten *tuhm ten* *that (one)* pron
tancovat *tuhn*·tso·vuht *dance* v
tanec ⓜ *tuh*·nets *dance · dancing*
taška ① *tuhsh*·kuh *bag*
taxi stanoviště ⓝ *tuhk*·si *stuh*·no·vish·tye *taxi stand*
teď *ted'* *now*
těhotná *tye*·hot·na *pregnant*
telefonní budka ① *te*·le·fo·nyee *bud*·kuh *phone box*
telefonní karta ① *te*·le·fo·nyee *kuhr*·tuh *phonecard*
telefonní seznam ⓜ *te*·le·fo·nyee *sez*·nuhm *phone book*
telefonovat *te*·le·fo·no·vuht *telephone* v
televize ① *te*·le·vi·ze *television*
tělo ⓝ *tye*·lo *body*
tělocvična ① *tye*·lots·vich·nuh *gym (place)*
ten ten *ten* *that* a
tenhle *ten*·hle *this (one)* pron
tenisový kurt ⓜ *te*·ni·so·vee *kurt* *tennis court*
tenký *ten*·kee *thin*
tento *ten*·to *this* a
teplota ① *te*·plo·tuh *temperature (weather)*
teplý *tep*·lee *warm* a
teta ① *te*·tuh *aunt*
těžký *tyezh*·kee *heavy (weight)*
tchán ⓜ *tkhan* *father-in-law*
tchýně ① *tkhee*·nye *mother-in-law*
tichý *tyi*·khee *quiet*
tiskárna ① *tyis*·kar·nuh *printer (computer)*
tisková agentůra ① *tyis*·ko·va *uh*·gen·too·ruh *newsagency*
titulky ⓜ pl *tyi*·tul·ki *subtitles*
tlumočník/tlumočnice ⓜ/① *tlu*·moch·nyeek/*tlu*·moch·nyi·tse *interpreter*
tlustý *tlus*·tee *fat* a
tmavý *tmuh*·vee *dark (colour)*
to *to* *it*

toaleta ① *to*·uh·le·tuh *toilet*
toaletní papír ⓜ *to*·uh·let·nyee *puh*·peer *toilet paper*
toastovač ⓜ *tohs*·to·vuhch *toaster*
topení ⓝ *to*·pe·nyee *heating*
trajekt ⓜ *truh*·yekt *ferry*
trampovat *truhm*·po·vuht *hike* v
tramvaj ① *truhm*·vai *tram*
tranzitní salónek ⓜ *truhn*·zit·nyee *suh*·law·nek *transit lounge*
trh ⓜ *trh* *market*
tričko ⓝ *trich*·ko *T-shirt*
turistická informační kancelář ① *tu*·ri·stits·ka *in*·for·muhch·nyee *kuhn*·tse·larzh *tourist office*
turistická třída ① *tu*·ris·tits·ka *trzhee*·duh *economy class*
turistika ① *tu*·ris·ti·kuh *hiking*
tužka ① *tuzh*·kuh *pencil*
tvrdý *tvr*·dee *hard (not soft)*
tvůj *tvooy* *your* inf sg
ty *ti* *you* inf sg
týden ⓜ *tee*·den *week*
typický *ti*·pits·kee *typical*

U

ubytování ⓝ *u*·bi·to·va·nyee *accommodation*
ucpaný *uts*·puh·nee *blocked*
účet ⓜ *oo*·chet *account · bill · check*
učitel(ka) ⓜ/① *u*·chi·tel(·kuh) *teacher*
ucho ⓝ *u*·kho *ear*
ukázat *u*·ka·zuht *show* v
ukazovat *u*·kuh·zo·vuht *point* v
úklid ⓜ *oo*·klid *cleaning*
ulice ① *u*·li·tse *street*
ulička ① *u*·lich·kuh *aisle (on plane)*
umělec/umělkyně ⓜ/① *u*·mye·lets/*u*·myel·ki·nye *artist*
umělecká řemesla ⓝ pl *u*·mye·lets·ka *rzhe*·mes·luh *crafts*
umělecké řemeslo ⓝ *u*·mye·lets·kair *rzhe*·mes·lo *handicraft*
umění ⓝ *u*·mye·nyee *art*
umýt *u*·meet *wash (something)* v
unavený *u*·nuh·ve·nee *tired*
úschovna zavazadel ① *oos*·khov·nuh *zuh*·vuh·zuh·del *left-luggage office*
ústa ⓝ *oos*·tuh *mouth*
ustaraný *us*·tuh·ruh·nee *worried*
úvěr ⓜ *oo*·vyer *credit*
užitečný *u*·zhi·tech·nee *useful*

V

v v *in*
vadný *vuhd*·nee *faulty*
vaření ⓝ *vuh*·rzhe·nee *cooking*
vařit *vuh*·rzhit *cook* v
váš vash *your* sg pol&pl
včas fchuhs *on time*
včera *fche*·ruh *yesterday*
včetně *fchet*·nye *included*
vdaná f·*duh*·na *married (woman)*
vděčný *vdyech*·nee *grateful*
večer ⓜ *ve*·cher *evening*
večerka ⓕ *ve*·cher·kuh *milk bar*
večeře ⓕ *ve*·che·rzhe *dinner*
večírek ⓜ *ve*·chee·rek *night out* • *party*
věda ⓕ *vye*·duh *science*
vědec/vědkyně ⓜ/ⓕ
   vye·dets/*vyed*·ki·nye *scientist*
vedle *ved*·le *next to*
vegetariánský ve·ge·tuh·ri·yans·kee
   vegetarian a
věk ⓜ vyek *age*
velikost ⓕ *ve*·li·kost *size (general)*
velký *vel*·kee *big*
velvyslanectví ⓝ *vel*·vi·sluh·nets·tve
   embassy
venkov ⓜ *ven*·kof *countryside*
venku *ven*·ku *outside* adv
veřejná telefonní budka ⓕ *ve*·rzhey·na
   te·le·fo·nyee *bud*·kuh *public phone*
veřejné toalety ⓕ pl
   ve·rzhey·nair to·uh·le·ti *public toilet*
vesnice ⓕ *ves*·nyi·tse *village*
větrák ⓜ *vye*·trak *fan (machine)*
větší *vyet*·shee *bigger*
více *vee*·tse *more*
videonahrávač ⓜ *vi*·de·o·nuh·hra·vuhch
   video recorder
videopásek ⓜ *vi*·de·o·pa·sek *video tape*
vidlička ⓕ *vid*·lich·kuh *fork*
víno ⓝ *vee*·no *wine*
visací zámek ⓜ *vi*·suh·tsee *za*·mek
   padlock
vítr ⓜ *vee*·tr *wind*
vízum ⓝ *vee*·zum *visa*
vklad ⓜ *fkluhd* *deposit*
vlak ⓜ *vluhk* *train*
vlasy ⓜ pl *vluh*·si *hair*
vlna ⓕ *vl*·nuh *wool*
vnitřní *vnyi*·trzh·nee *inside* adv
vnuk/vnučka ⓜ/ⓕ vnuk/*vnuch*·kuh
   grandchild

voda ⓕ *vo*·duh *water*
voda po holení ⓕ *vo*·duh po *ho*·le·nyee
   aftershave
volno ⓝ *vol*·no *vacancy*
volný *vol*·nee *free (available)* a • *vacant*
vozík ⓜ *vo*·zeek *trolley*
vracení peněz ⓝ *vruh*·tse·nee pe·nyez
   refund
vrátit se *vra*·tyit se *return* v
vstoupit *vstoh*·pit *enter*
vstup ⓜ vstup *entry*
vstupenka ⓕ *fstu*·pen·kuh *ticket*
vstupné ⓝ *fstup*·nair
   admission (price) • *cover charge*
všechno ⓝ *vshekh*·no *everything*
všichni *vshikh*·nyi *all* • *everyone*
vy vi *you* sg pol&pl
výdej zavazadel ⓜ
   vee·dey zuh·vuh·zuh·del *baggage
   claim*
vyfotit *vi*·fo·tyit *take a photo*
východ ⓜ *vee*·khod *east* • *exit*
východ slunce ⓜ *vee*·khod slun·tse
   sunrise
vyjít *vi*·yeet *go out*
výlet ⓜ *vee*·let *trip (journey)*
výměna ⓕ *vee*·mye·nuh *exchange*
vyměnit *vi*·mye·nyit
   change (money) v • *exchange* v
vynikající *vi*·nyi·kuh·yee·tsee *fine* a
vypůjčit *vi*·pooy·chit *hire* v
výron ⓜ *vee*·ron *sprain*
vysoký *vi*·so·kee *high (tall)*
výstava ⓕ *vees*·tuh·vuh *exhibition*
vystoupit *vis*·toh·pit *get off (bus, train)*
výtah ⓜ *vee*·tah *lift (elevator)*
vytápěný *vi*·ta·pye·nee *heated*
vývozní povolení ⓝ
   vee·voz·nyee po·vo·le·nyee *export permit*
vývrtka ⓕ *vee*·vrt·kuh *corkscrew*
vzácný *vzats*·nee *rare (uncommon)*
vzduch ⓜ vzdukh *air*
vzteklina ⓕ *vztek*·li·nuh *rabies*
vždy vzhdi *always*

Z

z z *from*
za za *behind*
zabít *zuh*·beet *kill* v
zácpa ⓕ *zats*·puh *constipation*
začátek ⓜ *zuh*·cha·tek *start*
záda ⓕ *za*·duh *back (body)*

zadek ⓜ zuh·dek bottom (body)
zadní zuhd·nyee rear (location) a
zahrada ① zuh·hruh·duh garden
zajímavý zuh·yee·muh·vee interesting
zakázka ① zuh·kaz·kuh commission
zákazník/zákaznice ⓜ/①
  za·kuhz·nyeek/za·kuhz·nyi·tse client
zákon ⓜ za·kon law (legislation)
zámek ⓜ za·mek castle
zaměstnání ⓝ zuh·myest·na·nyee job
zamknout zuhm·knoht lock v
zamknutý zuhm·knu·tee locked
zámoří ⓝ za·mo·rzhee overseas
zaneprázdněný zuh·ne·prazd·nye·nee busy
západ ⓜ za·puhd west
západ slunce ⓜ za·puhd slun·tse sunset
zápalky ① pl za·puhl·ki
  matches (for lighting)
zapalovač ⓜ zuh·puh·lo·vuhch
  cigarette lighter
zápas ⓜ za·puhs match (sport)
zápisník ⓜ za·pis·nyeek notebook
záruka ① za·ru·kuh guarantee
zasnoubení ⓝ zuh·snoh·be·nyee
  engagement (to marry)
zasnoubený zuh·snoh·be·nee
  engaged (to be married)
zásoby potravin ① pl
  za·so·bi po·truh·vin food supplies
zástrčka ① zas·trch·kuh plug (electricity)
zataženo zuh·tuh·zhe·no cloudy
zátka ① zat·kuh plug (bath)
zavazadlo ⓝ zuh·vuh·zuhd·lo
  baggage (luggage)
zavazadlová schránka ①
  zuh·vuh·zuhd·lo·va skhran·kuh
  luggage locker
zavírat zuh·vee·ruht close v
zavřený zuh·vrzhe·nee closed • shut v
zdraví ⓝ zdra·vee health
zdravotní sestra ①
  zdruh·vot·nyee ses·truh nurse
zdrhovadlo ⓝ zdr·ho·vuhd·lo zip (zipper)
zelenina ① ze·le·nyi·nuh vegetable
zelený ze·le·nee green
země ① ze·mye country
zima ① zi·muh winter
zítra zeet·ruh tomorrow
zkažený zkuh·zhe·nee off (spoilt)

Ž

zkusit sku·sit try (attempt) v
zlodějna ① zlo·dyey·nuh rip-off
zlato ⓝ zluh·to gold
zlomený zlo·me·nee broken
změna ① zmye·nuh change
zmeškat zmesh·kuht
  miss (not catch train etc.)
zmrzlina ① zmrz·li·nuh ice cream
zmrzlý zmrz·lee frozen
známka ① znam·kuh stamp (postage)
znovu zno·vu again
zpáteční jízdenka ①
  zpa·tech·nyee·den·kuh return ticket
zpěvák/zpěvačka ⓜ/①
  spye·vak/spye·vuhch·kuh singer
zpoždění ⓝ zpozh·dye·nyee delay
zpráva ① zpra·vuh message
zprávy ① pl zpra·vi news
zranění ⓝ zruh·nye·nyee injury
zraněný zruh·nye·nee injured
zrcadlo ⓝ zr·tsuhd·lo mirror
zrušit zru·shit cancel
zříceniny ① pl zrzhee·tse·nyi·ni ruins
ztracený ztruh·tse·nee lost
ztráty a nálezy ① ztra·ti uh na·le·zi
  lost-property office
zub ⓜ zub tooth
zubař(ka) ⓜ/① zu·buhrzh(·kuh) dentist
zubní kartáček ⓜ zub·nyee kuhr·ta·chek
  toothbrush
zubní pasta ① zub·nyee puhs·tuh
  toothpaste
zvyk ⓜ zvik custom

Ž

žádný zhad·nee none
žaludek ⓜ zhuh·lu·dek stomach
žehlička ① zheh·lich·kuh iron (for clothes)
železniční nádraží ⓝ zhe·lez·nyich·nyee
  na·druh·zhee railway station
žena ① zhe·nuh woman
ženatý zhe·nuh·tee married (man)
ženský zhens·kee female a
židle ① zhid·le chair
žiletka ① zhi·let·kuh razor blade
život ⓜ zhi·vot life
žíznivý zheez·nyi·vee thirsty
žlutý zhlu·tee yellow

The topics covered in this book are listed below in Czech. If you're having trouble understanding Czech, show this page to whoever you're talking to so they can look up the relevant section.

FINDER

don't just stand there, say something!

o see the full range of our language products, go to:
lonelyplanet.com

What kind of traveller are you?

A. You're eating chicken for dinner *again* because it's the only word you know.

B. When no one understands what you say, you step closer and shout louder.

C. When the barman doesn't understand your order, you point frantically at the beer.

D. You're surrounded by locals, swapping jokes, email addresses and experiences – other travellers want to borrow your phrasebook or audio guide.

If you answered A, B, or C, you NEED Lonely Planet's language products ...

- **Lonely Planet Phrasebooks** – for every phrase you need in every language you want
- **Lonely Planet Language & Culture** – get behind the scenes of English as it's spoken around the world – learn and laugh
- **Lonely Planet Fast Talk & Fast Talk Audio** – essential phrases for short trips and weekends away – read, listen and talk like a local
- **Lonely Planet Small Talk** – 10 essential languages for city breaks
- **Lonely Planet Real Talk** – downloadable language audio guides from lonelyplanet.com to your MP3 player

... and this is why

- **Talk to everyone everywhere**
  Over 120 languages, more than any other publisher
- **The right words at the right time**
  Quick-reference colour sections, two-way dictionary, easy pronunciation, every possible subject – and audio to support it

Lonely Planet Offices

Australia	**USA**	**UK**
90 Maribyrnong St, Footscray, Victoria 3011	150 Linden St, Oakland, CA 94607	2nd fl, 186 City Rd, London EC1V 2NT
☎ 03 8379 8000	☎ 510 250 6400	☎ 020 7106 2100
fax 03 8379 8111	fax 510 893 8572	fax 020 7106 2101
✉ talk2us@lonelyplanet.com.au	✉ info@lonelyplanet.com	✉ go@lonelyplanet.co.uk

lonelyplanet.com